Ewald Hein / Andrija Jakovljević / Brigitte Kleidt

Cyprus

Ewald Hein

Andrija Jakovljević

Brigitte Kleidt

Cyprus

Byzantine Churches and Monasteries
Mosaics and Frescoes

English Translation by
John M. Deasy

Melina

> The Greek text above the heads of the family in the illustration on the dust cover reads:
> 'Thou, O Redeemer, who hast created the spirit of Thine angels who render homage unto Thee like the flame of fire through the intercession of Thy Michael, the Taxiarchos, illuminate the souls of those who approach Thee, Presbyter Basil, the Founder, with his wife and his two daughters, and grant them forgiveness for their sins.' (Taxiarchos was a high Byzantine military rank).
> Below the donor portrait:
> 'The most reverend and divine church of the Archangel Michael was constructed from the foundation walls upwards at the cost of and through the great efforts of the most reverend Presbyter Basil Chamados ... (illegible passage) and was decorated Anno Domini 1474, 6983 years after Adam.'
> Between the Archangel's wing and abdomen we read once again that it is Michael.

Die Deutsche Bibliothek - CIP-Einheitsaufnahme

Cyprus - byzantine churches and monasteries : mosaics and frescoes / Ewald Hein/Andrija Jakovljević/Brigitte Kleidt. Übers. John M. Deasy. - Ratingen : Melina-Verl., 1997
Dt. Ausg. u.d.T.: Zypern - byzantinische Kirchen und Klöster
ISBN 3-929255-15-4

© Melina-Verlag, Ratingen 1998
Am Weinhaus 6, D-40882 Ratingen/Deutschland

The work has also been published in a German edition.

All rights of distribution, also by film, radio, television, photomechanical reproduction, sound storage and recording media of all kinds and reproduction in excerpt are reserved.

Cover picture: Fresco with the founders of the Archangel Michael Church in Pedoulas; photo: Papacharalambos Chouris

Organisation, photos (cf. individual illustration credits), plan of the location of the churches and monasteries: Ewald Hein

Author of the descriptions of the churches: Dr. Andrija Jakovljević

Layout, editing of the descriptions of the churches, author of the introductory section, appendix: Dr. Brigitte Kleidt

Translation: John M. Deasy

Lithos: Basis Druck, Duisburg

Printed by: MA-TISK d.d., Maribor, Slovenia

ISBN 3-929255-15-4

Contents

Plan of the location of the churches and monasteries 6
Preface 8
A History of Cyprus 11
Prehistoric period – The seafarers' world – On the way to Christianity – Under the wings of Byzantium – The Frankish-Italian era – Sword and Crescent – Under the Union Jack – Enosis and Civil War
The Byzantine Empire 31
New capital, new religion – Renovatio imperii – Hercules Herakleios – Survival through reforms – Iconoclasm – Emperor Basil I – The age of the Komnenes – Grandiose conclusion
History of the Orthodox Church 38
On the way to a state religion – Councils and schisms – The Church as a national institution
Characteristics of Byzantine Art 43
Mosaic and dome – The pictorial programme – The art of the Comnenes, Palaeologues and post-Byzantine period

The Monasteries and Churches

Nikitari: Panagia Asinou 55
Galata: Panagia Podithou 61
Kakopetria: St. Nikolaos tis Stegis 66
Lagoudera: Panagia Araka 71
Platanistasa: Stavros tou Agiasmati 77
Lazanias: Machairas 80
Palaichori: Metamorphosis Sotiros 82
Louvaras: St. Mamas 84
Monagri: Archangel Michael 88
Monagri: Panagia Amasgou 90
Pelendri: Church of the Holy Cross 93
Trooditissa Monastery 97
Pedoulas: Archangel Michael 98
Moutoullas: Panagia Moutoulla 100
Kalopanagiotis: St. Lampadistis 103

Kykkos: Panagia Kykkotissa 107
Chrysorrogiatissa Monastery 111
Monastery of St. Neophytos 112
Geroskipos: St. Paraskevi 117
Vavla: St. Minas 121
Kato Lefkara: Archangel Michael 122
Stavrovouni Monastery 124
Kiti: Panagia Angeloktisti 127
Larnaca: St. Lazarus 131
Kellia: St. Anthony 133
Pera Chorio: Church of the Apostles 135
Peristerona: Barnabas and Hilarion 137
Nicosia: St. John's Cathedral 138
Morphou: St. Mamas 140
Myrtou: St. Panteleimon 143
Lamboussa: Acheiropoietos 144
Bellapais Abbey 145
Koutsoventis: St. John Chrysostom 147
Kalogrea: Christ Antiphonitis 148
Tremetousia: St. Spyridon 154
Monastery of St. Barnabas 155
Trikomo: Theotokos 157
Lythrankomi: Panagia Kanakaria 162
Monastery of St. Andrew 165

Appendix

Cyprus in the Bible 171
The Archbishops of Cyprus 172
Lists of rulers 173
Chronological Table 175
Saints 179
Glossary 187
Literature 193
References 198

Cyprus
Location of the churches and monasteries

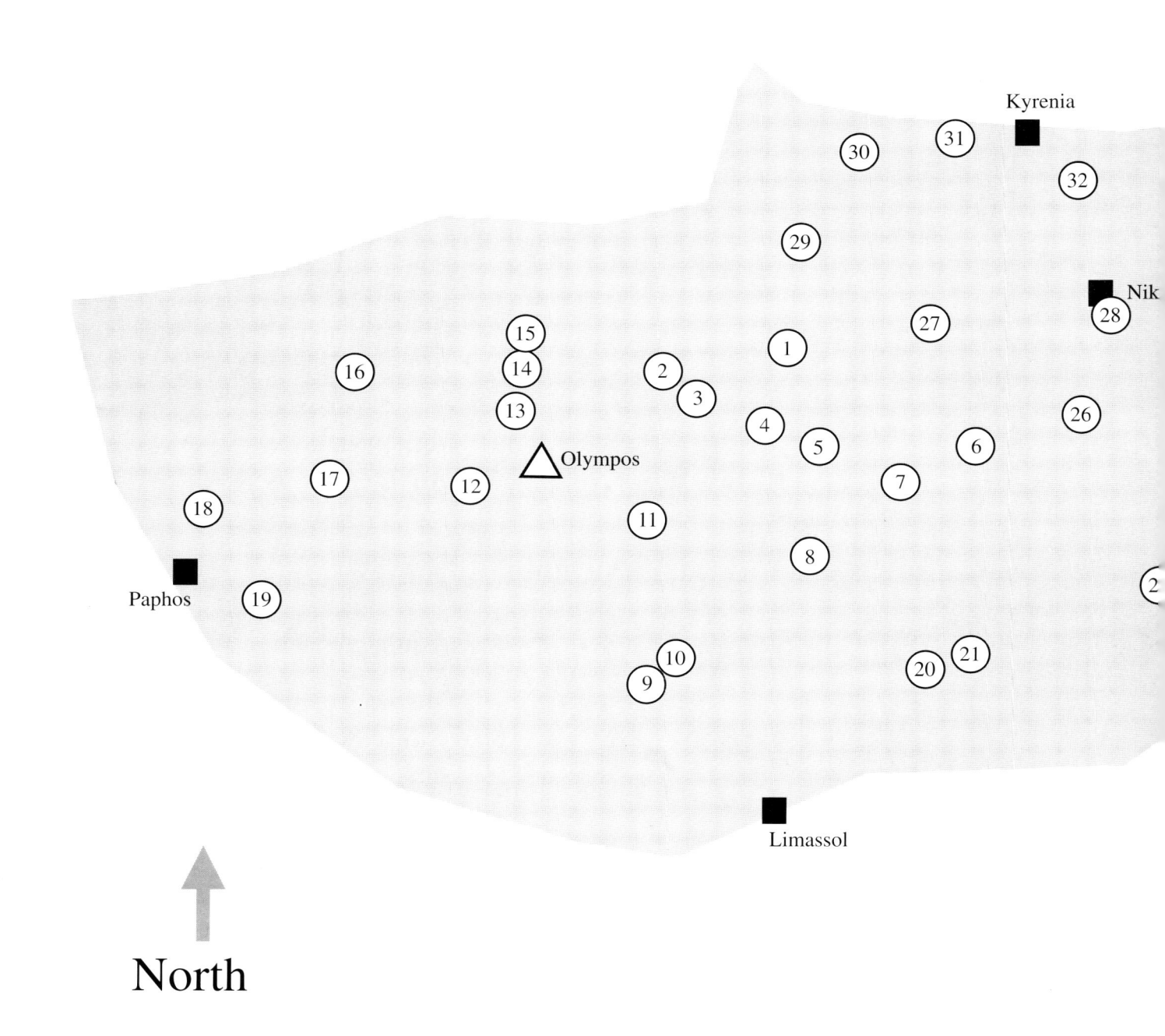

North

Kap Andreas

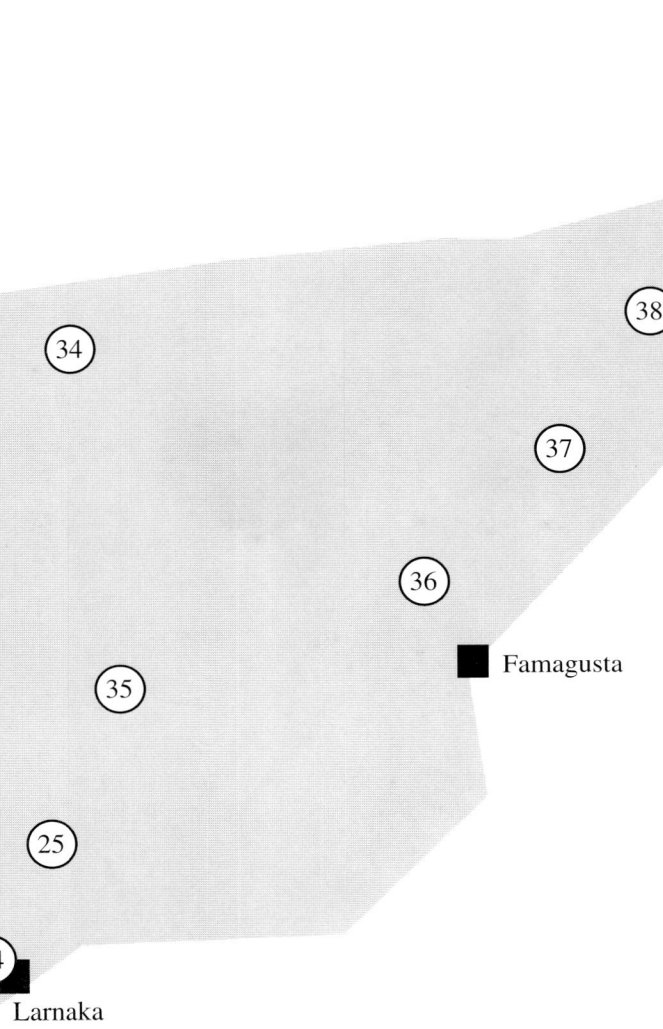

1. Nikitari: Panagia Asinou (p. 55)
2. Galata: Panagia Podithou (p. 61)
3. Kakopetria: St. Nikolaos tis Stegis (p. 66)
4. Lagoudera: Panagia Araka (p. 71)
5. Platanistasa: Stavros tou Agiasmati (p. 77)
6. Lazanias: Machairas (p. 80)
7. Palaichori: Metamorphosis Sotiros (p. 82)
8. Louvaras: St. Mamas (p. 84)
9. Monagri: Archangel Michael (p. 88)
10. Monagri: Panagia Amasgou (p. 90)
11. Pelendri: Church of the Holy Cross (p. 93)
12. Trooditissa Monastry (p. 97)
13. Pedoulas: Archangel Michael (p. 98)
14. Moutoullas: Panagia Moutoulla (p. 100)
15. Kalopanagiotis: St. Lampadistis (p. 103)
16. Kykkos: Panagia Kykkotissa (p. 107)
17. Chrysorrogiatissa Monastery (p. 111)
18. Monastery of St. Neophytos (p. 112)
19. Geroskipos: St. Paraskevi (p. 117)
20. Vavla: St. Minas (p. 121)
21. Kato Lefkara: Archangel Michael (p. 122)
22. Stavrovouni Monastery (p. 124)
23. Kiti: Panagia Angeloktisti (p. 127)
24. Larnaca: St. Lazarus (p. 131)
25. Kellia: St. Anthony (p. 133)
26. Pera Chorio: Church of the Apostles (p. 135)
27. Peristerona: Barnabas and Hilarion (p. 137)
28. Nicosia: St. John's Cathedral (p. 138)
29. Morphou: St. Mamas (p. 140)
30. Myrtou: St. Panteleimon (p. 143)
31. Lamboussa: Acheiropoietos (p. 144)
32. Bellapais Abbey (p. 145)
33. Koutsoventis: St. John Chrysostom (p. 147)
34. Kalogrea: Christ Antiphonitis (p. 148)
35. Tremetousia: St. Spyridon (p. 154)
36. Monastery of St. Barnabas (p. 155)
37. Trikomo: Theotokos (p. 157)
38. Lythrankomi: Panagia Kanakaria (p. 162)
39. Monastery of St. Andrew (p. 165)

Preface

Fig. 1: Two angels - fresco from the monastery Agios Neophytos near Paphos.

How many names are used to designate an island which has been at the point of intersection of historical developments for millennia? Alesija, Iatnana, Cyprium: between these designations lies a span from the Neolithic period to the Roman Empire. And the name by which it was finally to be known for centuries comes in more than one spelling: Cyprus, Kibris, Kypros – one often has to consult three different volumes in alphabetically arranged works of reference before finding what one is looking for! And often enough the findings are paltry, because the island does not just lie at the point of intersection, but in the shadow of the peoples who developed their own history on it and around it.

The bewildering variety of names of place and peoples reflects the genesis a little further: Greek sound shifts (*hagia, agia, ayia, Barnabas* or *Varnavas*) and Roman superimpositions (*Kition* or *Kitium*, endings in *-os* or *-us*) lead to several correct variants.

In addition there is the juxtaposition of Greek and Turkish designations which are, admittedly, rarely to be found together on one map. The mosques of the Moslems and the churches which were or are used by Latin and Orthodox Christians testify to the inhabitants' religious differentiation. The fact that these houses of God not infrequently stand on the ruins of ancient shrines tells us something of the structures of power, just as much as the fact (about which more anon) that churches were converted into mosques and – sometimes – were returned to the Christians again.

Many lords ruled the country, gods and kings, archbishops and the emperor's representatives, pilgrims, crusaders and warriors, noble women and semi-degenerate figures have left traces in part weathered, often enough no longer decipherable. The periods of independence were somewhat rarer.

On the voyage of discovery into past greatness, the present remains insistently alive, particularly in Cyprus with its painful 'green line' which does not at all fit in with this colour's customary ascription of hope. The island state is too much a part of Europe, lying too far in the most easterly corner of the Mediterranean for it to remain spared from the conflicts between Orient and Occident. But a conflict dating back thousands of years only knows victors superficially.

The twenty-year long partition of the island is too present in its inhabitants' emotions, a constant thorn of sadness and anger. Too many have fled from North to South, from South to North; too many have lost their house and home; it is just too unnatural to look over to the other side and yet not be able to travel there. Because in contrast to tourists, it is not possible for Cypriots to cross the demarcation line.

Although it is possible to see the sea from nearly every point, Cyprus is the third largest island in the Mediterranean followed by innumerable other ones right down to uninhabited rocks. It is itself the ruler over sandy, palm-lined beaches, cliffs on which the waves can break in frothy foam – the foam out of which Aphrodite, the ancient goddess of love is said to have been born – through winters in the mountains rich in snow and the summer air shimmering in the heat. Its cedar groves are as beautiful as the Biblical regions of the Lebanon. Even the over-exploitation by pre-Christian peoples with their well-nigh insatiable demand for construction material for ships was unable to completely destroy this wealth, whereas elsewhere all round '*mare nostrum*' the soil of the cleared forests has become irretrievably karstified.

On Cyprus, not only do the sun, mountains and sea promise recreation, there is much to be discovered here, much to experience. The rich tradition and superb landscapes do not only cast their spell on the culturally interested. And this book has information and suggestions ready for a trip into the past, helping when uncovering the treasures and deepening knowledge about what has been seen. It shows and explains the finest and most important architectural monuments from one of the formative epochs, not only for Cyprus, but for the world of the Eastern Church as a whole: from the age of an Empire which lasted for over a thousand years – Byzantium.

One point should be explained: all the terms which play a role in this book should never be confused with similar or even homonymous political designations; they are used exclusively in accordance with their art historical meaning.

In addition to numerous individuals who are named in part in the Appendix of this book, our thanks are due to the Cyprus Ministry of Education and Culture, the Press and Information Office and the Archaeological Museum, all of which are located in Nicosia. We would also like to express our gratitude to the Cyprus Department of Antiquities for permission to photograph the frescoes in the churches in Cyprus.

A History of Cyprus

Cyprus's history is marked by a dynamism of its own. The island is, if one disregards some exceptions, too small to be able to maintain real independence. It has therefore always been at the mercy of external power constellations. It is possible to observe alternations taking place in long cycles. Sometimes Cyprus was a border area and lay between power blocs; then its strategic importance became significant. For long periods, however, it was to be found within a power bloc, dependent on the development of a foreign state. Under Roman and Byzantine rule, it experienced a lasting boom and prosperity, under Ottoman rule it was left to decline slowly in keeping with the agony of the empire as a whole. The island has never held a really decisive role, either militarily, culturally or economically. But it was important: rich in mineral and other resources, in principle capable of supporting itself, and with the tenacious way of life of an indigenous culture. Despite the regular domination of foreign elements, it preserved something of its own and assimilated the outside influences. In this ambivalence lies its strength and its tragedy.

Preliminary remarks

In the case of all languages written in a different script, and especially in the case of languages such as Greek and Latin where there is already a long tradition with respect to the adoption of words from them into English, the question of transcription arises. It would be comparatively simple if it just involved certain letters. But many old names have themselves gone through a long history; the names of ancient cities (e.g. Caesarea/Kayseri) or historical persons, for example. In the case of letters, it is possible to agree on a solution – in this work the Greek φ is transcribed with *ph* instead of with *f* as is often the practice of late; χ as a rule with *ch* (Christ, Machairas), etc. Admittedly, in the case of names there are always versions which have become accepted and, in view of such usage, there are great difficulties in consistently adhering to a form of spelling once selected. This present book thus represents a compromise. It does not succeed in maintaining a form of the transcription of sounds right down to the smallest detail; the authors would ask the reader's forbearance for this.

Prehistoric period

Neolithic period

Cyprus's history extends far into the past. Already in the Neolithic Age there was human life on the island. But, apparently, there was no continuity in this for thousands of years and it consisted of various independent cultural phases. The first settlement coincided in time with one of the greatest changes ever, the "Agrarian Revolution", the last stage in the transition from a collector and hunter existence to a settled agricultural form of existence. Well organised groups landing in Cyprus in about 7000 before our era brought seeds for domesticated plants, domestic animals and fallow deer with them. Tools have been found, idols and the remains of settlements. The oldest and largest is Choirokoitia, lying close to the coast half way between Limassol and Larnaca on a mountain slope, and protected against attacks by a wall. These settlements remained isolated culturally, and rooted in their traditions; they vanished without leaving any apparent successors.

The pottery epoch began for Cyprus around 5250 BC without its being possible to ascribe the findings to a

Fig. 2: Chalcolitic cross figure made of steatite.

particular culture. They were uncovered during excavations dealing with the Sotira Culture dated about 4500-4000 BC and named after the site located to the west of Limassol. It left settlements following a uniform pattern and with richly decorated clay vessels, the styles of which allow one to assume several epochs. There were regional differences and technical improvements. Of the 30 known villages, only a few were still inhabited in the next period; why the others were abandoned is not known.

Copper Age

With the Erimi Culture, Cyprus entered into one of the longest phases in its history; an age in which metal was used and trade links with the mainland were developed, social structures formed and the Cypro-Minoan script introduced. Thus between 4000 and 2500 BC a very great deal must have happened, but we do not know how these changes took place. Objects made of copper have been found, but it is unclear whether they were imported or made out of Cypriot ore. Ornaments and cruciform female figures were made out of picrite, a greenish stone occurring in copper deposits. They were worn as pendants or used as grave-goods (cf. fig. 2).

The standardised pottery in the west of the island allows one to conclude that it was produced at just a few places and distributed from there. Seals and large storage vessels in excavated houses make it highly probable that food was centrally administered, something possibly forced on the authorities by an exhaustion of the soils. Grave chambers and complicated burial ceremonies developed: signs of a society which was becoming differentiated.

The Seafarers' World

Bronze Age

Bronze, the collective name for various copper alloys, but mainly for those with tin and copper, made it easier to manufacture objects than from pure copper. Weapons, ploughshares, clasps for clothing and balance weights for spindles made of bronze have been found in Cypriot burial fields. Together with gold, this material stands for a new stage in civilisation.

The epoch was probably brought about by a period of destruction by the migratory movement of the Indo-Europeans. From the second millennium BC, they pushed south-westwards, thus setting off population shifts in several waves. One of the first of these led to the settlement of Cyprus. With it began the systematic exploitation of the copper deposits. Cyprus, which at that time was probably called Alashiya, became the most important supplier of copper – *cyprium aes* – in the old world, and for a time held an important position in maritime trade. The north, where the ore deposits lay, prospered. External relations with Egypt (at times as a vassal), the Aegean Islands, Palestine, Syria (Ugarit) and Babylon can be shown to have existed. Minoan traders from Crete established colonies on Cyprus and conducted their trade from there. Towards the end of the epoch, fortresses were established close to the coast which show traces of violent destruction. It is not known whether internal disputes or attacks from outside were the cause of this.

Indo-European tribes which had entered Greece (Ionians and Achaeans) merged – quite certainly not always peacefully – with the original Mediterranean population creating the Mycenean culture. The highest class formed a warrior caste. Why their palaces and cities were destroyed or abandoned at the end of the twelfth century has remained a riddle down to the present. At all events, their culture was not apparently continued. Mycenean traders took the place of the Minoan ones who had previously been established in Cyprus and utilised the island, among other things, as a trading post for luxury goods. It became the melting-pot for the artistic styles in the Levant and Aegean. This period of peace and economic growth ended in the thirteenth century BC. What has survived is correspondence between the king of Alashiya and the king of Ugarit who warns his neighbour about foreign ships – but it helped neither of them, their countries were ravaged, like wide parts of the Mediterranean area, by the "Peoples of the Sea" disaster. This wave of peoples known to us from Egyptian sources, was due to a new thrust in Indo-European migration. Trading centres on the coast were destroyed and reconstructed again later – larger and finer than before. But yet once again a 'dark' age, an age of transition began about which we know little. Homer's Odyssey bears witness to it in a literary coded form.

Iron Age

Iron, known already in the second millennium, is harder than bronze, but it rusts. From the twelfth century BC on it was used ever increasingly for weapons and tools which needed to be sharp, and armed conflicts occurred increasingly frequently. The Dorians drove the Achaeans out of their territory so that the latter came to Cyprus as refugees and settlers, initiating the Hellenisation of the island. Towards the end of the twelfth century, the Arcadian dialect had ousted the indigenous language, but the independent Cypro-Minoan script lasted until about the third century alongside the more practical alphabet employing letters adopted from the Phoenicians which the Greeks had enriched with signs for vowels thus creating the basic form for European scripts.

The Achaeans also brought the typically Greek political structure of the city state with them, admittedly not the democracy which later came into being in the mother country. The island thus had the predominant ethnic population it still has, the Greeks. All subsequent alien rules and immigrants did nothing to change this. There continued to be, of course, strong elements from surrounding peoples, for example the Phoenicians founded a colony in Kition (later Larnaca) in the eighth century. It was one of the seven to ten small kingdoms which were to shape Cyprus halfway through the millennium. Little is known about their social structure.

On the surrounding continents, the various empires came and went. Assyrians, Egyptians and Persians had little trouble with the Mediterranean island which was so important for trade and warfare. For many centuries, it had to accept vassal status with only brief periods of independence. The events of this time are only recorded in outlines, any dates are followed by many question marks. In the seventh century, Cyprus came under Assyrian sovereignty for about 40 years, however the minor kings apparently did not have to completely give up their autonomy. In the mid-sixth century it was briefly annexed by the Egypt of the Pharaohs which was experiencing its last climax. The age-old kingdom rose to be a sea power in the eastern Mediterranean and cultivated good relations with the Greek colonies in its vicinity. Admittedly, alliances against the Persians failed. In 525 BC Egypt became a Persian province, a fate which had befallen Cyprus about 20 years earlier. The inhabitants of the island rebelled against the foreign lords several times, but at times they also fought with them. At the beginning of the fifth century, Onesilos of Salamis risked a coup d'état against his brother and joined the revolt by the Ionian cities. The revenge of the superior Persians was not long in coming. Ten, twenty years later, the Greek city states recently allied against Persia devastated Cyprus, more or less while sailing by, and then took course for Byzantium. The Cypriots fought on the Persian side against them. In the middle of the century, they joined the Athenians who, under Pericles, were conducting an initially successful offensive against the Persians and Spartans simultaneously, but in the end they

Fig. 3: Traces of the Roman past: the gymnasium near Salamis in which men and boys were able to engage in sports under the supervision of instructors. In classical antiquity this was done on principle completely undressed, hence the name of the institution – 'gymnos' means naked. The majority of the pillars were brought here from the theatre during a restoration in the early Byzantine period.

lost. In the Peace of Callias, the hotly contested island was once again annexed by the Persians. Only Alexander, who destroyed the Persian Empire of Xerxes, liberated it – once again for just a short time. After Alexander's death in 323 BC, his empire disintegrated, decades of struggles followed over his inheritance. It was the age of the Diadochi and it was the age of Pyrrhus. In his name, these battles have become a proverbial symbol: victories followed by downfall in the next moment, because the price for the victory had been too high. Cyprus with its important resources, timber and copper above all, was drawn into bloody disputes between Antigonos (Asia Minor) and Ptolemy (Egypt). In 295 BC, it fell once again to Egypt, and Ptolemy took his vengeance on those who had sided with Antigonos. The minor kingdoms had to make way for a central administration, only the cities were granted a certain autonomy. In the Ptolemaic epoch occurred one of Cyprus's most significant contributions to European intellectual history. Zeno of Citium established the Stoic school in Athens, a philosophy which it is impossible to imagine life of the late antique period being without.

On the way to Christianity

From the mid-second century BC on, Rome did not miss any opportunity to exploit the disputes between Syria and Egypt and those which broke out among the Ptolemies themselves to her advantage. In the epoch of the Roman civil wars, Cyprus fell to the expanding empire which was being transformed, step by step, from a republic into a monarchy. In 58 BC, Marcus Portius Cato conquered the island. He was an upright republican and with this move he was removed for the moment from the political stage in Rome. He administered Cyprus studiously correctly for two years. In 51/50 BC, Cicero was governor of the island. In his case too, his proper conduct of official business was in stark contrast to the ruthlessness of the businessmen and officials. They granted 'loans' at horrendous rates of interest. In 47 and 36 BC, Caesar and Anthony gave the island as a present to Cleopatra with whom they had had affairs. In 31 BC, Octavian conquered it back. In 29 BC, Cicero's son, Marcus by first name, was appointed governor. With the division of the Roman provinces into imperial and 'public' provinces, it came to Syria which was directly subordinate to 'Augustus' (the title the Senate had conferred on Octavian) because troops had to be deployed for its protection. In 22 BC, Cyprus became a senatorial province, a sign that the situation had stabilised. It was administered by an annually changing proconsul.

After an initial phase of the most brutal exploitation, Roman rule brought the island an effective infrastructure and, as an unintended side-effect, the Christianity which, for the Greek-speaking Cypriots, became the most important feature of their identity alongside their language. Cyprus lay on the route of the first missionary journey of the apostles Paul and Barnabas. In 45 AD, they crossed the island from Salamis to Paphos. Barnabas, a Cypriot Jew by descent, returned in 51, continued preaching the gospel and died a martyr's death.

Greek remained the vernacular on the island, as elsewhere in the East of the Roman Empire (the official and administrative language, however, was Latin), Cyprus was divided into four districts and 12 or 13 smaller administrative units, each allotted to a city. With two exceptions, all administrative centres lay on the coast. Roads, aqueducts, public baths, theatres and other public institutions ensured a comfortable life which was, admittedly, seriously disrupted by frequent earthquakes. In 15 BC, Paphos, the capital, was destroyed. In 76 AD, Paphos and Salamis. Particularly bad was an earthquake in 164 AD in which almost all cities on the island were severely damaged. The political peace was seldom disturbed. Only in 116 AD did the Jews, many of whom had fled to Cyprus after the fall of Jerusalem, rise against Roman rule. As there were hardly any troops stationed here, they were able to cause a blood-bath among the inhabitants, whereas in other parts of the country they were quickly brought under control. All in all, according to the – quite certainly exaggerated – report of an ancient historian, 240,000 persons are said to have been killed on Cyprus, including all non-Jewish inhabitants of Salamis. The revolt led to brutal suppression and the expulsion of all Jews from the island under Emperor Trajan.

The offer of Roman citizenship, which went out to all provinces in 212 representing an attempt at holding together the disintegrating Empire by an inner sense of belonging together, apparently found little echo on Cyprus. Despite the civilisatory achievements, the imperial power ultimately remained alien to the people here. During the administrative reform by Emperor Diocletian at the end of the third century, the island was allotted to the diocese of 'Oriens' in which it remained until the next reform under the Byzantine Emperor Justinian I in the sixth century. The 'Praeses' was subordinate to the 'Comes Orientes' with his seat in Antioch. Apart from an incursion by the Ostrogoths in 267, Cyprus was spared from the invasions by the Barbarians who struck the Roman Empire ever more frequently, finally leading to the division and the fall of the western half, but not from the famines and economic disasters, such as the galloping inflation of the third and fourth centuries which was only stopped by the coinage reform of Constantine the Great. In addition there was a whole series of earthquakes which destroyed the island's most important cities, and the plague which had spread from Ethiopia since 250.

Under the wings of Byzantium

Roman transformation

Christianity and the survival of the Roman Empire in the east are the decisive forces marking Cyprus's next epoch, the Byzantine one. Emperor Constantine I transferred the capital from Rome to Byzantium, thus shifting the main focus of the Empire to the East; in addition, he tolerated Christianity. In 395, Theodosius divided the Empire among his sons, Arcadius received the western half of the Empire, Honorius the eastern half, to which Cyprus also belonged. This 'temporary' division introduced for practical considerations and by no means for the first time, proved to be final and has influenced European history right down to the present. Both parts passed through different developments. In the West, through the fragmentation, an organisation of society from below, individualism and competition became possible. Through its superior economic strength, the East was better able to resist the attacks by the 'Barbarians' and preserved the political structures of late antiquity.

Cyprus was ruled from Constantinople from 330 on and was incorporated into the capital's administrative system. From there came the decisive cultural and economic impulses; the master builders and painters who worked in Cyprus were trained there, the decisions on questions of faith in the Orthodox church were taken there. The governors of Cyprus resided in the new capital Constantia replacing Paphos which the Romans had preferred. Emperor Constantine had Constantia, that was named after him, erected on the ruins of Salamis which had been destroyed in earthquakes in 332 and 342, dispensing the surviving inhabitants from tax for four years.

Little is known about the period between the fourth and sixth centuries, apart from the struggle by the church for its autonomy. One of the Byzantine governors, Kalokairos, is said to have brought cats to Cyprus so that they would check a plague of snakes; it is possible that he attempted to make himself independent of Constantinople, but his coup was rapidly suppressed. Basically, not much changed by comparison with the Roman period, but here, even more than elsewhere, it is only possible to draw a line between both epochs with great difficulty. Inner stability and economic well-being mark the centuries from the turn of the era until the seventh century. By comparison with the other areas of the Mediterranean world, Cyprus thus had a privileged fate, because all the others were ravaged by wars and subjected to a fundamental transformation of political conditions.

Cyprus profited from the short-lasting period of peace in the Mediterranean which came about through Justinian I's conquests. Indeed, as a lucrative source of taxes it even enjoyed special attention during the construction of roads and defensive installations. Magnificently furbished churches and public buildings were commissioned.

The centralist economy introduced by Justinian I provided for the export of wine, cereals and textiles by Cyprus; copper and timber declined in significance. The agrarian structure of the island was enriched by the introduction of sericulture which Justinian had had spied out from the eastern neighbours.

However, Justinian I's policy exhausted the state coffers and East Rome was hardly equal to the onslaught of the Slavs in the Balkans in the seventh century. At the same time it had to defend itself against the Persians on a second front. A cautious policy of safeguarding assets marked these centuries, Cyprus still preserved its internal peace and profited from the regeneration process under Herakleios who admittedly had just defeated the Persians only to find himself confronted with a new danger shortly before his death: the adherents of the new religious faith, Islam, from the desert wastes of the Arabian peninsula developed a meteoric expansionist force.

Between the Emperor and Caliph

And Cyprus was not spared from this danger. Unlike the Persians, the Arabs quickly learned the techniques of navigation. With the former Byzantine territories, they conquered the prerequisites with respect to technology and personnel for a navy. With this they were able to pit themselves against the Byzantines on land and at sea, and they invaded, plundered and pillaged Cyprus which was no longer protected by the sea. In 647, they destroyed Constantia, killing and deporting many inhabitants and demanding tribute payments from the others. The Imperial troops drove them out, but scarcely six years later they repeated the bloody game and an Arab garrison secured the conquest for thirty years. At the time of this invasion, the foster-mother of the Prophet Mohammed accompanied her husband. She fell from a mule and was mortally injured. Above the scene of the accident – it is by the salt lake near Larnaca – the Moslems later constructed a mausoleum and mosque. It is one of the most important Islamic shrines.

Emperor Justinian II was not in a position to defend his widely threatened Empire as a whole, he had to restrict himself to what was feasible. One of the means adopted were compulsory resettlements. In 691 he compensated in this manner for the dramatic losses in population caused by Arab attacks on Constantinople. Cyprus lay too far away anyway for its defence to have been a priority for the weakened Empire. So many Cypriots, together with their Archbishop, moved to the shores of the Sea of Marmara, albeit to a marshy and infertile area. Heavily decimated, they returned home a little later.

Cyprus became something of a no-man's land. Until well into the tenth century, it was dominated by both powers, at times by the Arabs, at times by the Byzantines, at times by both, never by neither. In some periods, the arch-enemies lived in peaceful co-existence, sometimes even a high regard for the opposing civilisation predominated; but ultimately confrontation decided the relationship. The island remained their bone of contention for over 300 years and was able to secure a kind of neutrality for itself at times. The iconophiles fled here, those adherents of religious images who did not want to allow every figural representation to disappear from churches and that the Mother of God or Jesus Christ should no longer be venerated in their pictures. In the economic field, a free-trade area, so to speak, came into being, a place of transshipment for the transport of goods from East to West and vice versa. But taken as whole, they were needy and difficult times. At least eleven Arab invasions – just raids as well as attempts at occupation – resulted in constant destruction; the uncertainty did not allow the inhabitants to engage in continuous economic activity. The Cypriot coastal cities were destroyed, the population gave preference in future to the safer locations further inland; Nicosia gained in importance.

Around 872, Cyprus passed to Byzantium for seven years, a sign that the Empire was gradually in a position to dictate the theatres of war and Arab expansion was abating. The position only improved lastingly with the 'final' reconquest of Cyprus. Already in 910, Byzantine troops led by the Logothete Himerios occupied the island. They were intended, just like the operation in 965, to prepare the conquest of Cilicia and Syria. But the Arab fleet was still superior to the Byzantine one.

On his retreat in 912, a renegade governor, Leon of Tripolis, destroyed Himerios's expedition corps. The Moslems' expansive force declined in the next decades as a result of internal quarrels; the Caliphate split into several rival territories. For about two centuries, Byzantium returned to the political stage in glittering style before it was slowly crushed between the North Italian mercantile republics and the Ottomans.

Byzantine renaissance

Niketas Chalkoutzes took possession of Cyprus for the Emperor in 965; together with Crete, reconquered in 961, it was now part of the most southerly outpost of Byzantium which was at the zenith of its medieval power. A chain of Imperial forts protected Cyprus from attacks from the sea. Whereas in Asia Minor, ever new armies of horsemen undermined the Empire's strength, it was possible to maintain prosperity and peace on the island for two centuries. Prosperity admittedly only for a small upper class; the extreme partition of Cypriot society into wretchedly poor land labourers liable to pay taxes and a very small upper class was one of the main constant features for centuries. There were only very few craftsmen or other 'bourgeois' who could have mitigated the differences between the two groups. For churches, monasteries and cities, the middle-Byzantine epoch was just as fruitful as the period up to the sixth century. Brisk construction activity changed the island's appearance. There were many new foundations, but many settlements already existing in antiquity were also revived. Cities, such as Paphos or Karpasia, were re-established a few kilometres away from the coast. The re-conquest by the Byzantine Empire meant, on the one hand, relative security but, on the other hand, subordination to a state with the highest tax burden and the most effective tax collectors. There was tension between the basically secular administration and the Cypriot church which had not lost any of its ability to function during the Arab invasions and rule, and had gained greater freedom and more influence without regimentation by Constantinople. Archbishop Mouzalon in particular opposed the Byzantine governors Boutoumites and Philokales.

The island's economy recovered relatively quickly. In addition to the salt which was taken from the lake near Larnaca in summer, wine became the main export good. Thanks to new weaving processes for silk, Cyprus became one of the centres of Byzantine textile production. In addition, trade with the Levant flourished once again in the eleventh century. The island also participated intellectually and culturally in the renaissance under the Macedonian Emperors; the most important frescoes date from this period.

The cross with the Crusaders

After the establishment of the French-dominated Crusader states in Syria and Palestine in the year 1098/99, Cyprus became caught up in the wake of this movement. Almost inevitably the interests of the Crusaders, which by their nature were directed against Byzantium, were intent on tearing the geographically exposed island, which was so strategically important for the conquest of the coast of Palestine, away from Constantinople. On the one hand, the schism in 1054 between the Latin and Greek creeds had put the parties into opposing camps. On the other, the Crusaders' demands were too particularistic by comparison with the interests of the Byzantine Empire; the Middle East was a small frontier area, and from Constantinople's viewpoint a not particularly important one. And not infrequently, the Crusaders themselves deviated from their declared objective. Not only the tightly organised Normans were concerned above all to expand their own power. In addition there were the contradictory economic interests: it suited Venice, Pisa and Genoa only too well to have the competition on the Bosphorus eliminated. Finally, the indigenous populations were often subject to outrages in which the local Christians, Jews and Moslems were massacred, plundered and enslaved without distinction. These circumstances led more than once to Byzantine alliances with the Arabs or Turks.

Ever more frequently, military clashes took place on Cyprus. In 1099, a fleet from Pisa attacked; the governor Philokales was able to repel it with some losses because he received help from Constantinople in good time. Rénaud of Châtillon, a French nobleman who had risen to become Prince of Antioch, led a surprise attack against the rich Levant island. The governor, John Komnenos, a nephew of the Emperor, was unable to do anything against the superior strength, as in Constantinople the authorities were not in a position to act because of their own problems. For three weeks the intruders wrought havoc at will, burning the fields, destroying villages and cities, killing the inhabitants. In 1157, Cyprus experienced a severe earthquake. In 1158, Egyptian pirates plundered the land. Two years later, another Frankish nobleman, Raymond III of Tripoli, recovered his losses on its coast. Cyprus took a long time to recover from the devastation.

In 1184, a nephew of the Byzantine emperor arrived in Cyprus with falsified documents. Thanks to his family name, Komnenos, his claims did not at first arouse any suspicion. Isaac Dukas appointed a patriarch, had himself crowned Emperor of Cyprus by him, but quickly proved himself a tyrant. In the course of his revolt against the central Byzantine government, he was supported by the fleet of William II, king of the Norman realm of Sicily. Later he allied himself with the Armenians, then with the Egyptian Sultan Saladin. Isaac brought about his own downfall by providing the English King Richard I, Coeur de Lion, with a pretext for conquering the island while on his way to the Holy Land. He allowed his troops to capture the ship of the English king's bride which had run aground between Limassol and Amathous, taking the travellers prisoner. In less than a month, Richard had deprived the Byzantine of power, married in Limassol and enriched himself with Isaac's goods, and levies which he demanded from the island's inhabitants. Two of his followers were intended to rule Cyprus, but while Richard was engaged with the conquest of Acre, a revolt broke out on the island. He thereupon sold it to the Knights Templar who quickly also incensed the inhabitants against themselves. Finally, Richard appointed his loyal follower Guy de Lusignan from the family of the Counts of La Marche from Poitou as regent, not without letting himself be paid once again for this favour.

The Frankish-Italian era

Latin and Orthodox Christians

In 1192, Cyprus thus passed into the hands of a Catholic French aristocratic family. The transfer of power was facilitated by the peace signed between Saladin and

Fig. 4: Crusader castle, the 'Grande Commanderia' near Kolossi. The wine grown in this region takes its name from it.

the Crusader state of Acre. Guy de Lusignan endeavoured to expand the basis of his power and generously granted fiefs to Frankish nobles. There were enough candidates through the losses of territory in Syria. He died childless in May 1194. His brother, Amalric, consolidated the rule of the Lusignan dynasty by adopting the constitution of *'Outremer'* without copying its weak points. In Frankish Cyprus there were no over-powerful barons who might have disputed his power in the ruling council. He consolidated his position by adopting the title of king. The Hohenstaufen Emperor Henry VI became his overlord. Amalric was crowned in Nicosia in 1197. In addition, he expanded his secular power through the spiritual power of the Roman Catholic Church. For the next centuries, Orthodox and Latin hierarchies existed side by side, mainly to the disadvantage of the indigenous office-holders. When Amalric died in 1205, he left a minor son; Cyprus passed under the regency of one of the barons, Walter de Montbéliard. He broke the peace with the Moslems in 1206/1207 by an attack on the coast of Asia Minor, enriching himself so much that he was sent into exile in 1210. At the age of 13, Amalric's son married Alice of Jerusalem and assumed the reins of government as Hugh I at the age of 15 and died at 23 at the wedding of a half-sister in Tripoli. His wife Alice delegated the regency.

The dynastic relationships of these centuries were not infrequently marked by the rapid sequence of princes in their minority with their mothers, regents and young kings. Again and again there was a vacuum of power revealing the exposed nature, the strange irreality of this realm. Such situations opened the door to outside intervention. In addition, in the long term, the existence of the Latin kingdom on Cyprus was not to be separated from the

Fig. 5: Frankish noblewoman from a donor's portrait in the narthex of Asinou. She is wearing the black veil usually worn by the ladies after the fall of Acre as a sign of mourning for the end of 'Outremer'.

idea of liberating the Holy Land. Without supplies and support from the West, this regime, which never really came to any arrangement with the Greeks, despite certain concessions and a certain degree of assimilation, but always remained an alien element, was unable to survive permanently. In the first hundred years of its existence, the Frankish dynasty was directly involved in the crusades. And as all the crusades, apart from the first one, remained unsuccessful, it was thus involved in a chain of defeats involving heavy losses.

Hugh I, who had participated in the Fifth Crusade alongside his liege lord, the Emperor Frederick II, with his own troops, also left a minor son at his death. His queen had entrusted the government to a member of the most powerful family in Frankish Cyprus, the Ibelins. Frederick II, Emperor of the 'Holy Roman Empire', one of the three leaders of the Crusade, triggered off a civil war on the island by deposing this regent in 1228 and appointing people acceptable to him. The uprising did not last long; on 14 July 1229, the renegates were defeated in a battle near Nicosia. They fled into the Pentadaktylos Mountains, but had to give up in 1230. Frederick II again sent a marshall who was intended to press his claims. In the year before the prince would be able to take up the reins of government, fighting broke out again which the young king – Henry I – was only able to decide in his favour with the help of the Genoese. The Genoese claimed Famagusta as a base and from then on interfered considerably in the island's politics. Pope Innocent IV dispensed the Cypriot king from his feudal oath in 1246 so that the German emperors were no longer able to interfere in Cypriot affairs.

In Summer 1248, the Seventh Crusade led by Louis IX, later Saint Louis, assembled in Cyprus. As the French king was hoping that the Mongols would attack the Saracens from the land side, the war society spent the winter in Famagusta, setting off by sea for Egypt in May 1249, conquering Damietta and then suffering a disastrous defeat near El Mansûra. The Crusaders' position in the Holy Land became ever more precarious; without Cyprus as a supply base and source of food, the collapse would have taken place even more quickly.

In 1260, the soldier dynasty of the Mamelukes took power in Egypt. The last bastions of Christianity in Palestine collapsed before their military superiority.

The power of the losers

In 1289 Tripoli fell, in 1291 Acre. A flood of refugees fled to Cyprus. With them came a very great deal of money into the country, because the Genoese, Venetians and Pisans had amassed huge fortunes with their trade with the Arabs which they had continued even during the war. But others had lost everything and brought nothing with them except their wretchedness and the plague. The Latin element on the island was strengthened, but with the aristocratic families settling, resistance to the Lusignans' absolutist assertions also grew. The ending of the obligations towards the Holy Land and the independence from the Western as well as the Eastern emperor meant that the money earned by trade remained in Cyprus for the first time in centuries. The position directly on the front-line to Islam was a two-sided matter: on the one hand, trade with the Orient was left to the island's inhabitants, on the other hand, they had to reckon constantly with attacks.

The Knights Templar, who had moved their mother house to Nicosia, and Cypriot barons helped the brother of King Henry II to power. Civil war broke out once again. Whereas the Templars had long been suppressed and put on trial in France, they were able to survive for a while in Cyprus. With Henry II's return to the Cypriot throne, they were then also put on trial here; their property fell to the Knights of the Order of St. John of Jerusalem who had their mother house in Limassol from 1291 to 1308, but then withdrew to Rhodes.

In 1324, Henry II once again became the victim of the over-powerful Frankish-Cypriot barons; they had him arrested and deposed. Admittedly, Henry's successor curbed the power of the nobles energetically. Hugh IV, who was 24 years of age when he acceded to the throne, was an absolutely modern ruler, intent on efficiency. Under his leadership, the country experienced the climax of its economic prosperity which, admittedly, only those who were already rich anyway were really able to enjoy. The indigenous Greeks lived in poverty. Apart from the poll tax, they had to perform villein service twice weekly and hand over one third of all their agricultural products.

The island became an experimental field for the cultivation of oriental plants. In addition to cotton and bananas, sugar cane grew particularly well. The Lusignans, the Knights of St. John and a Venetian family of importance in Cypriot history, the Cornaros, maintained extensive plantations and refineries. The finely chopped and crushed cane was pressed out once again in a mill, then boiled up two or three times. The molasses was then filled into funnel-shaped clay vessels, dripping out inside. When it had dried out, it was freed from its clay casing. Until the discovery of America and the development of loose sugar, the sweetener was sold in the shape of a hat. In addition, luxury textiles, such as Lefkara lace and gold brocade, which are still familiar today, were manufactured on Cyprus for export.

With Peter I, who was crowned in 1359 and murdered ten years later, the island acquired a dubious fame. Peter was obsessed with the crusade idea and from 1362 on travelled throughout the whole of Europe to fire the Emperor and kings there with enthusiasm for his idea. By 1365 he had indeed assembled a large number of troops who sailed with 150 ships to Alexandria, the Seventh Crusade. The city was conquered, but the majority of the participants were intent only on booty. The idea of holding the city and regaining the Holy Land from there was one which apparently only the King of Cyprus cherished. Seen as a whole, the expedition was a disaster which Peter followed up with several expensive and senseless incursions on the Syrian coast. More successful was the conquest of the Turkish city of Attaleia which had already been completed in 1361; the city remained Cypriot for 60 years.

Genoa and the downfall of the Lusignans

After Peter I had fallen victim to an assassination by the Frankish nobility, his 18 year old son was crowned Peter II. He was at the mercy of the Genoese trading interests. In 1373, they occupied Famagusta with 14,000 men – the financing had been carried out by a private trading company – brought the king into their power and starved him out until he left the city to them. His uncle James had to go to Genoa as a hostage. He was only able to succeed Peter II, who had died at the age of 30, with difficulty. His son Janus, who had been born in Genoa and named after the mythical founder of that city, remained there as a hostage; he was only able to ransom him in 1385.

Cyprus had been brought to the edge of ruin by mismanagement. The Genoese had taken the export trade away and the royal house was heavily indebted to them and the Venetians. Now the island also lost its transshipment role for trade with Syria because in 1372 the Pope lifted his ban on trading with people of other faiths.

At about the same time, the last Christian bastion, apart from Cyprus, in the Levant, the kingdom of Armenia, was overrun by the Turks; the danger which they threatened became ever more apparent, however not apparent enough to cause the Christians to abandon their internal disputes in favour of a common defence. The power of Byzantium had been undermined by the Seljuks for three centuries. Its decline in importance was to the benefit of the Italian mercantile republics, especially Venice and Genoa, which thus became the lords over the Levant. With the rise of the Ottomans, they lost this growth in power once again and with the shift of global trade brought about by the discovery of America, the Mediterranean area became a region of subordinate importance from a power politics point of view.

But the galleys of the North Italian merchants still dominated and when in 1381 Genoa also lost a long war against Venice, it retained Famagusta until 1464 and raked in tribute payments from Cyprus. In 1426, the island was struck by the Egyptians – a late act of revenge for Peter I's attack on Alexandria – and also had to pay annual duties to them. In 1427, the exorbitant burdens which had been passed on to the population led to a peasants' revolt which was put down violently. While the serfs had hardly the wherewithal to eke out their existence, regardless of what was happening, the rulers indulged in hunting with falcons, hounds and leopards which were cared for by their own servants.

In 1453, Byzantium fell, and the kingdoms in the Balkans which could have held up the advance of the Ottomans were weakened and torn by inner conflicts. Europe was drawn into the defensive action against the Moslems. There was no time to think about the defence of an island in the remote Middle East which had become unimportant. The fall of Constantinople also brought a burgeoning dream to nought: The Cypriot King John II married as his second wife Helena, daughter of the Despot of Morea and Duke of Sparta from the Palaeologue dynasty. She ensured a better status for the orthodox church, Greek became the second official language alongside French and the natives had fresh hope of a renewed link with Byzantium, especially after the uncle of the queen, Constantine XI, ascended the throne in Constantinople in 1448. The dream lasted scarcely five years. After the defeat of this still largest city of the Christian Middle Ages, just as in the case of the Latin Christians after the fall of Acre, the Greek element was strengthened by the many refugees. Helena made sure of an honourable reception for them until her own and John's death in 1458; afterwards Latin suppression dominated again.

Helena's and John's daughter Charlotte held her own on the throne for just two years. Then a 'Bastard', the son of John II and his mistress Marietta Flatri, succeeded in usurping the throne with the help of the Mamelukes. Charlotte held on to Kyrenia for a further four years, but the hope that her European relatives would support the reconquest from this port city was dashed. In 1474, Charlotte left Rhodes where she had found shelter with the Knights of St. John. From 1478 to 1481 in Cairo, she asked unsuccessfully for help for her return to the throne. In 1485, she abdicated officially and died in Rome in 1487.

Her adversary and half-brother, James II, himself fell victim to a plot which the Venetians contrived with their usual cunning; he became engaged to the Venetian merchant's daughter Catharina Cornaro whose parents owned large estates on Cyprus. The last king of Cyprus dealt with the Genoese alone whom he starved and then drove out with a carefully arranged campaign. But he needed a powerful ally against the Turks. So it was of little help to him that he was fully aware of what was at the back of the Venetians' minds when he finally married Catharina in 1472 after hesitating for a long time; he and his scarcely one year old son died in 1473 in unclear circumstances. In 1489, his widow abdicated after fifteen years of sham rule. Venice, which had 'adopted' her in 1474 and had ruled in fact since then, now officially annexed the island.

Under the yoke of the Signoria

The impoverished Frankish nobility, a group of some 300 persons, lost their influence, if not also their estates. The Venetians administered their property with an ingenious system of offices. The highest officials were replaced every two years so that, despite the distance,

Fig. 6: The 'Othello Tower' in Famagusta, a legacy of the Venetians. Above the gate can be seen their heraldic animal.

complete control was ensured. The governors acted solely in the interest of the Lagoon City; they took no account of local sensitivities; each inhabitant was regarded as suspect. Unlike the Franks who shared certain of the country's interests if only on account of their link to their fiefs, the Venetians were concerned only to draw money from the island and to safeguard the military strategic use. The exploitation of the rural population, which had already been considerable under the Lusignans, now took on unscrupulous forms.

In 1517, the Ottomans also advanced to Egypt and Cyprus was surrounded by the expanding state of the Turks. Venice reacted with the strengthening of the fortresses: Kyrenia, Famagusta and Nicosia were protected by bastions; the old castles in the Pentadaktylos were razed, Paphos and Limassol abandoned. The defence measures had to be financed by the population and implemented by means of compulsory labour. The resentment felt about these burdens exploded in a revolt in 1562 which remained just as unsuccessful as the two previous ones. When less than ten years later Lala Mustafa arrived on the island with a large army, the indigenous population was more for the Turks than against them, and despite the extensive fortifications the Republic of St. Mark was able to hold the island for scarcely a month. Only Famagusta put up resistance for a certain period of time. In 1571, Cyprus was incorporated into the Ottoman Empire.

Sword and Crescent

First relief and disappointment

The Ottomans governed Cyprus no differently from their other conquests, and that meant they integrated the island into the existing empire. In general, the Moslems

Fig. 7: The gothic St. Sophia Cathedral in Nicosia, constructed 1208-1326, coronation cathedral of the Lusignans, partially destroyed by earthquakes in 1491 and 1547. After the Ottoman conquest, the minaret and the prayer niche pointing towards Mecca were added. Still the Selimiye Mosque today.

by no means forced Christians to convert, they 'just' had to pay a poll tax. The Orthodox Church received its old position back, the Metropolitan took up his see in Nicosia again and had a certain influence on the decisions of the new ruling powers. Serfdom was abolished, the land of the Frankish nobles was distributed among Greeks. The Ottoman structures which were determined by Islamic law and had made the state the strongest power of that time in the European, as well as the North African and Asia Minor areas, were transferred from the mainland to the island. But when Cyprus came to the Ottoman Empire, the world power had already passed its zenith. The last victory in open battle had been won in 1541, the great expansions of the territory of the state were a thing of the past. The empire's military organisation was based on the Janissaries in the capital and a cavalry distributed around the countryside, both of whom were rewarded with livings. If it was no longer possible to award any more new livings, the existing ones had to be divided up. But then they no longer fulfilled their function, because an increase in rural productivity was not in sight under the conditions prevailing and any increase in duties was only possible at the risk that there would no longer be any incentive for the peasants to produce. In so far, the economic strength of the Ottoman Empire was dependent on gaining land; without any new domains, it was no longer possible to maintain the superbly trained elite troops. Therefore, the end of the expansion at the same time meant the end of economic stability. In addition, world-wide changes had had negative influences. With the discovery of America, but also on account of the constant wars in the Mediterranean, the main trade routes shifted to the Atlantic and Pacific. As well as this, there were the huge quantities of silver and other precious metals which the Spaniards in particular found in their colonies, undermining the value of the Turkish silver currency. A chain of various factors caused prices to rise about 250% within a period of 20 years; that for its part indirectly brought about an increase in the tax burden of 600%.

These economic difficulties above all led to a decadence in the formerly so successful Ottoman system. Bribes balanced out the office holders' losses in income, but the corruption led to an extremely rapid decline in competence. A downright sale of offices, later indeed an auction of offices set in, even among the troops. It was no longer the trained, capable persons, deployed according to their performance, who were given the posts, but those who produced the most money. One example for the at times strange effects which the influence of men linked with this, who had no longer undergone the traditional training in the Janissaries or been through Islamic centres of education, was the conquest of Cyprus. The campaign was undertaken at the advice of a Jew, Joseph Nassi, who had had to flee from po-

Fig. 8: The aqueduct near Larnaca financed by Abu Beke, the only pasha of Cyprus about whom the chronicles report good things. Nowadays it stands in the middle of a prosperous new housing area. It was still in use until the thirties in our century.

groms in Spain and had found refuge in the Ottoman Empire. Against the doubts of the Grand Vezir who was actually responsible for the business of government, he convinced Sultan Selim II that he should pocket the last Christian bastion in the Eastern Mediterranean which had virtually become an Ottoman inland lake.

Under the rule of Selim II, corruption and the purchase of offices assumed disastrous proportions. Both methods, which were intended to cover the growing financial demand, allowed the crisis at the end of the sixteenth century to develop into a permanent problem and brought about a feudalisation of society. Whereas in Europe early-capitalist conditions were beginning to show their dynamism, the successor empire to Byzantium stagnated, and in a strangely parallel development local big landowners became ever more powerful while the central government had ever less influence. The state controls failed, the impoverishment of large sections of the population took its course. Many left their hereditary place as peasant, soldier or craftsman and joined renegade bands. Many revolts assumed such proportions that it was not possible to bring them under control even with the greatest deployment of military force. At times, the government had to come to terms with the insurgents.

This development applied for the whole Empire. Immediately after the hostilities ceased, newly conquered Cyprus had first-hand experience of the decadent conditions. The sigh of relief was of short duration. Not only did the hoped-for regeneration fail to materialise, the privation grew worse and led to a rapid decline in population. But land without people to till the soil brings no profit. In this respect, the highest Turkish administrative authority, the Divan, solved two problems at one stroke. Peasants were brought in from Anatolia so that the land would be cultivated, but also to take the edge off the anger there which was being repeatedly vented in uprisings.

A time of agony

With the settlement of twenty thousand persons from mainland Turkey, a problem was created, from the effects of which the island suffers today. From the outset, the immigrants lived spread over the whole of Cyprus and this mixed settlement structure remained until 1974. Hatred between the two ethnic groups only developed in the course of time. In general, national conflicts only gained in explosiveness after 1800, whereas in the seventeenth and eighteenth centuries Turks and Greeks suffered too much under the same repressive measures and hardships for them to be at enmity with one another. As the Greek clergy had already allowed themselves to be roped in at a profit to themselves in 1589 to carry out Ottoman directives, which were concerned for the most part with skimming off taxes, it was more the authorities which were the object of anger. Admittedly, the fact that Christians were legally in a worse position and in practice at a considerable disadvantage, ensured resentment right from the outset. However, the religious antagonism was eased by the comparatively generous attitude of the Moslems towards Christians. Even the poll tax should not just be regarded as a means of bringing pressure to bear. Originally, it was a kind of substitute for military service which the Moslems had to perform whereas those of other faiths were not allowed to participate.

Economic decline and political circumstances in the Ottoman Empire led to a steady decline in the number of inhabitants. In the mid-eighteenth century there were about 84,000 inhabitants, 44% Christians and 56% Moslems. Uncertainty and unrest marked the age. There were no impulses, no incentives, at the most a period of respite now and again for a few decades. It was of little help that, in addition to their fiscal levies, the bishops were conceded a right of intervention directly with the Grand Vezir in Istanbul; ultimately, it was still just money which counted which the pasha entrusted with running Cyprus had to send to the Sublime Porte, the Sultan's palace in the capital. A century later, in 1754, the Archbishop of Cyprus was recognised as Ethnarch, thus as the leader of the Cypriot Christians. Admittedly, this was only official confirmation of the position which he already held in fact. Hardly ten years later, a doubling of the tax burden triggered off a revolt which was borne equally by Greeks and Turks; they murdered the Turkish gover-

nor without succeeding in bringing about a fundamental change in conditions.

Army reform and civil rights

In the meantime, admittedly, the balance of power on the world stage had changed fundamentally. Russia had become an important nation and Catherine II was throwing a greedy eye at Turkish territory from Asia Minor to India. In order to achieve this ambitious conquest, she wanted to talk Austria, Venice and France round to concerted action. In the course of this, Venice was to receive Cyprus among other territories as booty. In view of the threatening gestures by the Orthodox tsarist realm, the Sultan decided on an attack on the Russian fleet in the Black Sea. Only Austria supported the tsarina, but, on account of the effects of the French Revolution, it had to break off its campaign in 1791 without having achieved anything, while Russia was able to push its frontier forward a little, even though by nothing like the intended amount. In addition, the Turkish fleet was practically destroyed with the result that the Russian fleet was able to cruise in the Eastern Mediterranean while the Cypriots not only groaned under the special taxes ordered on account of the war, but in addition had to pay for the expansion of the defensive installations.

The renewed defeat of the Turkish forces, one of many, now finally led to the insight that reforms were necessary in the Ottoman Empire – admittedly first of all only by Selim III. The young sultan found himself confronted with massive resistance and, in addition, was surprised by Napoleon's campaign against Egypt. The country on the Nile was albeit in the meantime more just formally subject to Ottoman sovereignty. The Sultan allied briefly with the British against the French and won this war. But the reforms fell by the wayside; Selim was deposed and strangled by the Janissaries.

A little later, Mahmud II acceded to the throne, he too was willing to make reforms, but more cautious. Schools on the western model were established, high authorities renamed into ministries and the wearing of European clothing was ordered in cities. There was still a lack of any insight in the administrative apparatus into the need for essential reforms. Mahmud for his part found

Fig. 9: Troodos landscape with reafforested areas – a legacy of the British who thus increased the wooded area from 2% to 18% of the island area. For the most part Aleppo pines were planted, at higher altitudes cedars.

himself confronted with the burgeoning nationalism of the peoples within his Empire which gave new force to the uprisings. The last wars, in their turn, had led to an increase in the burden of duties and with the impulse given by Western Europe there were uprisings by the Serbs and Greeks. The latter succeeded in establishing a Greek state in the Peloponnese which was able to count on West European support. In passing it may be observed that there was a fundamental misunderstanding between the volunteers from the North and the Greeks. The Europeans still thought of ancient Greece, but the Greeks meant the Byzantine Empire when they dreamed of the restoration of their territory. Before the spark of liberty jumped over to Cyprus, the governor of the island organised a massacre of Orthodox inhabitants which nipped any revolt in the bud. The archbishop, three bishops and over 500 Greeks were executed and murdered in July 1821; confiscations and terror lasted for weeks. After the preliminary works under Mahmud II, his son and successor Abdülmecid I proclaimed the abolition of tax farming in 1840, and thus the introduction of tax burdens fixed by the state which were intended to be free of the arbitrariness of office holders. Jews and Christians were granted the same rights as the Moslems by law, the judicial system was reorganised, the boundaries of the provinces were redrawn on the French pattern, a newspaper and a bank were established. But the measures were not implemented efficiently, either in Egypt, where in the same year Talaat Effendi arrived specially as new governor, or in the Ottoman Empire as a whole. The second attempt in 1856 also brought only partial successes. The reforms seeped away in official channels; anyone who had previously profited from the system, procured weapons for himself or protested to the highest authorities. But internal administrative reason also led to a withdrawal of or delay in enforcing the firmans. Nevertheless, conditions did improve: on Cyprus schools and hospitals were constructed; hygienic innovations made their appearance so that the population nearly tripled. The economic problems, inflation and unpredictable burdens remained.

The conflict between the Ottomans and Russia flared up again and again, bringing the weakened Empire new defeats, such as in 1853/54 in the Crimean War. In 1877/78, the Sultan signed a disastrous peace treaty in order to save his capital. Now, admittedly, the Russians became too strong for the British who saw their trade routes in danger. Up to then, the Ottoman guild economy, which had remained on a medieval level and was thus uncompetitive, had brought them huge profits. Otto von Bismarck offered himself as an 'honest broker' at the Congress of Berlin in 1878, and in return for their moderate policy towards the Ottoman Empire, the Sultan ceded control over Cyprus to the British. The island passed formally into the British Empire in November 1914 when it was annexed after Turkey entered the war on the side of the Central Powers. In fact, the year 1878 is decisive; the sea route to India ran past Cyprus through the Suez Canal, which had opened in 1869. In addition, the British Empire was laying claims to the Middle East and Egypt. All this gave the island its strategic importance back for a short time.

Under the Union Jack

The greatest gain from British rule for the Cypriots was the legal security which came to the island with the British, and the ending of nepotism. Already in 1882, Cyprus received a constitution, completely in the tradition of British colonial policy. Linked with this was a new system of courts with civil and criminal jurisdiction, as well a supreme appellate instance. The administration worked efficiently. The cadastral land survey as the basis for taxation was reorganised in accordance with modern standards. The peaceful transfer of sovereignty was also fortunate, there was no devastation through fighting as there had been at previous changes of rule.

Otherwise, however, there was little cause for pleasure. Ottoman penal law was not abolished until 1928, the land law only in 1946; the tax system remained as it had been. Levies which burdened the island's budget disproportionately still had to be paid. The Ottoman gendarmerie was also taken on. Relatively little of the money which the island earned was invested here. As a result, agriculture in particular only recovered slowly. Once again the inhabitants had believed in a liberator but yet another exploiter had come to rule the island in accordance with requirements which did not correspond to those of the natives.

Cyprus was only ruled by military governors at the beginning. The first high commissioners, Sir Garnet Wolseley and Sir Robert Biddulph, were appointed by the Foreign Office; their successors, civilians, were under the Colonial Office. The island's military importance waned with the conquest of Egypt in 1882.

The infrastructure was gradually improved. Roads, bridges and railways were constructed, the ports improved, reafforestation projects were implemented and public health and hygiene expanded – the bases for the economic upswing. An important decision was taken in the education sector: classes were held in Greek or Turkish respectively; the education system and curricula were based on the Greek or Turkish model.

Initially the Greeks, who accounted for about three-quarters of population at the time of the British takeover, hoped that Britain would allow them to unite with Greece just like the other Greek islands. With the argument that the agreement with the Sultan would not allow this, their request was refused and any real right to take a share in political decisions was prevented. There was, it is true, a nationally mixed 'Legislative Council', but the High Commissioner with his right of veto was able to rule at any time in London's sense.

Union with Greece was contrary to the interests of the British who used the island as a base and source of revenue and did not want to grant it independence. Great Britain did, it is true, offer Greece Cyprus in 1915 in return for Greece's entry into the war – but, firstly at that time the Greeks wanted to preserve their neutrality and, secondly, the gesture was dictated by the concrete interests of a particular historical moment: The offer was provoked by Bulgaria's entry on the Austro-Turkish side. When Greece did indeed enter the war a year later on the British side, the latter did not repeat their offer.

Against this background, co-operation between the British and Turkish-Cypriots developed almost inevitably better than that between the British and the Greek-Cypriots. Here, as so often in their colonies, the British exploited the differences between the ethnic groups in the sense of 'divide et impera' – divide and rule. They treated the Greeks and the Turks in each case as Greeks and Turks, and by no means as Cypriots.

After the 1914-1918 war, the world had changed: the Ottoman Empire gave way to the Turkish Republic; tensions with the Greeks living on the Aegean coat of Asia Minor led to corrections to the agreements made at the end of the war which were fixed in the Treaty of Lausanne of 1923. One of the results of this treaty was that the Turks laid no further claim to Cyprus. The British argument against the union of the island with Greece was thus no longer valid, but that did not cause them to change their opinion.

In 1925, Cyprus became a crown colony with the political rights of the inhabitants becoming more restricted rather than expanded. Also the share of Cypriot taxes levied on the island originally as a tribute to Turkey still had to be paid. This was accepted very reluctantly so long as Cyprus still profited from the world-wide economic upswing of the 'golden twenties'. But after it collapsed here as everywhere else in 1929, the readiness for violent action spread. The cause of the disturbances was the 1931 budget; the Greeks were no longer willing to accept the tribute payments. On 17 October, the Bishop of Larnaca proclaimed union with Greece and called for civil disobedience. He founded a radical party representing the Enosis idea (*enosis:* Greek for unity). In Nicosia, insurgents burned down the colonial administration buildings. British soldiers brought from Egypt quickly suppressed the revolt, the leading figures were sent into exile and the Greek Cypriots had to pay for the damage caused. Civil rights were restricted, the press censured, the see of the Archbishop who had died in 1933 was not refilled. All this did not prevent the Greek

Fig. 10: The once so busy beaches of Famagusta are nowadays deserted, the hotels unused – except for one from which the complex lying opposite was photographed.

Cypriots with the Orthodox Church at their head from continuing to strive for union with Greece.

At the end of the thirties, the situation relaxed a little. Britain took cautious steps towards democracy and in 1941 permitted political parties. In the meantime, through the founding of the Turkish Republic, Turkish national awareness increased; they founded pro-Turkish organisations. The polarisation of both ethnic groups took on irreversible dimensions.

After the Second World War too, the hopes of political self-determination were disappointed. The new Labour government in London did, it is true, endeavour to create representative governments in the colonies, but the Greek Cypriots were not striving for independence, but wanted union with Greece. The Archbishop elected in 1947, Leontios of Paphos, coined the slogan 'Enosis and only Enosis' and rejected every other solution. An officer of Cypriot extraction, George Grivas, who was serving in the Greek army organised armed resistance (EOKA) from 1950. Training camps and arms caches were established and in 1955 bloody disturbances broke out. EOKA's explosives blew up the colonial relationship, but did not lead to union with Greece.

Enosis and Civil War

After some tactical manoeuvres, the British came to the conclusion that military bases on Cyprus would suffice and they therefore did not need the whole island. They secured two bases for themselves with a total area together of some 150 km², both are still British sovereign territory right down to the present. In November 1959, Archbishop Makarios III was elected first state president and Dr. Fazil Küçük vice-president. In August 1960, Cyprus became independent. The first years were marked by a considerable upswing in the economy, but Cyprus had a constitution the unalterable nature of which was laid down in the treaties with the United Kingdom, Greece and Turkey, and proved difficult to implement in practice. The state president was always to be a Greek Cypriot, the vice-president a Turkish Cypriot. The prescribed proportional allocation of offices applied at all levels down to the communal administration. Both sides had a right of veto; only too often the Turkish side used it to bring the government's work practically to a standstill. In the army and police, the Turks were intentionally disproportionately represented measured by their 18% share of the population with a 40% and 30% share respectively, a provision which was not implemented. Both sides formed secret armed units. Military forces from Greece, Great Britain and Turkey were stationed on the island. All this did not help to reduce mistrust.

In 1963, Makarios's attempt at supplementing the constitution failed with Ankara's brusque rejection anticipating a reaction by the Turkish-Cypriot side. In the inflamed atmosphere, a small incident led to an escalation of violence. There were over 1000 dead, mainly on the Turkish side. Despite economic disadvantages, about one quarter of the Turkish Cypriots withdrew into enclaves. UN troops have been on the island since that time.

In 1967, the military in Greece organised a putsch; a junta now ruled in Athens which believed it could solve the Cyprus problem in no time at all in the sense of enosis. The crisis came to a head again, but diplomatic activities succeeded in saving the situation once again. The enosis idea lost in popularity in Cyprus. In 1965, 18% of the Greek Cypriot inhabitants were for union with economically weaker Greece. But enosis activists, such as Grivas, continued to fight for it. They regarded Makarios as a traitor; on 15 July 1974, Greek units attacked the Presidential Palace and proclaimed a counter-president. Five days later, Turkish troops attacked Cyprus and occupied over a third of the island's territory. Some 180,000 Greek Cypriots fled to the south, about 40,000 Turkish Cypriots went to the north. Since then, communication between the two parts of the country has been practically broken off, the situation has become bogged down, and the hope that both communities might come together again appears a woolly-headed fantasy. The free part of the republic coped with the enormous economic problems quickly; in the Turkish north they lasted longer as the economy there is almost completely dependent on Turkey. But in both parts, nobody forgets what has happened; the longing, sadness and anger about events which overwhelmed the people here remain.

The Byzantine Empire

Three centuries after the conquest of Constantinople, Edward Gibbons wrote a six volume History of the Roman Empire dealing with the period from 180 to 1453 AD. With two key words in the title, he expressed a still familiar estimate exactly: decline and fall are said to characterise the empire. The ever diminishing territory and an emperor who, shortly before the destruction of his empire, which had been reduced to a mere city state, had to beg for help from his European neighbours, seemed to confirm this judgement. But what other empire has had a historically decisive influence for over a millennium?

The Roman Empire reached its greatest extent around 115 AD. The enormous area and the innumerable languages, cults and customs apparently exceeded the dimensions of what it was possible to maintain as a whole. The tribes immigrating from the north-east, revolt against Roman uniformity, but also internal power struggles led to an incessant sequence of wars and insurrections subjecting the economic and social structures to hard endurance tests. The Greek eastern half, which had come to the empire relatively late and was economically stronger, was better able to stand these problems than the West; by means of fundamental reforms it succeeded in reviving state unity several times. This ability to create something new from ruins, reviving what had been earlier in form and its conception of itself, is the fascinating aspect of Byzantine history. The conservative trait, which is so especially noticeable for us in Byzantine art, should not mislead us about the profound changes. It was the strength for creative adjustment to completely changed conditions which made it possible to build up a tradition. The link with the idea of the Roman state was preserved visibly in the Greek form of the word 'Roman'. The Byzantines described themselves as *'Rhomaioi'*. Never was the idea of restoring the Roman Empire as a whole completely abandoned. Even in times of the greatest difficulties, it was the ideal of Byzantine policy.

The continuation of the notion of the Roman state makes it impossible to state clearly from when the Byzantine Empire existed. From a legal point of view, the continuity of the Roman Empire, until Byzantium ceased to exist, is clear. But, in keeping with historical reality, sometime between the laying of the foundation stone for Constantinople and the revival of the Empire's fortunes under Herakleios, the changes had reached such an extent that the Classical Imperium had become a Medieval Empire.

One of the decisive events on this way was the division of the Mediterranean area by Islam. At almost the same time, the West made itself independent, a process which led to a first major stir with the crowning of Charlemagne as emperor. Out of the confusion of the migration of the peoples and the buried Roman tradition in Europe grew a third centre of power, religiously different despite the profession of Christianity, that initially adopted culturally decisive impulses from the East. However, the constant struggle for the claim to leadership opened up intellectual rifts which were scarcely less deep and dangerous than those to Islam. The third important factor for Byzantium was the advance of the Slavs into the Balkans. After the main wave of the migration of the people had already ebbed away, they pushed forward like a wedge between the Greek East and the Latin West; a process which also fell in the period between the seventh and ninth centuries. The Slavonic occupation and settlement of the land is one of the reasons why the Islamic expansion was not experienced as a common threat to the West and defence was not co-ordinated. The changes forced fundamental changes onto the Byzantine administration and army that represented the main support for the emperor against the claims of the land-owning aristocracy which were tearing the Empire apart. So long as it was possible to maintain a balance between these forces, however tricky, Byzantium remained a great power.

New capital, new religion

There are two decisions dating back to Constantine the Great to which Byzantine history owes its continuity to a considerable extent. The first one concerns the choice of a new capital. Constantine raised the old Greek city of Byzantion to the seat of government which was solemnly consecrated as the city of Jesus Christ on 11 May 330. And that already touches on the second decision: the link with Christianity which began under Constantine. The anchoring of the emperor's absolute rule in the universal religion, the legitimisation of the one emperor through the one God created an ideal basis for the coherence of the Empire.

At the same time, the unity of Christendom became a central problem for the state. It affected government power so directly that the pressing problems of the young religion could not be left just to the ecclesiastics. But the imperial interventions often only settled the conflicts in a rough and ready way; at times they even fomented them. This is true especially for the North African and Middle Eastern parts of the Empire with the oldest episcopal sees, Jerusalem, Alexandria and Antioch, which claimed the power to decide on matters concerning the faith for themselves and did not always back council resolutions from the capital. The difference in opinions between Oriental and Greek territories remained virulent until the Arab conquest, also promoting the latter.

In addition to internal church disputes, Imperial decrees also regulated the suppression of paganism. Whereas the followers of Jesus of Nazareth had been subject to persecutions until the recognition of Christianity, now things changed. Between 319 and 435, again and again ever sharper laws were promulgated against the pagans and the exercise of the ancient cults. There were anti-pagan riots in the fifth century, even systematic persecutions. On the other hand, numerous ancient customs and opinions found their way into Christian rites. The victory of the new religion was a protracted, tough process which dragged on for many generations and had still not been completed even in the 6th and 7th centuries.

After the fall of the western Roman Empire, the new capital had no competitors; created as capital of a state already in existence, it developed, unlike European capitals, independently of its hinterland. This fabulously rich metropolis with the imperial palace, the aristocrats' houses and the often concealed luxury of its merchants and officials admittedly contained enough social explosive to endanger even the emperor's position from time to time.

Renovatio imperii

At a first glance, a brilliant start, at a second, however, the seed of the deep crisis of the 7th century, is the to a large extent successful restoration of the Roman Empire as a whole under Justinian I. He was able to build on the consolidation of the state finances under his predecessors, he quelled an uprising by the lower classes in Constantinople and made peace with the Persians who had been threatening the eastern frontier for centuries. After that, he concentrated all his forces on the subjection of the Teutonic kingdoms in Italy, Spain and North Africa which did, it is true, nominally acknowledge East Roman supremacy, but did not, however, want anything to do with an actual dominance by Byzantium. Corresponding to this, in modern terms, foreign policy objective of a '*renovatio imperii*' was the ultimately failed restoration of inner order, prohibition of the buying of offices, the struggle against the growth in the nobility's power, and much else. The real and surviving brilliance of the Justinian epoch is based on the great construction activity giving new impulses, especially in the field of church construction.

The extraordinary successes of Justinian's military campaigns obscured the omissions. The danger which threatened the Empire through the immigration of the Slavs was recognised too late; the peace made with

Fig. 11: The originally Byzantine fortress near Kyrenia, one of many which were further used and changed structurally by the Franks, Venetians and Turks. Accordingly little is left of the original structure.

Persia was bought for too high a price and did not last long. The religious conflict between the Monophysitic provinces (in particular Egypt and Syria) and the Orthodox ones put the Empire to a severe test which from its violence may be compared with the wars between Protestants and Catholics in the 16th and 17th centuries in the West. The achievement of a balance between the social classes and the revival of production and trade failed because the monetary requirements prevented any sensible limit on the collection of taxes. After Justinian's death in 565, the Empire disintegrated within a few decades.

In 602, a general, Phocas, came to power by a coup. Under his regime of terror which led to a civil war, Byzantium slid into a catastrophe. In the Balkans, Slavonic and Bulgarian tribes established their own states, while in Asia Minor the Persians stood before the gates of Constantinople. The age of imperial greatness was irrevocably over, although the Empire did recover again from this almost impossible position to become a considerable power factor in the early Middle Ages.

Hercules Herakleios

In 610, Herakleios, the son of the governor of Carthage, a Byzantine military province in North Africa, arrived and deposed Phocas. This further usurpation marks the beginning of a new, transformed Byzantine state. Herakleios needed twelve years in order to prepare the remains of the Empire for a counter-offensive. He was helped in this by Byzantine diplomacy with its rich tradition and the progress made in military techniques, but also a reform of the administration and command structures. The reasons for his huge success are unclear on account of the poor position with regard to sources, but he apparently recognised the signs of the time and was also an excellent strategist. In order not to expend himself in a war on two fronts, he made peace with the enemies in the West. Avars and Slavs had besieged Constantinople for months in 618 and 626 simultaneously with the Persians; admittedly, their fighting power had suffered so much as a result that Herakleios was able to negotiate tolerable terms for Byzantium. Instead of now fighting skirmishes with the Persians for each individual tract of land, Herakleios moved his headquarters to the Caucasus and attacked the Sassanids at the centre of their power. In 627, the old main enemy had to accept its last, final defeat.

Herakleios led Byzantium to a new climax. Admittedly, the territory which he had now won was reduced to a third of its size even during the period of his rule. The year in which he had started the Byzantine counter-offensive was the year of the *Hegira*, the beginning of the Islamic era, 622 AD. The development of the third monotheistic religion was so rapid that it completely escaped the Byzantine spies. The first attack in 630 was regarded in Constantinople as an unimportant border incident. In 638 Jerusalem was Moslem; in 640 Syria became part of the Caliphate, in 642 Egypt. Within six years, Herakleios lost his economically strongest, also intellectually rich provinces, and war on two fronts remained the fate of Byzantium: in the north-west against the Slavs and Bulgarians, in the south-east against the Arabs. For 200 years the confrontation maintained the character of a struggle for very existence of the empire.

Survival through reforms

The Byzantines succeeded in adapting to the requirements of a permanent state of war. Justinian I had already abolished the separation of civil and military power typical for the late Roman Empire in the newly acquired provinces of Italy and Tunisia. His immediate successors, especially Maurice, continued spinning this thread and were thus able to record some successes against the Slavs. Herakleios also further expanded the theme system. It reached its final form under his successors. A theme was an administrative district which was under the rule of a military commander (*strategos*). The term *thema* may probably be traced back to the bundle of files in which the soldiers within a province were recorded. The *Strategos*, that is a Byzantine title, was the military commander and administrative head in one. He was able to act independently in many things and did not have to waste time obtaining permission beforehand. The short decision-making paths made the state elastic without seriously threatening the Emperor's claim to final leadership.

The governor levied the taxes for his district and used the money for the expenditure incurred there. The Emperor financed the central bureaucracy and the palace from the surpluses which the state monopoly enterprises earned, as well as from customs duties and special levies. The pay for the soldiers in the relatively small but superbly trained army was saved by means of the Stratiot system. A stratiot received land and from what he earned from that he had to pay for his equipment and his livelihood. He was employed for the defence of the area in which this piece of land lay and therefore had – in contrast to a purely mercenary army – a personal interest in the outcome of a battle. In addition, these soldiers' settlements served the population policy. There were repeated compulsory resettlements of whole tribes, Slavs, Armenians, Cypriots, etc. were transplanted to areas which had become depopulated as a result, for instance, of plague epidemics or military campaigns. This was also intended to take people away from the enemy.

In addition to the stratiot units came the fleet which was provided by two maritime themes. The Byzantine navy was the decisive means of warfare, already because no other state in the Middle Ages had such a long coast. Against the Arabs, who quickly acquired an effective fleet of their own through the Monophysites in Syria, the Byzantines were able to use an invention which was kept so secret that its exact composition is unknown even today. This was what was known as 'Greek fire' by which a petroleum mixture was thrown onto the sea by a siphon and then ignited so that the enemy ship caught fire. Without this weapon, Constantinople would hardly have survived the frequent Moslem sieges. The fact that the Empire collapsed in the 13th century under the onslaught of the Crusaders was due above all to the decline of the fleet, the result of the insidious financial haemorrhage.

Iconoclasm

Among the curious features of Byzantine history is the linking of efficiency and iconoclasticism in this period of resistance. Herakleios's successors warded off the simultaneous advance of Slavs and Arabs with varying and towards the end of the seventh century very moderate success. In the Balkans, the Empire of the Bulgarians came into being, a powerful and aggressive enemy, and summer after summer Moslem armies invaded Asia Minor.

In 717, a man from northern Syria came to the throne through a revolt, Leo III. He too was an excellent military leader whom soldiers trusted unquestionably. He and his son and successor, Constantine V, succeeded in stopping the Arab advance. The power of the provincial governors, over a hundred years after the introduction of the theme system, had reached an extent which was becoming dangerous for the central power, and Leo countered this by splitting the themes up into smaller units. He also strengthened imperial power over the Empire in other ways. He took money for his campaigns – among other things – from the Church. Leo was convinced that portrayals of holy persons were idolatrous and utterly reprehensible. He therefore banned all figural imagery in religious art. This was in keeping with original Christian opinion and met with approval among many subjects. The majority, however, loved and revered the pictures and ascribed miraculous powers to them. A deep split resulted which lasted until into the ninth century. Especially under Leo's son Constantine V iconophiles were banned and executed.

One of the 'side products' of iconoclasm was the crowning of Charlemagne as emperor already mentioned above. Irene, the wife of Leo IV, who had left a ten year-old son at his death, succeeded in securing her rule as regent. She reintroduced the cult of images against great resistance; when her son took over rule, he withdrew this decision. On account of the scandal of his second marriage, Irene succeeded in having him deposed, had him blinded and ruled alone. But that allowed the Pope and the Frankish ruler the interpretation that the imperial throne was vacant, an interpretation which Constantinople naturally rejected. But Byzantium's position in Italy was completely undermined, so all that remained was the weak means of diplomatic protests. With the existence of two emperors, a part of the old world collapsed which had been based on the assumption of a universal empire.

The end of the iconoclastic controversy led to the first flowering of Byzantine art since Justinian I. Three hundred lean years were followed by three hundred fat ones. The loss of the south-eastern provinces, the militarisation of life through the themes and the permanent commitment of funds for defence expenditure had brought about an impoverishment of culture which was now surmounted. The adjustment had been successful and unleashed forces for creative processes. The mission in the Balkans and in Russia allowed the Orthodox Church, and with it Byzantine culture, to become the historically formative force there. The monk Cyril contributed particularly to this by developing the script named after him. It is used throughout the area of the Eastern Church, with the exception of the Greek areas.

Emperor Basil I

It was once again a usurper who brought the Byzantine Empire to new brilliance. Basil I entered the service of Emperor Michael III as a groom and succeeded in rising to the top. He became co-regent, a common procedure in late Antiquity and the Middle Ages to secure the succession, and had his predecessor murdered on 24.9.867.

After this unkind act, he proved himself an excellent ruler. He began to tackle the overdue legal reform and had the legal codes, which until then had still been compiled in Latin, revised in Greek and adapted to the considerably changed social realities since Justinian. In the course of this, the division of tasks between Church and Emperor was fixed. The patriarch was responsible for the salvation of the subjects' souls, the ruler for their physical well-being. The Greek language became binding for court titles, the emperor was called '*Basileus*' from then on, the Greek equivalent to the Latin '*Imperator*'.

Basil I laid the foundation for the military successes of his sons who led the Empire to its greatest expanse in the Middle Ages. In contrast to him, who had worked his way up from humble conditions, his children received an excellent education and were early initiated in the business of government.

Leo VI, who, after the death of his father in 886, continued his work, was given the epithet 'the Wise' already during his lifetime. Leo completed the legal reform and strengthened the position of the Emperor in the course of this. While a senate, as a vestige of Roman tradition, had still retained certain rights up to then, this institution was now abolished. Only the ruler could promulgate laws, even if he was himself still bound by those laws. The inner strength of the Empire permitted a restructuring of the themes which were made even smaller and deprived of their sub-units. Their leader was not so respected in rank as a commander of a unit of troops in the capital.

After Leo's death, the continuation of the dynasty was at risk. His son, Constantine VII, who had been born in a special purple red chamber in the palace, and thus received the epithet '*Porphyrogennetos*', was still too young. Leo's brother Alexander was luckless in his actions. After he too had died, the Bulgarian Tsar Simeon raised claims to the Byzantine throne and marched up to the walls of Constantinople with an army. Once again, the strategic position of the city proved a blessing; both parties started negotiations during which the acceptance of the title of a Bulgarian Tsar and the betrothal of Simeon's daughter to Constantine eased the tension. These concessions led to a palace revolt as a result of which the Empress-Mother Zoe came to power. With her intransigent attitude, she provoked new campaigns by the Bulgarian, involving heavy losses especially for Greece. The position was critical, the army weakened by several bitter defeats.

A man who was of humblest origin and had become an officer in the navy through a brilliant career struck while the iron was hot: Romanos Lekapenos rendered Zoe harmless, married his daughter to Constantine and became co-emperor. Tsar Simeon and his daughter had no chance against the agile upstart who pushed the young Constantine to one side and wanted to found a dynasty of his own. He was the first Emperor who wanted to get to grips with the problem of an over-powerful aristocracy with a law, but drought disasters and epidemics thwarted the success of the measure. In the war with the Bulgarians, he was able to impress with diplomacy and the military, so that in the end Simeon's son married Lekapenos's daughter. Conversely, Byzantium recognised Bulgaria as an independent ecclesiastic area, thus as an autocephalic archdiocese. The peace on the western front released forces for the eastern frontier.

In 944, Constantine VII overthrew Lekapenos and from 950 on reconquered the greatest part of Herakleios's territory. He was a scholar who wrote excellent history works; under his rule, the Empire did not just gain in territory, but also in intellectual greatness. Under his son, Romanos II, Nikephoros Phocas achieved decisive victories and married Romanos II's widow. As a result, a representative of the aristocracy came to power; and even if he was soon murdered: scarcely fifty years later the power of Byzantium was torn to threads by internal struggles for leadership.

The age of the Komnenes

The feudalisation of the themes, i.e. the servitude of the erstwhile military farmers who were no longer soldiers, and the absolute power of the nobles in their sector, took their course and undermined the state. After 200 years, the dynasty of the Macedonians became extinct with the death of Theodora in 1056 and officials took over the throne. The capable strategos Isaac I Komnenos was unable to reverse the development, and under his successor the danger, which five hundred years later was to mean the final end, became recognisable: The Turkic Seljuks went over to the offensive leading to a catastrophe during the reign of Romanos IV Diogenes. The defeat at Mantzikert in 1071 put an end to Byzantium's world-historical phase. In 1080, the nucleus of the later Ottoman state came into being.

At the same time, the tribe of the Pechenegs threatened the Empire in the north, the Normans in the west, the latter being especially dangerous as they had an army *and* a navy at their disposal. Through their enemy's internal dissensions they had an easy game so that Byzantium lost its possessions in Italy. That the Empire did not collapse is attributable solely to the skill of Alexios I KOMNENOS. Having come to power through a revolt, he was able to stabilise the position with Venetian assistance. In the hope of further assistance from troops, he promoted the idea of crusades, but then had to use his entire diplomatic skill to ensure that Byzantium did not disintegrate under this array of forces.

His successors did not succeed as well with their manoeuvring between the fronts. Manuel I plunged himself into the hazardous project of reconquering Italy and squandered valuable forces in the process. His pro-Latin ecclesiastical policy alienated him from his subjects. Temporary successes seemed to mark a change in trend, but in reality they accelerated the decline because the funds expended for this overtaxed the economic potentialities. Andronikos, who eliminated Manuel's son, arrested the collapse for a further moment. But his regime ended in 1189 in a reign of terror out of which the dynasty of the Angeloi succeeded to the throne shortly before the first collapse of Constantinople in 1204. The Byzantines were scattered among various small part empires, their former capital formed the centre of a Latin Crusader state. In Asia Minor, with his centre in Nicaea, Theodore Laskaris was able to consolidate his rule so far that he continued the East Roman tradition.

Grandiose conclusion

Once again, the Byzantines' masterly use of tactics triumphed. The Empire was restored from Nicaea and at the same time the last Byzantine dynasty, the Palaiologoi, came to power by a coup. Their age is marked by a cultural flowering completely untroubled by the political and economic decline. From no other period has so much evidence of art and science been preserved. It is impossible to imagine the Italian renaissance without the Greek element.

But the state of Byzantium, which attained European rank again for a last time and just for a few years under Michael VIII, failed to flourish any more. In the fourteenth century, the Balkans were lost to the Bulgarians and Serbs, Greece was devastated by the Catalans, Asia Minor conquered by the Ottomans. The inner strength was broken and disintegrated through civil wars, unrest and social tensions. The Empire now consisted only of its capital.

The Church stepped into the state's shoes. Monasteries and clergy gained more and more power; and after the second fall of Constantinople on 29.5.1453, they became the bearers of Byzantine culture, of the identity of the Greeks under Turkish-Ottoman rule, of the art of icons and frescoes. In it, Byzantium lives on in a new and revived form.

Fig. 12: Emperor Alexios I Komnenos is blessed by Christ. Miniature from the parchment manuscript 666, fol. 2r. in the Biblioteca Apostolica, Vatican, 12th century.

History of the Orthodox Church

Christianity traces itself back to the life, work, death and resurrection of Jesus of Nazareth whom many Jews regarded as the long-awaited Messiah, thus giving him the epithet '*Christos*', the Greek word for 'anointed one'. The historical Christ was born about seven years before the era bearing his name and crucified at about the age of 37. A community of followers came into being in Jerusalem who, in addition to their ties with the Jewish religion, believed in him as the Redeemer. Among them were many who spoke Greek, Jews who had returned from Greece and took a critical stance towards the Mosaic Law. Their leading exponent was Stephen who, according to the report in the Acts of the Apostles, was stoned to death by the Jews, thus becoming the first Christian martyr. With the expulsion of his comrades-in-arms from the city, the first wave of missionary work began, also among the Gentiles. A sharp conflict developed between Jewish and Gentile Christians which, after the destruction of Jerusalem in 70 AD, ended in the Gentile Christians' favour. The Jews' enmity towards the new religion was directed, among other things, against the notion that redemption could also be attained without complying with Mosaic Law. In the first century, it led to the most martyrs among the Christians, costing, among others, Barnabas in Cyprus his life. An anti-Christian attitude was also initially adopted by Paul who, after an experience leading to his conversion in about 31/32 AD, became the most important preacher of Jesus's message, although he had not got to know the founder in person.

Forty years after the Crucifixion, the first reports appeared setting down Jesus's work in writing; the Gospels were written down between shortly before 70 and shortly after 100 AD. The first Christians had still lived in the expectation that Christ would come again very soon. The longer this event was delayed, the greater the need for an organisation of their own became which would guarantee the faithful tradition of the message of redemption. As a result, the term 'church', which was derived from the Greek word *kuriakos* meaning 'of the master' and was originally used to mean the community, was transformed. It now became an institution. The existence of the office of bishop is documented from the turn of the first century; he was regarded as a successor to the Apostles and thus traced his authority indirectly back to Christ. He was to ensure the unity of the community. But for this purpose, Jesus's message had to be set down clearly, and as there was a considerable need for interpretation here, Christian teaching came into being, also in dispute with the pagan outside world, as apologetics, as defence not infrequently following the principle that attack is the best form of defence. A creed was formulated, about the correct form of which there was to be much discussion. Taking the reports about Jesus, an attempt was made to obtain directions for a righteous life. This included the sacrament of the Eucharist by which His memory was to be kept alive. From this developed gradually the third, now first meaning of the word church, the house of God in which the Eucharist is celebrated.

On the way to a state religion

Christianity initially spread especially in the East of the Roman Empire. From the mid-third century on, Christians were persecuted and suppressed several times, but at the beginning of the fourth century Emperor Constantine promoted the new religion. For the Roman state as well as for the early Christian church, the linking together meant a turning point. The link did not result in-

Fig. 13: Ruins of an early Christian basilica on Cyprus – Soli.

evitably from the previous development, but was the result of Constantine's far-sightedness. Considerable corrections were required – once again both in the state and in the church – so that the unequal parts would fit together. It was already an audacious venture to link together the pompous cult of the emperor with the doctrines of charity, selflessness and non-violence. Eusebius of Caesarea developed the theological justification for the omnipotence of the emperor in his argument from analogy. The *one* emperor corresponded to the *one* God. Emperor Constantine I let himself be buried as the 13th apostle, and alongside his throne a place remained empty for Jesus, whose deputy and co-regent he and his successors claimed to be. In contrast to the West, in the Orthodox area the Emperor retained his sacral competence; the theory of the two powers, which Pope Gelasius developed in the fifth century to differentiate from Constantinople's claims, did not correspond with the political reality in the East. In this lies one of the most important differences between East and West: the interpretation of the institution 'church' drifted ever further apart.

Whereas in the West it was able to achieve autonomy for itself owing to the lack of a central power thus forming a counterweight to state power, in the East it remained under imperial control. Even in the modern period, the idea of the separation of Church and State has not been able to gain acceptance.

Councils and schisms

At the time when the church became a state organ, the internal development of the organisation and the teaching was far from complete. Thus, especially in the initial phase, violent controversies occurred. There was the matter, for example, of the attitude towards Christians who did not accept the fate of a martyr during a persecution, but later wanted to return to the bosom of the church. This was settled in favour of a mild position. Another point of dispute was the question whether an ordination or baptism given by such an apostate might be recognised; here too a positive decision was taken. However, the majority of problems was caused by the differentiation from polytheism which was close to the

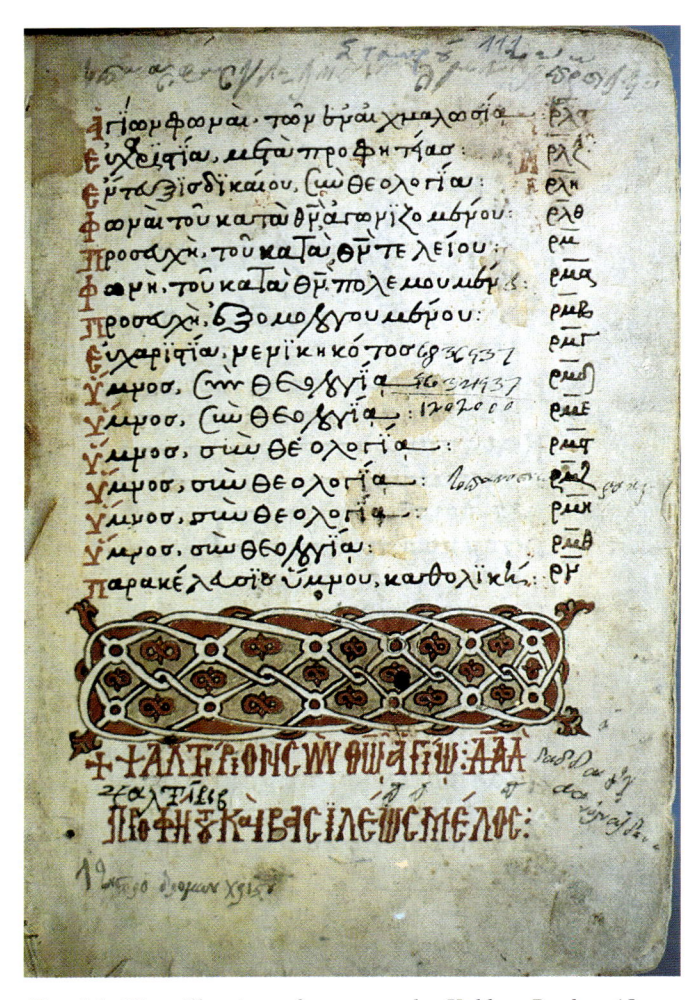

Fig. 14: First illuminated page on the Kykkos Psalter (Jerusalem, Stavrou, 111) from the year 1472, written by Symeon of Kykkos, Graeco-Byzantine.

doctrine of the Trinity of the Father, Son and Holy Ghost, and the question of how the interplay of man and God in Jesus Christ is to be understood: Was He above all a man who was inspired by God, but not Himself divine, because created by God, thus also not eternal? If the second answer had been accepted, known as Arian after the Alexandrine presbyter Areios, then for many believers the expectation of salvation, the redemption of the world, would have become doubtful. On the other hand, it was an understandable interpretation, and many endorsed it, including several emperors. The Church, however, rejected this solution. At the first ecumenical council in Nicaea, the problem was solved by the differentiation into being and hypostasis, form of appearance: Christ and God are one being with two forms of appearance. Arianism still lived on for a long time, it had not been eliminated by the council's decision, thus showing that questions of faith are not to be resolved, at least not always, by decree.

The dispute was by no means over with the pure equality of being of God and Christ; one could, as the Antiochian school did, regard the incarnation as the indwelling of God in the man Jesus, but also, as in Alexandrine teaching, also emphasise the divine part of His nature so much that the human part disappeared. In the solution of this question, the West stepped on the stage in the form of Pope Leo I who distinguished two natures in the one person Jesus Christ which existed alongside one another unmixed in Him, but working together. This complicated view had no chance in Egypt or Syria; there the decision of the Council of Chalcedon in 451 was rejected. The Orthodox church never overcame this Monophysitic split, the problem was only resolved with the Islamic conquest of these areas as it was favoured by its affinity in content to Islam. For several further centuries the Eastern church in the Caliphate played an important role. The indigenous Christians there only fell into discredit in the course of the crusaders' devastations.

The Emperors attempted several times to win back the renegade provinces by means of compromise solutions, but as a result it came to a separation from the West. The first schism between Pope and Patriarch lasted from 482 to 519. It was the prelude to an ever more profound alienation which had its background in competing claims for primacy. The spark which set off the next schism was the question whether pictures were idolatrous or harmless ecclesiastical tradition. Here too, the question of Christ's nature played a role, admittedly it was not a question of its doctrinal expression, but the meaning of the portrayal. All parties were agreed that the divine aspect could not be portrayed. For this reason, until the fourth century the Church had stood for a strict ban on portrayal. After the legalisation, many new believers came to church and as a concession to this mass, which was not thought out well theologically, the decoration of churches with images and pictures for per-

Fig. 15, 16: Initials 'O', 'T' from the prayer book for the St. Basil liturgy, MS 13 (now in the Library of the Monastery of St. Neophytos) from 1693, fol. 28r, 45v, written in Kykkos.

sonal piety on wooden boards, the icons, were initially tacitly tolerated and later promoted. Initially, the iconophiles had only educational arguments for this usage: the pictures were intended to consolidate what faith taught. Only in the course of the almost 150 year long dispute did John of Damascus in particular develop the theological justification: Christ was to be understood as the first image of God, and therefore all images were legitimate. The incarnations repeated in pictures preached grace and revelation. The iconoclasts, on the other hand, insisted on the sameness of nature which must exist between an image and original and which one could not ascribe to paintings on wood or limestone. But the view that the veneration of a picture was not intended for the picture, but the original, ultimately prevailed and temporarily restored unity with the West once again. On the Roman side, there had never been any support for iconophobe attitudes.

The breach with the West in the schism of 1054 came more by chance considering these profound differences, it remained almost unnoticed by contemporaries and was, at all events, not regarded as final. It was more the result of personal antipathies than a difference in substance. The unleavened bread used by the West for the Eucharist had to do for the accusations which the Patriarch of Constantinople, Michael Keroularios, made against

Rome, and, namely, because he wanted to harm the Byzantine governor in southern Italy. In view of the Norman attack on Sicily, an alliance between Byzantium and Rome would have seemed the obvious answer which Cerularius sought to prevent because it would have helped his personal enemy.

Nevertheless, the discussions of the following centuries prove that this separation was not the result of a chance rivalry, but in keeping with the intellectual divergences in both directions. Whereas in the West, with Thomas Aquinas, a rational theology, a theology on a high scholarly and intellectual level developed, the East was impelled by mysticism. Hesychasm found many supporters, particularly among monks. The word comes from the Greek *hesukhos,* quiet, and stands for mystical practices which were intended to make it possible to view God already on Earth. Hesychasm found its most eloquent representative in Gregorios Palamas. He differentiated between God's being and His energies which acted in the world and which human beings, as they are themselves the 'product' of these energies, can observe if they prepare themselves accordingly. By this, Palamas lastingly influenced the spiritual alignment of the East and its turn away from the West.

From the thirteenth century on, in view of the danger from the Turks, the Byzantine emperors attempted to achieve a reconciliation of standpoints between the two churches. The climax of these endeavours was the Union Council in Ferrara and Florence in 1439. But the union set down on paper remained worthless because the Orthodox clergy would not implement it and the military situation led to the catastrophe too soon for these measures to have been able to save Byzantium.

The Church as a national institution

Under Ottoman rule, the religious affiliation of the subjects determined their legal position. In this connection, the national unity already developed by the Orthodox Church was to its advantage. It was able to maintain a limited autonomy and look after the personal legal matters of the faithful (e.g. marriages), but also take on state tasks, such as tax collection. Important was the cultivation and continuation of the Greek language which formed the main identification element for the Orthodox in the area of the medieval Byzantine state.

Directly after the fall of Constantinople, the representatives of the Church concentrated on the maintenance of tradition and endeavoured to continue their everyday life and rites as uninterruptedly as possible. Towards the end of the sixteenth century, an attempt started in theological thinking to adapt the currents from the West and compensate for the deficits in scholarly treatment. With a time lag, in the age of European renaissance, a religious humanism was cultivated in which in particular schools and printing houses promoted the innovations, while the disciples of Palamas emerged as an element of constancy. In the seventeenth and eighteenth centuries, one can observe the increased reception of scholasticism; under the influence of the religious wars in the West, an attempt was made to ascertain the Church's own standpoint in the field of tension between the religions. Until the outbreak of national independence which the Greeks were the first to achieve in 1821, the confrontation with the Enlightenment led to a return to awareness of their own sources.

This of course only touches on the main trends within the Church. In people's everyday life they were hardly reflected with this clarity. Only the very fewest were even aware of the intellectual trends of the times, because they were unable to either read or write and were much too pre-occupied with survival. In Cyprus, for example, in the nineteenth century the village teacher still enjoyed extraordinarily great prestige, because his competence, however slight it may have been in individual cases, was viewed with awe.

In contrast to the earlier disputes of the Orthodox Church's own, these discussions were also no longer reflected in Art. If the various problems of the early period had at least led to change in iconography, if not indeed to destruction or an enormous upswing in pictorial decoration, from now on one was content to continue in the tradition prevailing in the fifteenth century.

Characteristics of Byzantine Art

The beginning and end of Byzantine are determined not by Constantinople, but by the 'Province', although this term is not really apt for centres such as Antioch and Alexandria. They were provincial cities in the organisational sense of the division of the Empire, but intellectually and culturally, on the other hand, metropolises unequalled in their way. Only in the fifth century was Constantinople gradually able to assert itself against this competition, the influence of the capital grew, culminating in the first flowering in the sixth century which was never to be repeated again as far as architecture was concerned.

The decline in artistic activity during iconoclasm also diminished Constantinople's aura; with the revival of Byzantine power, it regained its dominating role as a political and intellectual centre in the Empire for several centuries until the Komnenes' rule. The art of the Palaiologan period only reached the periphery after a lag in time and second hand because the political link had been interrupted; with the wave of refugees in 1453, Byzantine painting ebbed away in those provinces held by Latin conquerors and thus not yet Turkish. As the art of the Orthodox Christians it has lived on into our own century, but the strength for a reviving change was broken for a long time; the in part oppressive living circumstances gave no room for artistic impulses.

What applies for the relationship of Byzantine history to the Roman Empire, applies also for the relationship of Byzantine art to Classical art: it developed gradually over a period of several centuries out of the Roman-Hellenistic tradition. Oriental elements became interwoven in it. But the decisive feature was the adaptation of the Christian element in plastic arts, despite the sharp protest of the Church. Even at the end of the fourth century, the Cypriot Archbishop Epiphanios campaigned against the portrayals of Christ without succeeding in achieving a change. Over and above the depiction of ambiguous and therefore innocuous symbols, the monumental decoration of the communal rooms had long since become customary.

With the third century then began the scenic reproduction of Biblical events. Only sculpture was never able to become established on account of the closeness to the Classical idol in the East. Painting found its models in the heathen surroundings. The first bath of Achilles becomes the bath of the new-born Christ; Jesus Christ is modelled with the features of Orpheus.

The pictorial decoration of churches became politically necessary through the integration of Christianity into the state. Frescoes and mosaics acquired a second task and adapted themselves to the new requirements. Pictures of Christ were originally free of every imperial claim; Jesus sat as a teacher in the midst of his disciples who, engaged in relaxed dispute, formed a semicircle around him. After Constantine I had promoted the transfer of Roman imperial symbolism to the Son of God, the speaking gesture with which Jesus had originally turned to His disciples changed into a sign of authoritarian pronouncement of the new world order. The apostles now stand and acclaim, i.e. they confirm the new ruler in accordance with the act laid down for this in court ceremonial. In the sixth century, the picture of Christ in majesty, originally just a loan from the picture of the Emperor (also called Cosmocrator, ruler of the world), was regarded as a form of portrayal to which only Christ was entitled. Under the designation Pantocrator, after the turn of the millennium it formed part of the fixed programme of decoration in churches.

Parallel to the adoption of Classical picture schemes,

Fig. 17: Despite many reconstructions and additions, most Byzantine churches retain a uniform exterior. Here is the Panagia Angeloktisti in Kiti from the rear. The main church has a tambour with windows below the tiled dome, the apse is surrounded by a second ring of tiles protecting the second wall added later from rainwater.

the formation of two trends of style came about which were to accompany Byzantine art from then on with varying intensity: a modified retention of Hellenistic illusionism on the one hand and a deliberate dispensing with central perspective, plasticity, natural distribution of light and much else in favour of a ceremonial-sacral conception on the other.

The Classical inheritance was inaccessible in the West for centuries, among other things on account of the linguistic difference; with Italy as pioneer, there was only a return to the Greek source again in the time of the renaissance, which takes its name from this process. In the Hellenistic East, on the other hand, Classical literature, science and art remained a living tradition and thus one may only speak in a limited sense of renaissances in Byzantine art: in the sense of a return to their own roots after a period of external or internal threat. Such returns to the inheritance took place in the sixth century after the consolidation as 'half' a Roman Empire (Justinian) or in the ninth century after the threat by Islam (Macedonian/early Komnenian), in the twelfth after the destruction by the Crusaders (late Komnenian) and in the fourteenth century in view of the threat by the Turks (Palaiologan). In addition, there is the epoch of iconoclasm, although its own vocabulary of forms has only survived in a few examples with mat colours, undecorated crosses and ornaments. The most important effect of this period is the theological formulation of the pictorial language and arrangement inside the church building which marks the period after 845.

Fig. 18: Ground plan of the Church of the Archangel in Lakatamia, a village in the Nicosia district. Late 12th/early 13th century. The circle represents a dome, the semi-circles represent vaults. The two naves each end in the east with an apse.

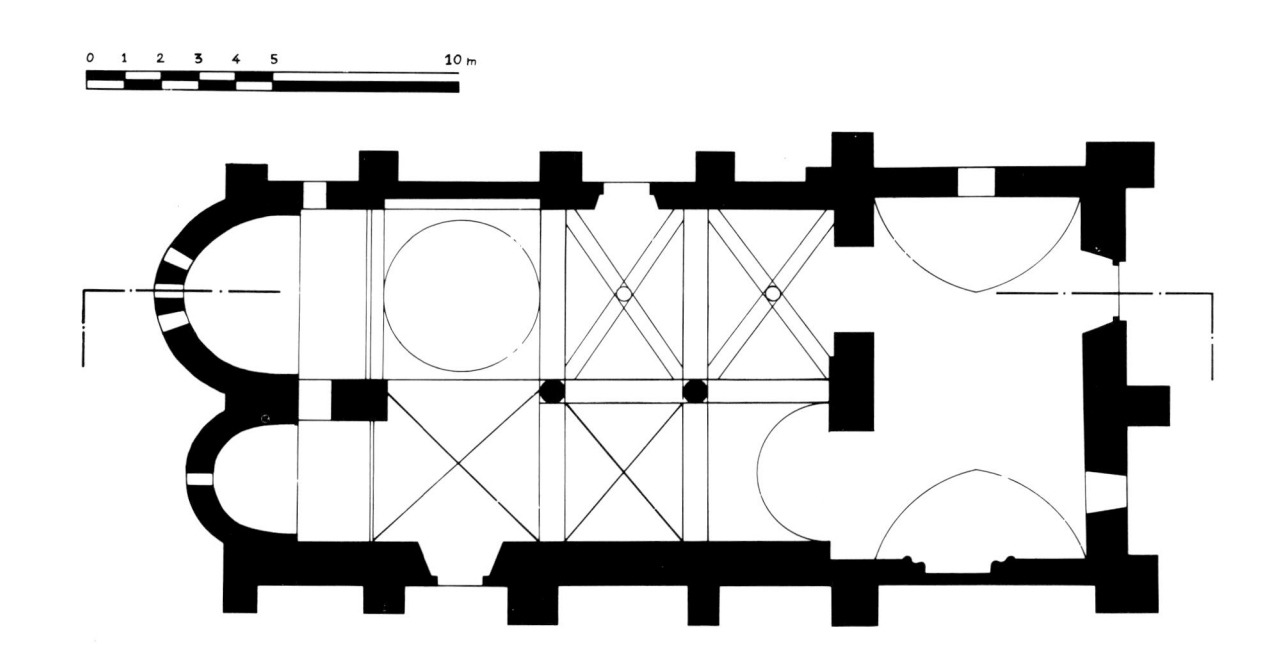

Mosaic and dome

Justinian's attempt to restore the Roman Empire may be regarded as a first 'renaissance'. In art, the revival of the Roman past aimed at by the emperor led to a fundamental renewal. In two fields in particular, solutions came into being which were long to be retained by the following generations: in church construction and mosaic art.

Until the fourth century, the multiple-aisled basilica formed the dominant structural type used for churches. The centre nave was higher and wider than the side aisles, but this form of emphasis did not satisfy Justinian's main idea. The central or round form handed down for baptisteries and the Church of the Holy Sepulchre corresponded just as little to the new need for representation. It found its fulfilment in the synthesis of the renowned Hagia Sophia. The central-plan building and basilica amalgamated into a gigantic interior above which rose semidomes and niches in several steps. A gigantic dome spans the entire interior. The room acquires an almost boundless dimension, the roof construction with its numerous windows spreads out like the firmament over the visitor. This milestone in architecture remained an unrepeatable ideal, but the idea of the domed central-plan building which contrasted the contemplative persistence of the purposeful basilica and is of unparalleled majestic effect, lay ready together with its technical solution.

The main problem was the technical development of the transition between the dome and the rectangular groundplan. In the case of the possibility preferred in Byzantium, the cruciform base of the dome was inscribed inside a square (cf. fig. 18). For this, four pillars or also walls were required which bear the lower concave corner points of four triangles. These pendentives meet together with the corners not resting on the pillar, thus describing a circular line on which then the hemisphere of the dome either rests directly or supported by a tambour (cf. fig. 18). This construction permits the inclusion of numerous windows through which light can flow into the sacred area and can be employed in a variety of ways. It can also be combined with the basilica type, as in fig. 18.

The mosaics serve the same purpose. They are based on a tradition dating back to the fifth century before Christ. These were brightly coloured pebbles which were laid out on a floor initially to form geometric-floral motives, later also as complete picture compositions. This

Fig. 19 (above): Early Christian floor mosaic with a swan from Soli; for the whole site today, cf. fig. 13 p. 39.
Fig. 20 (right): Wall mosaic from the period before iconoclasm, Archangel Gabriel from the apse conch in Kiti. He carries an orb decorated with a cross as a symbol for the fact thvat the scene is removed from earthly criteria.

decoration was also used in the early Christian basilicas (fig. 19), but not continued after the sixth century; so much attention was no longer paid to the floor. The mosaic art lived on particularly as wall decoration. In this way it was possible to imitate valuable tapestries and reduce the heaviness of the walls. Just as in the case of the domes, one wanted to avoid a massive, oppressive impression.

With pieces of coloured glass, which could also be backed by gold leaf, and mother-of-pearl, light materials were found which held to the still moist mortar against the force of gravity in the vertical and namely also in the dome or the semi-dome of an apse. Artists soon learned to compensate for the effects which come about through domed surfaces by distorting the drawing correspondingly. They took account of the optical refraction of the mosaic stones and set them at certain angles to one another in the plaster. This technique could lead both to works of the priestly, ceremonially reduced style, known as hieratic (fig. 176, 199, p. 164) and to an enraptured illusionism depicting the holy persons naturalistically and yet full of allusions so that there is no doubt about their removal to heaven (fig. 20). Where sufficient money was available for these lavish murals, preference was given to mosaic art. Their existence always indicates the presence of a patron who commissioned them on behalf of the state. If it was necessary to manage with more modest means, then it was possible to fall back on frescoes which had a similar, tapestry-like effect, albeit nothing like so magnificent. As Cyprus was at that time one of the richest and most peaceful provinces, it is possible to find relatively many remains of mosaics from that period here (cf. Kiti, Lythrankomi).

In the sixth century, the stylistic characteristics of Byzantine art are clearly marked. The frontal presentation of the main figures brings about a distancing; the emphasis on the lines is an abstraction, a denaturalisation corresponding to the Christian hope for the vanquishing of earthly things. Many of the schemes of the later canonical plan of composition, such as Mary *Orans* be-

47

Fig. 21: Fresco from the Komnenian period: Mary enthroned with Jesus and a guard of angels, Asinou, 1105/1106.

tween the Archangels Michael and Gabriel are already fully developed and change only in details.

The pictorial programme

As a result of the repulsion of iconoclasm, the number of theologically fixed composition schemes rose and their place within the church was fixed. With this is linked, of course, a check on the painters by the bishops. Their work was regimented by numerous rules. At the end of the development were the painters' manuals of the sixteenth century, the oldest of which was ascribed to an author who had lived one hundred years earlier, a certain Dionysios of Phurna, thus backdating it to 1468 to give the work greater legitimacy.

The definition of the thematic distribution of pictures envisages that Christ Pantocrator dominates in the dome (the representation of heaven). Beneath him, the four archangels, the choir of angels with cherubim and Preparation of the Throne and the twelve prophets of the Old Testament form the transition to the earthly. The transition is reached with the four Evangelists who belong in the pendentives. Supporting architectural parts are reserved for saints, monks and bishops as representatives of the earthly church. In addition to this vertical arrangement, there is also a horizontal one telling the story of Christ's life and sufferings starting out from the apse; in the eastern half, the Annunciation and Birth of Christ, in the west the Crucifixion of Christ and the Dormition of the Virgin; in between, the New Testament cycle develops in the traditional sequence. By comparison with the West, iconoclasm led to a greater emphasis on the incarnation of Christ which was the main argument against the iconophobes: A man may be portrayed, Christ became man, so anyone not believing in the portrayability of Christ denies His incarnation. The veneration and portrayal of the Virgin Mary are based on this teaching and were adopted by the West with a certain delay. Come to that, major impulses for the art of northern Europe came from the East through the then still for the most part Byzantine Italy. This is especially true for the age of the Saxon emperors during which Byzantine art experienced a brilliant climax under the Macedonian and Komnenian emperors, to match which the West had nothing comparable to offer.

The art of the Komnenes

The political and economic upswing in the tenth and eleventh centuries permitted the construction of numerous new churches. Over 200 were constructed in Cyprus alone until the year of the Latin conquest (1191), 40 of which are still more or less well preserved until today with their fresco decoration. Following the model of Constantinople, the 'inscribed cross' became a particularly frequent groundplan type. In this, a cross with equal arms is extended by a square. A special develop-

Fig. 22: The same topic as in fig. 21 in a fresco from the late Comnenan period, Lagoudera 1192.

ment of this is the five-domed church in which each section of the cross bears a dome. More frequent are three-domed churches in which the nave is emphasised by domes. However, a hall church consisting of just a nave with a timber roof is typical for the Cypriot mountain region. This is in keeping with the modest means and the weather conditions in Troodos. The side arms of the cross are just hinted at with arch-shaped niches (cf. fig. 61 p. 79). The decoration of the dome is omitted, the remaining pictorial programme was, however, transferred without difficulties.

In Constantinople, at the end of the ninth century, the epoch called the 'Macedonian Renaissance' after the ruling dynasty began. It continued without a break into the early Komnenian phase. The increased self-confidence as a result of many decisive victories over Islam finds expression in an elegant way of painting; the victory over the iconoclasts is reflected in enormous productivity. Following the destruction by the iconoclasts, painters founds a great field of activity awaiting them. The deliberate turn towards the past, to the period preceding the dispute about pictures of God, took place in depictive art without problems. The models from the Justinian era which had already been transmitted are taken up again. Outlines, garments, gesture and facial expressions are marked by lines, then modulated within the areas created by colour. Hair and beard are carefully elaborated. The nose is usually exceptionally long and bent to a slightly aquiline shape, the eyebrows form symmetrical arches meeting above the root of the nose in a V-shape. The pictorial programme was extended by the *dodekaorteon* (cycle of the twelve main festivals). Now *acheiropoietoi* also appear. One of the most important victories which the Byzantines achieved near the Anatolian city of Edessa is attributed to a cloth with the face of Christ which was found in the city wall and brought to Constantinople in a triumphal procession. From this cloth are derived the *Mandylia* which from now on decorate numerous walls above apses. In addition, the legend came into being that the Evangelist Luke had prepared portraits of the Virgin already during her lifetime so that her appearance is handed down to us authentically . These pictures include the *'Kykkottissa'* and the *'Machairotissa'* on Cyprus.

The island was reconquered at the climax of the Macedonian epoch and immediately very closely linked with the central government. Remains of fresco paintings from this period have been found in Kakopetria, Geroskipos and Kellia. Considerably more has survived from the period of the next imperial dynasty, Asinou, Trikomo and Koutsoventis are just the 'highlights' of the richly documented production of artists from the capital whose names are unknown. In the tenth and early eleventh centuries, a clear style of painting on a grand scale dominates, setting great store on elegance and classicisticity and not neglecting emotional qualities for all its restraint in expression of feelings.

Towards the end of the eleventh century, a fundamental transformation takes place. The two contradictory currents in Byzantine art – hieratic on the one hand and classical on the other – now appear alongside one an-

Fig. 23 (left): Fresco from the Palaiologan period, the Ascension of Christ. Excerpt. Pelendri, third quarter of the 14th century.
Fig. 24 (right): Fresco from the post-Byzantine period: Philip Goul's portrayal of Peter and Paul, Louvaras, 1495.

other within an epoch for the first time. The naturalistic-classical tradition is continued by painters in the courtly style, but at the same time, a more ascetic, harder method of painting comes into being in monastic circles which satisfied the ceremonial, sacral requirement better. The direct juxtaposition of both styles can be experienced in the St. Neophytos Monastery. The hieratic style is characterised by stronger linearity, more pronounced frontality and a flatter treatment of colour, whereas the classical style prefers soft lines and gently graded, in part pastel colours. A new pleasure in relating becomes apparent; the scenes are filled with many details, new topics come in addition, mainly from the life of the Mother of God and that of her parents Anna and Joachim.

The austere nature of the monastic style is meant for distance, whereas the courtly one develops mannerist tendencies. In Lagoudera it is readily possible to comprehend what that means: Excessively long figures, abrupt, dramatic gestures, folds shaped by agitated lines, flowing garments which billow in forms which even a whirlwind cannot have created. Basically, the same trend is shown in this expressive form of painting, apparently contradicting the monks' austerity of form. Mysticism had changed the intellectual climate to a deeper spirituality.

Palaiologoi and Post-Byzantines

Just as between the Macedonian and Komnenian renaissance, the transitions from the late-Komnenian to the Palaiologan period are fluid. After the catastrophic conquest of Constantinople, the empire was limited to the areas around the capital. Cyprus which had fallen to the Crusaders already a decade earlier never returned to Byzantium and remained much longer in the western field of influence. In the meantime, relations began to reverse. Whereas earlier the West had profited from the art of the East, now western influences penetrated Byzantine art. This can be seen from the backgrounds which made increasing use of architectures which are not to be found in the manner of building employed in the East. Also scenes such as the Burial of Christ or the three Women at the Tomb are an import from the West.

The method of painting was determined by the hesychastic movement which wished to impart the ecstatic view of God symbolically. Bright colours begin to appear, a powerful blue being particularly popular. Human emotions are now to the fore, the dramatic, abrupt gesture, the flattering garments are retained, but the corporeality is reduced. It is no longer the modulated forms of mannerism which determine the portrayal, but the hard broken lines. The unusually long figures give way to compressed ones. In Cyprus these trends arrived with some delay and mixed with gothic influences on account of the separation from the political centre. Plasticity and movement, realistic portrayal and a perspectively correct illustration encounter – sometimes more, sometimes less assimilated – Byzantine two-dimensionality, canonical figures with their size proportions dependent on their importance and ceremonial stillness. But despite all the external models, shadows will never be found in Orthodox pictures; the light emanates from the persons and does not come, as a naturalistic portrayal would require, from some source.

Already in the period of the Ottoman conquest, art in Cyprus lost its aristocratic character, even if it was in the service of aristocratic Latin lords. A to a certain extent native rusticity dominated the production which, after 1571, was for the most part restricted to the monasteries. The iconostasis, which had developed since the twelfth century from a simple rood screen between the altar area and the nave, took on great importance from the fourteenth century on. Partitions made up of several rows of pictures, in part repeating the decoration programme, become usual. The carved supporting frame forms a new object of craftsmanship leading to some very fine examples in Cyprus.

The Monasteries

Nikitari: Panagia Asinou

Fig. 25: The Church of All Saints lies idyllically in thickly wooded mountains. The protruding structure on the left is the south apse of the narthex, the door originally here was walled up to make space for the fresco of St. George. To the right of it the reinforcing pier buttress for the vaulting concealed beneath the pitched roof. It apparently threatened to collapse.

The famous church of the 'Theotokos', the 'Mother of God' of Asinou or the 'Theotokos Phorbiotissa' (to quote an inscription in the southern apse of the narthex which was added later) lies in the north of the Troodos Mountains near the village of Nikitari. It used to belong to a monastery. Although the latter was still intact in the seventeenth century, only a few foundation walls have survived from its buildings; ruins by the small river Asinou, which dries out in summer like all water courses in Cyprus, must be from the former monastery mill. The interior of the Panagia Phorbiotissa is completely painted and the quality of the monumental decoration make it of more than just regional importance. The astonishingly well preserved, cleaned and restored frescoes are among the best and most graphic which Cypriot – and not only Cypriot! – art has to offer. In addition, this gem of Byzantine painting stands in the midst of enchanting scenery with a view into the valley.

Asinou is a very old name. It goes back to Greek refugees from the mainland in the eleventh century BC who settled here and named the place after their home city of Argolis. It still existed in the Middle Ages, but by that time it was only a village. There are two possible origins for the word 'Phorbiotissa'. It is probably de-

Fig. 26: The antechurch with St. George, the first fresco there, late 12th century, the donor left above it, cf. p. 20. The other frescoes mainly 14th C., left below Christ and John the Baptist as supplicant; in the apse arch the damned, cf. p. 60.

rived from the term for milkwort (Gr. *'euphorbia'*). This would then fit into the use of epithets for the Virgin taken from plant names frequently to be found in Cyprus. But it is also possible that it comes from *'phorbe'*, meadow or pasture.

According to an inscription in the south-west niche of the nave, a certain Nikephoros Ischyrios, said to be a 'Magistros' with the epithet 'the Strong', paid for the painting of the church. Nikephoros was the son the Constantine Ephorbenos, duke and regent of Cyprus in the years 1103 to 1107. 'Magistros' is a title which was fourth in precedence in the Byzantine ranks. The inscription fills one of the dividing coloured strips between two painted zones, above it in the lunette one can see the Emperor Constantine and his mother Helena with a cross between them, a reference to the discovery of the True Cross during a pilgrimage by the Emperor's mother to Jerusalem. The arch over the niche is decorated with medallions of martyrs (cf. fig. 30f) and several saints have also found their place in the lower zone: Thekla on the left intrados of the niche, Theodosios, Ephrem the Syrian and Arsenios in the return of the wall itself, Andronikos, Hilarion and Kyriakos on the opposite intrados. The text reads, in so far as it has not been covered by later rebuilding: 'The church of the Panagia Theotokos was decorated thanks to the donation and great desire of Nikephoros Ischyrios, Magistros, when Alexios Komnenos was Emperor, in the year 6614.' The Byzantines calculated from Adam; in our calendar this is the year 1105/1106.

A little to the left, a large picture of the donor fills the lunette above the southern door in the centre of the nave. Nikephoros had himself portrayed here in noble garments in keeping with his position. Admittedly, this part was painted over in the fourteenth century, and it is not clear whether in fact the original portrayal was left and just touched up or if just the gist of the scene was repeated. The inscription which, to judge by the text, must have been faithfully copied, between Mary, as intercessor, and Christ on His throne indicates the first variant: freely translated it reads: 'As I was blessed in life with so many things with which thou, oh Virgin, didst provide me, I, Nikephoros, Magistros, a wretched suppliant, erected this church with humility, and pray that thou, my patron, mayest pray for me in the terrible days of the Last Judgement'. According to Andreas Stylianou and his standard work in English *'The Painted Churches of Cyprus'* (to which our own book owes a great deal without its always being possible to indicate this), there are sources according to which, after completion of the church, the founder retired there, founded a monastery and became its first abbot under the name of Nicholas. He died in 1115.

In the portrait of the founder, behind Nikephoros we see a considerably smaller figure of a woman, splendidly dressed just like him. Above her head too is an inscription from which is to be learned that she died in 1099, but not, however, in what relationship she stood to the founder. Judging by the size, it might be assumed that she was his daughter. However, in Byzantine painting (just as in Medieval painting in the West), the size of a figure plays a quite different role, it tells us rather about the significance, the importance of the person portrayed. In this place it may equally well be reasons of space which led to the female figure of only half the size, because the arch and the wish to preserve their memory with an inscription forbade any further extension (fig. 27).

The illustration of the church in the picture of the founder shows it with a slanted roof without a narthex. It had three entrances. The window and door lintels are constructed out of bricks, the inside transverse arches perhaps too. The other walls are constructed of rough hewn stone blocks using just mud instead of the usual lime sludge as mortar. This was apparently responsible for structural damage which appeared at an early stage which – in addition to earthquake damage – made comprehensive renovation works necessary in the fourteenth century. The structure has a rectangular groundplan with

Fig. 27: The donor, a woman, who according to the inscription died in 1099 and whose relationship to Nikephoros Magistros is unclear (wife, mother or daughter?) and Mary as supplicant with a model of the church. It shows that the first structure already had a shed roof, almost a century before the conquest by the Crusaders – an important structural history detail. In the soffit of the arch Ambios, cf. fig. 31.

not only the nave, but also the side aisles vaulted whereby the vaults are supported by transverse arches. They divide the indoor area into three parts. The apse forms the end in the east, in the west a narthex only added in the fourteenth century. Originally the church walls were whitened with lime mortar onto which a pattern of stones was painted; the intention possibly was to conceal the poor masonry. It was probably improved during the renovation in the fourteenth century in the course of which the central pillars were reinforced on the outside and inside to nearly double their original size. The narthex is a cult room added quasi at right angles to the nave with an apse in both the north and south. Between these two semi-domes rises a whole dome. Of the three original doors, the south door was bricked up on account of the large picture of St. George. Beneath this fresco, an inscription attests that a second Nikephoros who is des-

Fig. 28 (above): Mary Orans, apse conch; fig. 29 (below): Dormition of the Virgin in the west of the naos over the door.

Fig. 30: Bacchos medallion, vaulted arch in naos, 1106.

Fig. 31: Ambios medallion, name to be seen from the inscription.

ignated 'Tamer of horses', financed this painting at the end of the twelfth century. It was originally even covered with gold leaf on the shield, lance and the halo, so that this donor must have been a very rich man. Indirectly, this allows conclusions to be drawn on the importance of horse-breeding on the island. Richard Coeur de Lion is said to have been particularly proud of a horse which he took as booty when he conquered Cyprus.

So not all the frescoes in the church belong to the early phase 1105/1106, although about two thirds do date from that time and are the more important ones with respect to their quality and significance. They give testimony of the close links with Constantinople and the imperial court. Emperor Alexios Komnenos (fig. 12, p.35), who is mentioned in the older founder's inscription, moved his residence to Cyprus for a time during his fight against the Saracens and Crusaders and with him came artists who worked not only in Asinou, but also in Trikomo and Koutsoventis. We thus have an example here of the 'avant garde' of those days, an art which was at the climax of that time. Its characteristic features become particularly clear in the exceptionally long figures of bishops in the apse with their elegantly draped vestments. The symmetrical arrangement, classicist tendencies, but also a very human way of relating which concedes feelings to the figures of the saints, marks this style. Admittedly, the accentuation is only brought to full flower about two centuries later; this can be seen in the happy facial expression of Mary Orans probably completed in 1250 (fig. 28) In the case of the paintings completed in 1106, it is more the highly expressive gestures than the mimic art which bring the seriousness of the event closer to the viewer. Imitation of the Apostle Paul who bows in mourning over the foot of Mary's deathbed and wipes a tear from his cheek with the corner of his garment (fig. 29) are to be found in miniature painting as far away as England. The portrait of Mary above the door leading from the vestibule to the naos is very similar to the portrayal in the apse in Trikomo; it was painted on the outside wall of the first church, protected by a canopy, and only became an inside painting through the extension.

The frescoes in the narthex are devoted primarily to the Last Judgement. In keeping with its main function as a baptismal chapel, the main emphasis is placed on the eternal salvation of man and the consequences of a moral

Fig. 32 (top), 33: Parts of the Last Judgement.

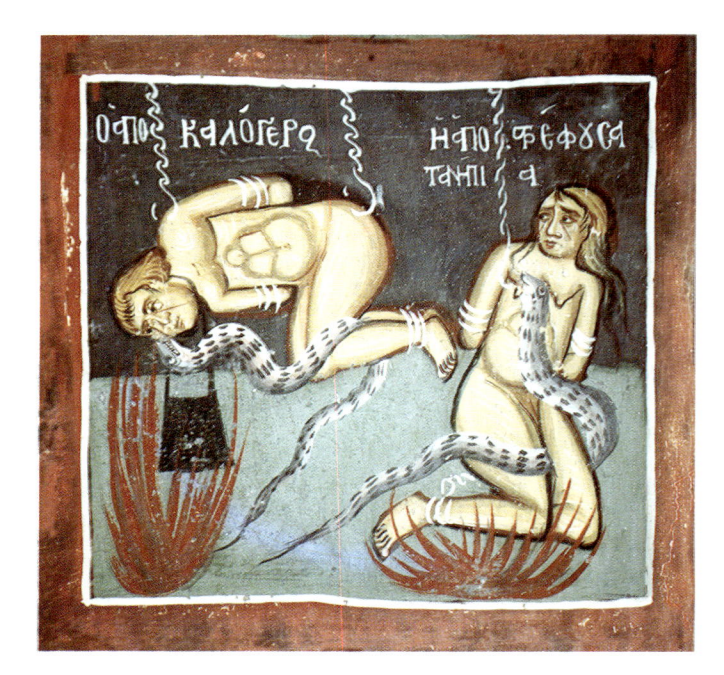

Fig. 34 (top), 35: Continuation under 32/33, the damned.

and a corrupt way of life. This includes the portrayal of the damned whose misdemeanours are stated exactly in the inscriptions: usurers, swindlers, millers who weigh falsely, spoilt children, faithless nuns, thieves and gossipmongers – the whole medieval cast of socially damaging transgressions is represented and is tormented naked with cords, serpents and fire (fig. 32-35). The good whose souls have passed on the scales are portrayed in or before Paradise. Unusual is the picture of two hounds and two mouflons, a scene taken directly from the nobles' favourite pastime: hunting in the mountains. As it is completely alien to Byzantine art, it must be due to the influence of the Crusaders.

Galata: Panagia Podithou

Fig. 36: Outside view of Panagia Podithou.

Just like the Asinou, the Klarios is a water course, dried out in summer, through which the water from melting snow and rain flows down from the Troodos Mountains to Morphou Bay. In its narrow valley lies the church dedicated to the Virgin Mary Eleousa tou Podithou. 'Eleousa' means 'to grant mercy', but the meaning of the word Podithou is still unclear. Like other churches in the mountains, the Panagia has a steep pitched roof resting on a second outside wall. It is thus enclosed in a protective shell.

The church was constructed in 1502, at the time of Venetian rule, close to the old town of Galata. Its origin lies already well into the post-Byzantine period. It is an important witness to the active further development of the classical East Roman style and the independent treatment of influences from the Italian Renaissance. To a certain extent, it thus reflects the situation of its founders, Demetrios de Coron and his wife, Helena. A Greek inscription at the lower edge of the western pediment bears witness to the fact that the church, together with the monastery to which it originally belonged, was erected at their expense. There were apparently further donors whose names have not, however, come down to us. Among the frescoes painted shortly after the construction phase are also portraits of the De Corons handing over a model of the church to the Virgin Mary. Demetrios, an old man at the time when the church

Fig. 37: King Solomon, connection above see fig. 40.

Fig. 38: King David.

was built, had been a soldier and a knight of the barony of Pendayia in his younger days. According to the sources, in 1461 the future church founder had been involved in the conflict between the Lusignan Queen Charlotte and her half-brother, the illegitimate James II. As a member of the Frankish nobility who had been deprived of their power by measures taken by the Venetians, Demetre, as his name was originally written, apparently moved closer to the indigenous Greeks, hellenised his name, married an Orthodox woman and himself spoke Greek.

The interior of Podithou was never completely covered with paintings. Frescoes are only to be seen in the altar area, thus the bema, namely in the apse, on both sides of the west wall and in the corresponding part of the north and south walls. The monumental decoration is executed in the Italo-Byzantine style which spread over the whole island under Venetian rule.

Fig. 39 (top): Mary enthroned in the apse conch – Fig. 40 (below) Archangel Gabriel, part of the Annunciation.

Above the portrait of the founders unfolds a portrayal of the Virgin Mary with reference to the Old Testament. Surrounded by ten prophets who have visions recorded on scrolls alluding to her virginity and incarnation, she stands with the child Jesus on her arm. The composition is to be found not only under the title 'The prophets predicted Thee' among the earlier frescoes in St. Paraskevi in Geroskipos, but also in a painter's manual, that of the monk Dionysios of Fourna. The Incarnation was one of the decisive arguments of the iconophiles that a portrayal of God and the history of salvation was not something reprehensible and every portrayal of Mary with Jesus in the Orthodox area is a symbol for this central element of faith and for the victory over the iconoclasts.

Right at the top of the pediment, the 'Ancient of Days' blesses the prophets and the Virgin Mary. 'I beheld till the thrones were cast down, and the An-

Fig. 41: The section below Mary in the apse conch – Communion of the Apostles, the Body of Christ. From left to right: Judas, Andrew, Philip, Luke, Matthew, Peter, Jesus, two archangels, Jesus, continuation see fig. 42.

cient of Days did sit, whose garment was white as snow, and the hair of his head like the pure wool: his throne was like the fiery flame, and his wheels as burning fire.' The portrayal is based on these words from the prophet Daniel (7, 9) and was developed from an early Byzantine predecessor. It symbolises the unity of God the Father and the Son of God, Jesus, replacing in some compositions the hand representing the Holy Spirit.

To the right and left of the apse, beneath the Annunciation (Gabriel, cf. fig. 40) are the prophets and kings of Israel, Solomon and David (fig. 37 and 38). One can see clearly how the figures are related to one another by the almost mirror-like arrangement of the composition. In the semi-cupola of the apse, the Virgin sits on an imperial throne flanked by two archangels clad in white (fig. 39). Jesus is sitting on Mary's lap looking at the viewer en face. This somewhat rare way of portrayal in a Byzantine context, perhaps adopted through the Italian influence, is called the 'Cypriot type'. This also includes the feature that the archangels wear sandals and not the red buskins adorned with pearls extending up above the ankles usual at the Byzantine court for persons right at the top of the hierarchy (cf. fig. 59, p. 78). The composition is a successful combination of eastern and western elements. Together with the Communion of the Apostles portrayed below (take, eat … in remembrance of me … fig. 41; 'Drink ye all of it … fig. 42) this is regarded as the best indigenous example for the Italo-Byzantine school. The fact that Judas is here portrayed with a slight beard is just as much part of the western influence as the fact that he turns away in accordance with the sentence in St. John's Gospel 'He then having received the sop went immediately out: and it was night.' (13, 30). We can admire a somewhat earlier version of the topic in the main church of the St. Neophytos monastery; Judas is not included there.

On the right side of the pediment, above the apse, we can see Moses kneeling and the Burning Bush, an

Fig. 42: Communion of the Apostles, the Blood of Christ. From left to right: two archangels, Jesus, Paul, John, James, Mark, Thomas, Simon. To the extreme right King David is just to be seen, cf. fig. 38.

unusual place for this topic. Here it is apparently a reference to the nearby village called Sinai, because the scene of the handing over of the Commandments took place, according to the Bible, on Mount Sinai. The north and south sides of the sanctuary are decorated with various scenes from the lives of Joachim and Anna, the literary basis for which is to be found in the Apocrypha.

It is unusual that the Anastasis, the victory of the Resurrected over Hell and its dark empire decorates the area over the main entrance on the western side. Particularly in a church dedicated to Mary, one would expect a Dormition, the death of the Mother of God. Instead, that is shown on the left of the entrance, to the right of it we see Christ. The Crucifixion scene, in complete contrast to the reserved, dignified manner of the Orthodox tradition, shows the event as a tumult. Soldiers in western clothing stand at the edge of the execution, the figures are garish and vivid in appearance, and the excitement which such a public enforcement of a judgment causes can be clearly felt. The inscription with the initials for 'Jesus Christ King of the Jews' is not affixed to the cross, but shown on scrolls.

Right at the very top of the pediment is a picture of the 'Mandylion', a Persian-Greek word coinage for 'small cloak'. According to the legend, the Messiah's face was impressed in its material; the western equivalent would be the veil of St. Veronica. The use of powerful colours in large parts of the compositions indicates an exact knowledge of Western painting which must have impressed the unknown painter of Podithou, despite all his faithfulness to Byzantine iconography.

The carved wooden iconostatis dates from the time of the construction of the Podithou church; it was regilded in 1783.

Kakopetria: St. Nikolaos tis Stegis

Fig. 43: Agios Nikolaos tis Stegis – the pitched roof from which the former monastery church takes its name is clearly to be seen.

Just like Galata, Kakopetria also lies on the Klarios, only somewhat further upstream. The best known church in this place is called Agios Nikolaos tis Stegis. The name refers to the second shed roof which was added at a fairly early stage as protection against the adverse weather in the Troodos Mountains (fig. 43). Nikolaos tis Stegis lies in a lovely pine forest about five kilometres outside the village, and belonged to a monastery until the nineteenth century. With the exception of high summer, the stream ensures a markedly fresher air, admittedly, the frescoes also suffer from the moistness of the ground.

Nikolaos tis Stegis dates from the early eleventh century. The church is of the 'cross-in-square' design. The interior has the form of a Greek cross with all arms of approximately equal length (like a plus sign). The corner rooms resulting between the arms have also been built around, but do not belong directly to the naos. This ground plan looks like a square in which a cross has been inscribed. The crossing, the point at which the four arms meet, is covered with a dome. This type of church is widely found in the Slavonic-Byzantine area. Admittedly, on account of the double roof construction, little light falls inside here in Kakopetria, either through the dome or through the side windows, so that the interior is gloomy and has to be lit artificially. In the early twelfth century, a domed narthex was added. In the following years, the second shed roof will have been constructed over the whole structure, which had now become longitudinal through the portico.

Nikolaos tis Stegis is completely painted, for a large part with the original frescoes from the early eleventh century. They are rustic compositions. Nevertheless, persons are portrayed sensitively, they have stern faces, restrained but significant looks. Although obviously stylised, they are of an indisputable naturalness which is emphasised by the warm, harmonious and mainly earthy range of colours used by the unknown master. The boundaries between the individual scenes are not always as strict as in other churches. For example, the Transfiguration of Christ and the Raising of Lazarus from the Dead are separated from one another only by a hint of a chain of mountains. The link between the two events is emphasised: only after His Transfiguration was Jesus able to raise the dead back to life; before He 'only' succeeded in healing the sick. One detail of the iconography of the Transfiguration goes back to the church of the Holy Apostles in Constantinople from the ninth century. The disciples present, John, James and Peter, are stylised as three ages of life. The youngest, John, faints, he lies thunderstruck on the ground. James, a man in his middle age, is entranced, and Peter, the old man, remains in rapt, glorifying admiration. The fact that James stands out between two mountains is the Byzantine way of indicating spatial depth. The drawing is, by the way, two-dimensional, even if the plasticity of the figures is suggested with some white lines and areas. The Triumphant Entry into Jerusalem, in which Jesus sits on the donkey almost as if on a chair, the fragmentary remnant of the Dormition of the Virgin in the western lunette, medallions of martyrs in the soffits of arches between the entrance and nave, the Descent from the Cross and Embalming of Christ in the northern lunette as well as the

Fig. 44: St. Nicholas portrayed as always in vestments with his left hand raised in a blessing gesture. On the left, below the donor, a monk, in the upper corners the Mother of God and Christ with a bishop's insignia. The features used here are characteristic for Nicholas. Early 12th century.

portrayal of several prelates date from the eleventh century. In the bema, frescoes from the fourteenth century have been removed (they are now in Nicosia) uncover-

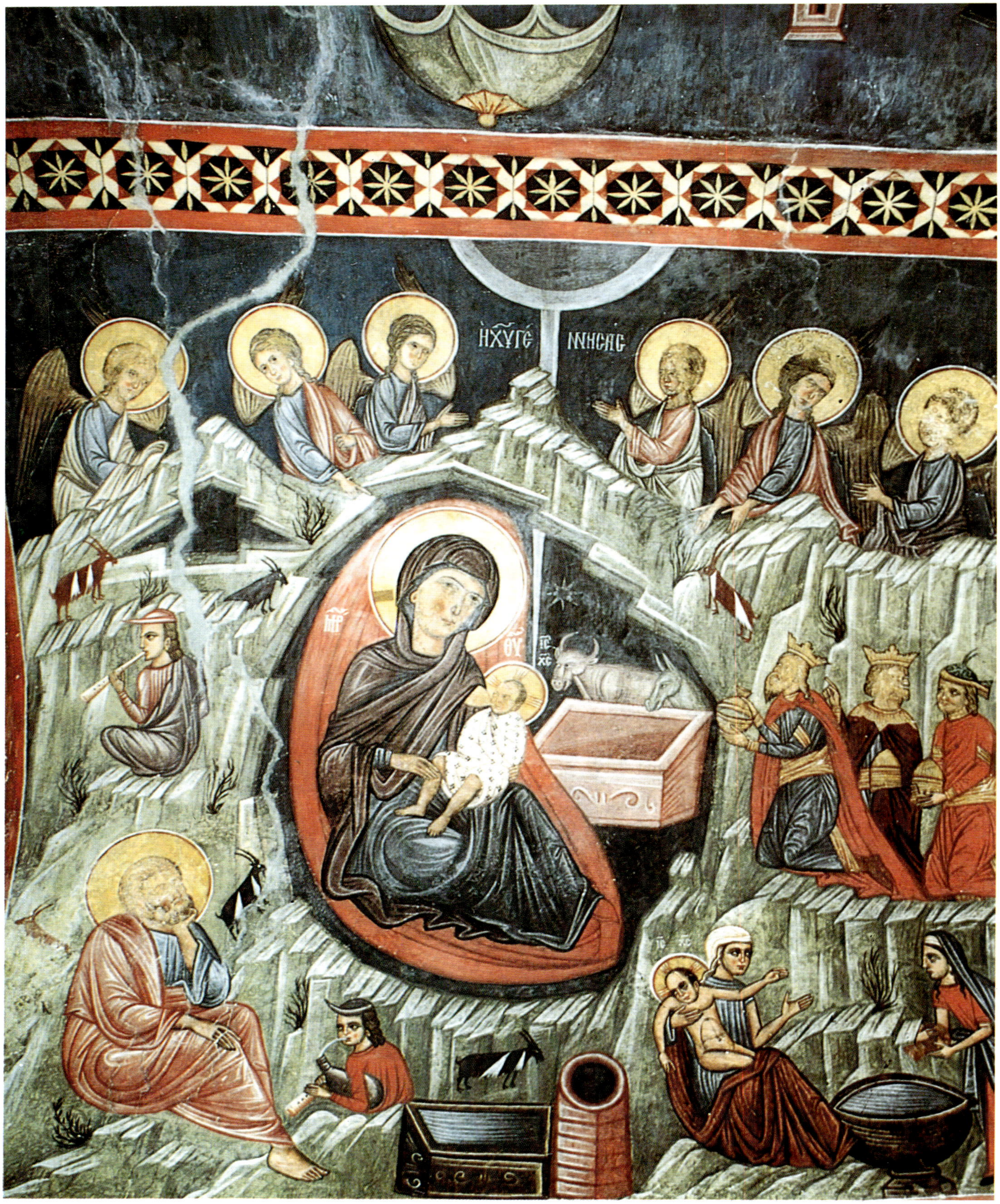

Fig. 45 (left) and 46 (above): Beginning and end of the cycle from the life of Jesus – Birth and Crucifixion. A unique feature is the fresco of Mary breast-feeding the Child.

ing ones from the early phase. The portrayal of the individual figures is influenced by the renaissance of the hellenistic-impressionistic way of painting which predominated in Constantinople in the tenth century; the faces with their wide open eyes recall the mummy portraits of El Faiyûm. In the opinion of M. Sotiriou, the frescoes in the oldest layer are like those of Haghia Sophia and the Panagia ton Chalkeon in Thessaloniki from the year 1028. They do not correspond with the style of the capital because they are coarser and designed with an almost naive charm. But they are thoroughly Byzantine which cannot be said of the later pictures here.

With the addition of the narthex, new frescoes became necessary, both in the narthex itself and also on the walls which had suffered from the construction activity. They were carried out in the Komnenian style of the early twelfth century and, although they make a slightly stiff and stylised impression, they do go back to influence from the capital. The Last Judgement is shown in the vestibule. On the north wall, six apostles sit in a row like jurors, behind them angels armed with rods. One sees people being led into Paradise and the angel of fire throwing the wicked into Hell. The Virgin Mary, 'pointing the way', is shown on the north-western centre column.

The Forty Martyrs of Sebaste shown in the south-western arch to the right of the entrance to the naos is an impressive composition (fig. 47). In the case of the majority of the men standing on the ice in long or short underpants, their necks are not to be seen, they have drawn up their shoulders, some are holding their arms before their bodies to protect themselves from the cold

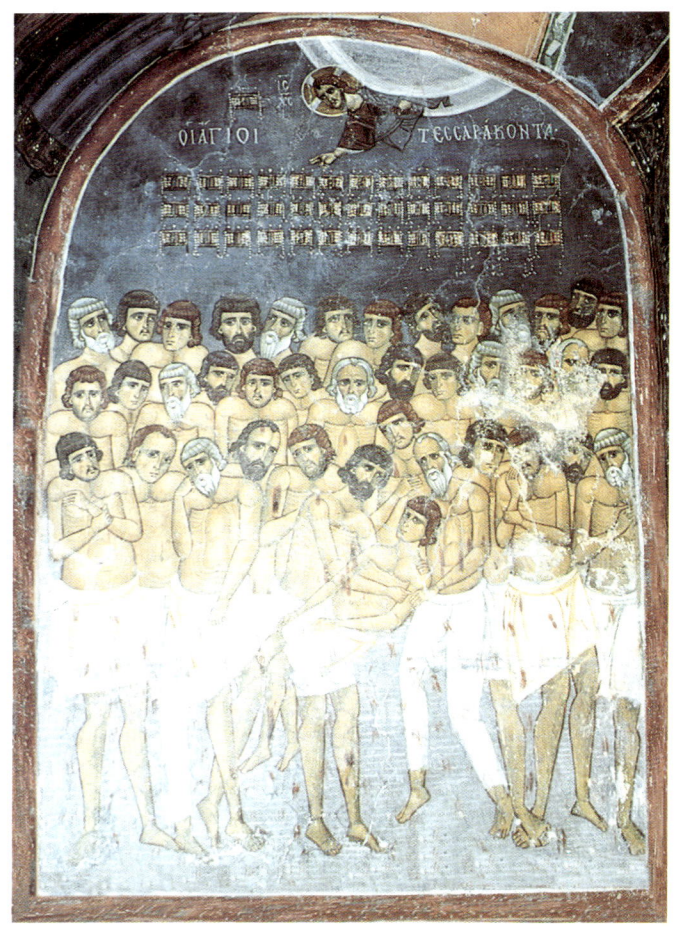

Fig. 47 (above): The forty martyrs of Sebaste, collective saints of the higher military ranks in the Byzantine army.
Fig. 48 (right): The soldier saints Theodore and George.

to which they will ultimately fall victim. Above their heads are suspended martyrs' crowns and Christ blesses them from a cloud.

The portrait of the patron saint above the entrance to the *diakonikon* is of high artistic quality. Nicholas is over life size, but the finish is fine in details; the work is by a master from Constantinople. In the inscriptions on this picture, the year is missing in which the donor of the painting, shown at the bottom left as a monk, made a gift of the work (fig. 44). Also over-life in size and of superb quality are the two soldier saints, Theodore and George, who are identically dressed and are only differentiated by the colouring. When making his drawing, the artist took care that the warriors' sword and spear point to the area, to the tip of the picture frame slightly distorted by the beginning of the arch, thus not allowing the glance of the observer to stray. The New Testament cycle, painted in the fourteenth century, represents a further highlight. The Birth of Christ in which Mary breast-feeds her son is one of the loveliest scenes (fig. 45). The background is not presented in gold, but with dark colours, the small figures are very carefully and skilfully painted. Architectural details here, just as in the Crucifixion (fig. 46), betray western influence. Several donors contributed further frescoes until into the seventeenth century, the last being the monk Philotheos in 1633.

Lagoudera: Panagia Araka

Fig. 49: A jewel of late-Komnenian frescoes, the church of the Virgin Mary with the Pea, lies protected from the wind on a slope.

The magnificent church of the Virgin Mary known as Panagia Araka is located between the villages of Lagoudera and Sarandi and lies a little way off the road leading from Nicosia into the Troodos Mountains. The origin of the epithet '*araka*' (pea) is unclear; it can only be presumed that it goes back to the discovery of a mysterious icon of the Virgin Mary in this agricultural area in which peas were cultivated centuries ago.

The church is a single-aisled, vaulted building with three niches in each of the side walls and a dome rising over the centre. The Panagia Araka also has the characteristic shed roof of churches in the Troodos Mountains; admittedly, here the dome is protected by a small extra roof (Fig. 49).

The frescoes in Lagoudera are nowadays considered to be among the most impressive examples of Komnenian monumental style. In the late twelfth century, outstanding painters were at work in many places in Cy-

71

Fig. 50: Iconostasis and pendentives with the Annunciation.

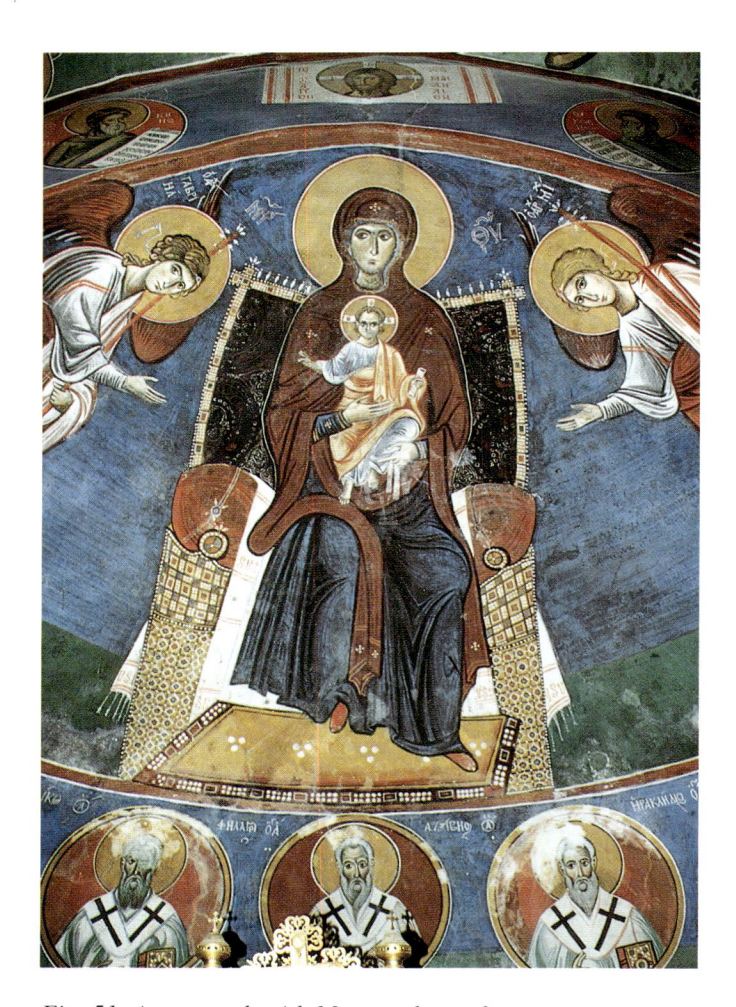

Fig. 51: Apse conch with Mary enthroned.

prus, but in the Panagia Araka they created frescoes of particular rank. They were donated in the year 1192 by a certain Leon, the son of the governor Authentes. This is recorded in two inscriptions: one of them is above the northern entrance, the other, in verse form, is to be found on the south wall on either side of the Virgin Mary 'Arakiotissa'. The church itself is probably older; it was presumably constructed a few years before the arrival of the Crusaders in 1191.

The monumental programme in Lagoudera begins with Christ Pantocrator – the King of Glory, the Ruler of the World, the Just Judge (fig. 56). He is shown in the dome against a purple background and surrounded by the Preparation of the Throne and angels in medallions. Below stand the twelve apostles. Each one is holding a scroll with the text of his prophecy which all refer to the fact that He as Redeemer will come down to us on Earth 'from there above'. The Annunciation was painted in the eastern pendentive (fig. 50). This is followed by the Presentation of the Virgin Mary to the Temple which is designed in accordance with the apocryphal account of her life: The high priest Zacharias receives the young virgin. She is accompanied by her parents, Joachim and Anna, and by seven maidens with silver earrings clad in colourful garments. In the portrayal of the Birth of Christ in the southern part of the west wall one can observe one of the most polished compositions on this topic; the three kings come from the right, three angels show the three shepherds the way, at the bottom right Jesus is given His first bath and at the bottom left sits a pensive Joseph (fig. 55). In the Presentation of Christ in the Temple, the aged Simeon, accompanied by John the Baptist, holds the infant Jesus. The child is here shown with a jewelled earring in His left ear – a strange, if also not

Fig. 52 (above): Dormition of the Mother of God over the west door, i.e. the opposite side to the view in fig. 50 and 51.
Fig. 53 (below left): Mary in the circle of apostles, fig. 54 (below right): Archangel Michael with Orb and Lance.

73

Fig. 55: The late Komnenian interpretation of the Birth of Christ, like the other frescoes in Lagoudera from the year 1192.

unusual decoration, the allegorical meaning of which has still not been completely clarified. Perhaps there is a link with an old Byzantine family custom. The picture of the Virgin Mary sitting upright on her throne is to be seen on the southern wall. Here the mother of Jesus is given the epithet of 'Arakiotissa' in an inscription. She is attended by two archangels and holds her new-born child – the Light of the World – in her arm (fig. 22, p. 49). Alongside, a huge Archangel Michael is to be seen in the robes of a deacon. In his left hand he presents an orb with an engraved cross – the symbol for God's rule over heaven and earth (fig. 54).

The splendid circle of frescoes in Lagoudera continues with the Baptism of Christ in the Jordan which is portrayed in the north-westerly niche. Christ stands naked next to John the Baptist. This scene refers to the concept of the divine power of Christ and the transience of worldly things. Opposite the Birth of Christ is a Resurrection. Stylistically, this fresco recalls a painting dating from 1183 to be found in the Enkleistra of St. Neophytos near Paphos. Christ's Ascension covers the whole eastern vault. Here Christ ascending is shown as a full figure in five concentric circles surrounded by the Apostles standing divided into two equal groups between whom the Virgin Mary and an angel stand. They form a rare stylistic whole (fig. 53). The polished scene of the Dormition of the Mother of God, filled with many figures, extends over the whole lunette in the southern central niche. It is a wonderful demonstration of the workmanship of the painter in Lagoudera and Byzantine art of the Komnenian age. In the dramatic facial expression of St. John who is bending over the breast of the dead

Fig. 56: View into the dome with Christ Pantocrator, numerous prophets, saints, the Annunciation and two scenes with apostles.

Virgin Mary and in the humility of St. Peter at her feet are to be seen what strength of feeling filled the artist during his work (fig. 52).

The second part of the painting consists of a larger number of individual figures. The Virgin Mary is depicted on the north pillar, Peter and Paul on the west column. The saintly brothers Cosmas and Damian are portrayed in the soffit of the north-western arch, the naked ascetic Onouphrios in the bema. The two stylites, Saints Symeon the elder and the younger, are to be seen on top of slender marble pillars with acanthus capitals. Lazarus of Bethany, the later bishop of Kition (modern Larnaca), is also shown in the south-western niche. Above the altar, as usual, is the Mandylion, while the Virgin Mary on her throne surrounded by the Archangels takes her traditional place in the semi-dome of the apse.

The saints in the lower part of the apse are notable for their more sharply contoured outlines, indicating the use of thicker brushes. Special mention should be made here of John the Almsgiver. He came from Cyprus and was born in Amathous in 560 and later appointed Bishop of Alexandria. He exercised this office from 609-615, but after the Persian conquest of Egypt, he returned to his native land. A second Cypriot among the figures of bishops in the apse is Tychon. In addition to these two, we see Nikolaos, Meletios of Antioch, John Chrysostom, Basil, Gregory and Athanasios.

Some frescoes in Lagoudera date from the fourteenth and fifteenth centuries when the church was extended. They show, among others, the hymn-writers Cosmas and John of Damascus. In addition Christ is portrayed sitting on a hill. A deacon by the name of Leontios painted a fresco of Mary Orans; it is to be found above the north entrance. The other paintings on either side of the niche are of more recent date.

Fig. 57: St. Cosmas, the physician saint; here with a turban.

Platanistasa: Stavros tou Agiasmati

Fig. 58: The Church of the Holy Trinity, surrounded all round by a protective shell and the pitched roof typical for the mountains.

The Church of 'tou Agiasmati' lies close to the village of Platanistasa in the north west of the island on the road to the Troodos Mountains. It is dedicated to the Holy and Venerable Cross and belongs to the Nicosia district. Its epithet means 'holy well'.

It is a single-aisled structure with a timber roof covered with tiles. The apse forms a semi-circle at the eastern end, but nothing is to be seen of this from the outside because a periapsidial aisle runs round the whole interior. From this vestibule three entrances lead into the naos. One lies on the north side, the other two are to be found in the west and south walls. Access to the ambulatorium is provided by three other entrances in the outside north, west and south walls. Two further entrances were breached in the eastern outside wall in 1967. Geometrically arranged niches are let into the north and south walls of the naos (cf. the north niche in fig. 61). The forms of post-Byzantine architectural style and the enormous craft skills with which they were constructed are to be seen on the interior walls. This gives the church the vitality and the strength of tradition which one finds everywhere in Cyprus.

The inscription on the outside above the southern door to the naos reveals to us that the most pious

Fig. 59: Mary Orans in the apse conch. The iconography is very similar to that in Pedoulas.

priest Peter Perates and his wife Pepane financed the church and the painting of the interior at the end of the fifteenth century, probably in the year 1494. The donor is shown in his priest's vestments together with his wife on the outside south wall. Both are handing a small model of the church to Jesus Christ and the Virgin Mary (just as in Asinou and Pedoulas). The inscription also names the painter, admittedly only by his epithet 'Goul'. Art historians identify him as Philip Goul, a Syrian by birth who had settled in Cyprus and was one of the best painters of that time here. Goul was also commissioned to paint the frescoes in St. Mamas in Louvaras.

On the south wall, close to the iconostatis, begins as usual the cycle of frescoes with the topics from the New Testament: the Birth of the Virgin Mary, the Evangelists Matthew and Luke, the Presentation of Mary in the Temple, Christ's Birth and His Presentation in the Temple. In the Baptism in the Jordan, Jesus is naked, without a loin cloth, but also without showing any genitals. Here we have an early example of a frequent method of portrayal in the late-Byzantine period (cf. fig. 89, p. 99). Then follow the Raising of Lazarus, the Entry into Jerusalem and the Transfiguration. The eastern pediment is dominated by the Transfiguration scene, the western pediment by the Crucifixion. At the bottom, John the Baptist is to be seen; his features are elaborated very sensitively. With a sorrowful expression he prays for mankind together with the Mother of God shown opposite him.

The Archangel Michael is portrayed quite traditionally in the southern niche. In the western pediment, the Crucifixion is followed by the Prophets, the Last Supper and below St. Mamas. Opposite the latter, sitting astride a lion with a lamb on his arm, we see St. George on horseback as a soldier holding a lance. He is riding through a river; fish spring around the hooves of his white horse. Instead of a lamb, he

Fig. 60 (above): Jesus before Pilate, scene from the New Testament cycle. Pilate washes his hands. A red cloth winds from a pillar to the architectural background around the Roman governor: a Palaiologan stage prop typical for the 'Macedonian school'.

Fig. 61 (right): The north-western niche with ten scenes on the discovery of the True Cross in Jerusalem. The portrayal in this form is unique, normally Constantine and Helena stand to the right and left of the Cross.

holds his hand protectively over a mysterious figure holding a sort of coffeepot and a striped napkin. This pillion rider is frequently to be found in mid-Byzantine painting in Cyprus without its being known what it really means. On the northern wall, the bound Jesus stands before Pilate (fig. 60); the Ascension, the Dormition of the Mother of God, John and Mark follow. Between the angels painted on the side walls of the niche are squeezed two small pictures of the Discovery of the True Cross (fig. 61). The Raising of the Holy Cross decorates the arch above. These topics are quite rare in Byzantine art, but, by contrast, frequent in Western art, especially at the time of the Crusades. A sure indication that Philip Goul knew the Latin iconography well. The eastern pediment shows Christ as a prelate and the Annunciation, the half-dome of the apse the Virgin with the Archangels Michael and Gabriel of the Blachernitissa type, in fact the finest fresco in Agiasmati (fig. 59). Below is the Communion of the Apostles. On the western wall, the Last Judgement, further scenes from the Bible and hagiographic persons are depicted.

The pictures in the Agiasmati show that Goul adapted the realistic style of the miniatures which informed him of the current trends in the West. He combined it with the Byzantine style of painting. Perhaps he had worked as a manuscript illuminator and adapted motives from the manuscripts on the wall, as had been usual for centuries. At all events, the arts of book illumination of his day were not unknown to him, just as little as the other creators of great monumental art in Cyprus. Philip Goul adapted his pictorial language to the forms and colours prevalent here while at the same time expressing a personal line and his experience with the perpetual contents of religious pictures.

Lazanias: Machairas

Fig. 62: The entrance with a view of the bell tower.

In the mountain forests of Machairas belonging to the Nicosia district there is a monastery dedicated to the Virgin Mary. It is called '*Machairotissa*' after a famous icon kept there. It lies at about 870 metres above sea level close to the village of Lazanias and was founded at the end of the twelfth century.

Its history begins with an unknown hermit. In the time of the iconoclastic dispute in Byzantium, he brought one of the 70 icons, which are said to have been painted by the Apostle Luke, secretly from Asia Minor to Cyprus. After his death, the icon of the virgin remained in its hiding place until the arrival of two other hermits from Palestine in 1145: Neophytos and Ignatios.

According to tradition, the two monks found the icon in a cave. In order to reach it, they needed a knife (Greek '*machairi*') so that they could cut away the undergrowth around the cave. It was given to them by 'divine hand'. Accordingly, the icon of the Virgin Mary was called 'Machairotissa' (and later also the monastery). After the death of Neophytos, Ignatios travelled with another monk, Prokopios, to Constantinople before the year 1172 where they succeeded in obtaining financial assistance from the Byzantine emperor Manuel Komnenos. Back in Cyprus, they constructed a small church which was enlarged by the monk Neilos in the early thirteenth century. He became the first abbot, later rising to become bishop of Tamassos.

The Angeloi emperors Isaac and Alexios granted the monastery new privileges at Neilos's request: it was dispensed from tax payments. The abbot drafted the first rules which have applied since then for the monastic community. He was followed by Ioakeim, later Ioannes and Konon took his place. They came from Asia Minor to support the Orthodox in the struggle against the Latin intruders in the period of Lusignan rule.

Leontios, a monk from Machairas and author of the comprehensive work 'Exegesis of the enchanting land of Cyprus', has left us written documents on the monastery and Frankish rule on Cyprus in the fourteenth century. According to an inscription on a stone slab, the monastery burned down completely in 1530. Just as in

Kykkos, only the icon of the Virgin Mary survived this fire.

Kleopas, a monk and calligrapher, makes mention of donations at the beginning of the seventeenth century. In 1697, during the period of office of Abbot Leontios II, the church was renovated. 23 years later, a monk of Arab origin, Parthenios, was elected abbot. He had come to Cyprus as a child and continued with the reconstruction of Machairas. Abbot Ioannikos (1766-1796) formed close spiritual, intellectual and economic links with Moldavia and Wallachia.

The Russian monk Basil Grigorovich Barsky visited the monastery in 1735, noting in his diary: 'Machairas is one of the largest and most famous monasteries in Cyprus that belongs to the jurisdiction of the archbishop. Located like Kykkos on uneven ground, on the tops of the mountains, above a ravine. The monastery is rectangular in layout and covered with a tiled timber roof. In addition, it has two entrances, one of which is the main entrance facing towards the east, the second looks to the west. The main aisle of the church has wonderful propylaea with columns on the western side. It is covered by a dome and the large tiled roof which extends over the whole church. Inside the church are icons, chandeliers, stone floors and frescoes. There are only 25 monks; they are extremely active and modest. They live mainly from agriculture and the donations of Christians. The monastery is surrounded by fresh air; one well inside the walls and another outside supply healthy and fresh water. It is, it is true, located in a remote spot, but through its wide-spread fame the ungodly Moslems do not cease to call on the monks in order to frighten them. In the main aisle of the church, a small icon of the miraculous Mother of God encrusted with gold and silver is to be seen. This icon portrays the Virgin without her child with her hands raised in prayer – in the same way as I would draw her.'

Both in the period of Turkish rule and later, the monastery was well-known as a centre of the national intellectual life of the Cypriots. Just as elsewhere in the Christian world, a school was opened there in the nineteenth century. Cyprus's folk medicine was practised mainly by the monk physicians Metrophanes and Charitos from

Fig. 63: The interior with the usual luxuriant chandeliers.

Machairas. Metrophanes is known as the author of an 'Iatrosophion', that is to say a work on the theory of medicine. In addition, especially in the recent past, the monastery was a centre for the production of liturgical books. Many of the works which came into being here are kept in the monastery library and the treasury.

The frescoes in the main part of the church were painted by Charalambos and Panagiotis Voulgaris from Amaliada in Greece in 1993; the mosaics on the right and left of the main portal of the church are by the contemporary Cypriot artist Arestis Stasis.

Palaichori: Metamorphosis Sotiros

Fig. 64: Transfiguration of the Redeemer.

Fig. 65: Pentecost, in the semi-circle the old cosmos.

Palaichori is a village in the Troodos Mountains about 45 km to the south of Nicosia. At the summit of one of the numerous curves with which the road threads its way through the village lies a small church. It is dedicated to the Transfiguration of the Saviour and dates from the early sixteenth century. From that time, one of the most comprehensive cycles of frescoes in the whole of Cyprus has been preserved remarkably well. The building itself is like many other churches in the mountains: it is protected by a steeply pitched roof under which there is no vaulting, apart from the conch of the apse. The visitor looks up directly into the timber roof. Vaulted niches arranged in parallel are let into the longitudinal walls marking the boundary to the sanctuary. As a result of a later L-shaped addition, the north and west walls became inside walls. The cycle with the most important events in the New Testament begins at the eastern pediment with the Annunciation. Opposite, on the western pediment, the Crucifixion is shown, the climax of Christ's Passion. The end is marked by the Descent of the Holy Ghost on the northern wall of the niche (fig. 65). Apart from the pediment, the story of the Life of Christ takes up the upper of two zones. In the lower zone, standing saints are gathered, so to speak, around the congregation which – unlike in the West – stands during the religious service. The life-size figures are painted especially finely and carefully, including four heavily armed soldier saints on the northern wall. Their richly decorated armour shows the continuing effect of the Macedonian school of the fourteenth century on the unknown painter of the Church of the Trans-

Fig. 66: The soldier saints Merkurios and Nestor who is portrayed as a young man in Byzantine tradition.

figuration. Merkurios supports himself on a spear and a sword; on his right arm hangs a shield. Nestor is standing in the course of a movement turning to the left so that his body forms a gentle S-curve and he is holding an arrow between the finger tips of his right hand and his left hand. The quiver is hanging on his left hip, on his right hip one can see the handle of a sword, the bow is suspended, somewhat detached, over his right arm (fig. 66). Although the garments allow one to recognise influence by the Macedonian school, the faces of the saints are clearly to be assigned to the Cretan school. At that time it was the latest trend in post-Byzantine painting and the quality of some portraits justifies the claim that Cyprus played a leading role in the development of this school. It is distinguished by numerous white lines which spread brilliance and brightness on the faces and give expression to feelings through their fine interlacing.

These features are particularly marked in the *Mary Orans* in the apse conch where she is portrayed without her Son. She is standing in the traditional attitude of prayer with her hands raised. Beneath her simply painted dress her slightly bent right knee shows physically. The Fathers of the Church in the lower part of the apse and the Communion of the Apostles above, whichist the only known example in Cyprus, shows 11 and 12 apostles respectively on both sides, are superb works. Many of the very crowded scenes recall pictures by Philip Goul which the painter here must have known. Several show western influences, such as architectural backgrounds of Italian inspiration or certain compositional features. The Byzantine *Anastasis*, for example, has been ousted by the western Resurrection: Christ pushes the rock to one side while three guards sleep in the foreground.

Louvaras: St. Mamas

Fig. 67: The small basilica with a shed roof dedicated to the martyr St. Mamas lies in the middle of the village.

Louvaras lies some 27 km to the north of Limassol and to the south of the Troodos Mountains. Here stands a church erected in the fifteenth century to the honour of St. Mamas with its steeply pitched roof still preserved. It manages with the smallest space, without a narthex and without any windows; the two doors are located at the centre of the south and west walls respectively. The floor is constructed of bricks. Above the west door, which nowadays connects the naos with the narthex added later, there is a large and well preserved inscription. It mentions the name of the priest Constantine as the founder of the church and the year 1455 as the date of its construction. In addition, it informs us about when and by whom the frescoes were painted. With respect to the year, there are two interpretations; in the second edition of his standard work 'The Painted Churches of Cyprus', Stylianou corrects his reading from 1465 to 1495. What is certain is that they were designed and carried out by

Fig. 68: View of the interior looking west.

the painter Philip Goul. This took place 'at the expense and through the great efforts of John, son of Kromides, and George, son of Pelekanos, as well as their wives Irene and Helena'. Goul portrayed the said persons on the right and left side of the wall inscription (fig. 68, directly above the door). Shortly after completing the works in Louvaras, Goul also painted the interior of the Church of the Holy Cross 'tou Agiasmati' in Platanistasa (p. 77 ff.); the frescoes there are in a better state.

The longitudinal sides in Louvaras are divided into three zones, the pediment walls into four which are separated from one another by coloured bands. The upper two and three zones respectively show scenes from the New Testament, while the lowest zone is decorated with a frieze of standing figures of saints. The Nativity and the Presentation of Jesus in the Temple, as well as His Baptism and Transfiguration, the Raising of Lazarus from the Dead and Christ's triumphal Entry into Jerusalem are among the most impressive scenes in the naos. In the central zone are the Healing of the Lame Man and the Blind Man, right at the bottom the four Evangelists. The lame man is shown with his bed on which he was brought to Christ. He is carrying it on his back while looking thankfully towards his healer. The blind man is to be seen twice in the miniature: once kneeling before Jesus with his arms crossed before his chest in which he his holding his blind man's stick, his eyes firmly closed and bent slightly forward towards the healing hand which half conceals his nose; in addition in a room which just appears in outline; with his eyes open he is disputing with a Pharisee (just to be seen on the left in fig. 68). The Crucifixion fills the pediment of the western wall. One zone lower, one can see the Last Supper (fig. 68), the Washing of the Feet with Peter embarrassedly scratching his head (fig. 69) and the Betrayal of Christ with Peter cutting off Malchus's ear (fig. 70). Alongside is shown the Denial of Peter in which at the same time Christ is shown before Annas and Caiphas (fig. 71).

Fig. 69 (left top): The Washing of the Feet. Peter sits unskilfully painted in front of Jesus, two further disciples are just taking off their sandals while the others crowd behind the bench.
Fig. 70 (left bottom): The Arrest of Jesus, Judas approaches from the right, below Peter cuts off the ear of the High Priest's servant which Jesus then puts back in place again...
Fig. 71 (right): Peter claims not to know Jesus: 'Verily, verily, I say unto thee. The cock shall not crow, till thou hast denied me thrice.' (John 13: 38). In the middle one sees Christ before the high priests Annas and Caiphas who prevent a soldier from continuing to beat Jesus.

Below, from the left seen from the viewer, alongside the donor portrait, is an unusual portrayal: Christ exorcises devils, two wild lads look at Him happily and the devils flee in panic into a suggested rocky landscape. Behind the two scantily clad men one sees hairy pigs running into the valley. Also unusual is the portrayal of the three saintly sisters mentioned in the inscription, Pistis, Elpis and Agape, martyrs of the second century AD, and at the same time the personification of faith, hope and love, the translation of their names. They are the Christian counterpart to the ancient topic of the Three Graces. Their mother Sophia, wisdom, who died with them during Hadrian's persecutions of the Christians, stands directly next to them on the south wall. In the middle of the exceptional scenes on the north wall, in the middle and upper zone, the Procession to Calvary, a large figure of the Archangel Michael, the appearance of the Holy Ghost, Ascension and the Dormition of the Mother of God are to be seen. Mary's death is filled with great depth. In the place of honour to the north of the icon wall, the titular saint Mamas rides his lion (cf. p. 141 and fig. 187 p. 184). In the lower zone of the bema follows the Sacrifice of Isaac, the Annunciation at the eastern edge, King Solomon on the right of the apse and the Virgin as usual in the apse conch, here of the Orans type, above pictures of the Fathers of the Church Tychon, Epiphanios, Chrysostom, Basil, Gregory and Spyridon.

The frescoes by Philip Goul in Louvaras are typical for his personal style: The compositions show many faces, but the expression is not always true to nature. The best in this respect is the portrait of John the Baptist in the south, next to the iconostasis. The heads are too large for the most part in proportion, the ecclesiastical vestments not particularly successful; these were apparently adopted from the Macedonian school. In many scenes, e.g. in the Healing of the Blind Man, Goul used prototypes from western miniature painting.

Monagri: Archangel Michael

Fig. 72: View of the propylea of the Monastery of the Archangel Michael.

Surrounded by orchards and vineyards, the Monastery of the Holy Archangel lies about 20 km to the north of Limassol, near to the village of Monagri. The main church with its iconostasis from the eighteenth century is small, it has just one nave with hexagonal side apses. Its vault is protected by a shed roof. In front of the entrance, a tiled canopy is built on a timber construction. It is borne by two marble pillars, fragments of structures from the pre-Christian period (fifth century BC). At the top, the shafts end in Corinthian capitals. Apparently there was an ancient Greek temple in the area in which the Church of the Archangel was later erected.

The century in which the monastery church was built is not known. According to one hypothesis, it dates from the twelfth century. One part of the original building is still to be seen in the north wall. The only entrance to the inside room lies in the middle of the western wall. Above it is a fresco showing the Archangel Michael. To the right of this is a portrait of Bishop Makarios of Kition (1737-1776) who had the church restored in the years 1740/44. He had to borrow the money for this from a Turk at an interest rate of 12%. According to the inscription to the left of the door, both frescoes are by Philaretos who also painted Agios Minas in Vavla. In addition to the portraits of the bishop and archangel, he enriched Monagri with a scene depicting God the Father with the

Fig. 73. St. Vachianos and St. Paraskevi.

Fig. 74: The Apostle Paul.

angels in the clouds. The Holy Ghost descends from the clouds and touches Christ's head with the Crown of Thorns. The Messiah here holds His hands crossed in front of His body. Philaretos painted the Archangel Michael once again in 1746 near the iconostasis on the north wall. The figures of Paul, Vachianos and St. Paraskevi (fig. 74, 73) are probably also by him.

A second painter, Savas Nikolaou, was involved in decorating the church. The figures of St. Lazarus, Basil, Christopher, Anthony and an unknown bishop and an unknown ascetic are by him. To judge by the feeling for colour and style of painting, he is the less important of the two artists. His relatively large inscription under the icon of the Archangel Michael on the iconostasis (on which the majority of icons are by him) allows one to assume that, in addition to his painting, he was a talented script writer.

Monagri: Panagia Amasgou

Fig. 75. Recently a convent has been under construction around the Church of the Mother of God near Monagri; the view into the lovely valley towards the Church of the Archangel Michael is still free. Fig. 76 (right): The partially destroyed portrayal of the Pentecost; the Apostles are marked by initials above their heads.

To the south-west of Monagri and about 32 km distant from Kakopetria in the south of the Troodos Mountains lies a single-aisle church made of Cypriot limestone with a timber roof, vaulted side niches and a semi-circular apse. It is dedicated to the Virgin Mary. The exact time of its construction is not known. However, research work, in particular the discovery of coins from the time of the Lusignan kings in a small window in the apse with three bull's eye panes, long since bricked up, indicate that it dates from the twelfth century. In the past, the church was renovated and improved several times.

Scholars have attributed the wall paintings to four periods. A few frescoes belong to the early twelfth century, and are thus the oldest. St. Spyridon in the lunette of the apse window, the deacon Athanasios Pentaschenites as a full figure to the right of the apse, and Athanasios from Mount Athos with another unknown saint on the adjoining side wall. From the second period – late twelfth century – come fragments from the festival cycle (vault and west lunette). An extract from a former Birth of Christ, the scene of the Bathing of the New-Born, from the early thirteenth century has survived in the southern middle niche. Alongside is a portrayal of Christ in the Temple. In this fresco, the Virgin Mary is wearing colourful garments; and the aged Simeon holds the Christ child (fig. 78). The Death of the Mother of God in its traditional place in the lunette of the west wall is severely damaged. Nevertheless, the fragments of this scene are remarkable on account of the ornamental treatment of the bed cover. Only Mark has survived of

Fig. 77 (above): Presentation of Mary in the Temple; right John the Baptist.
Fig. 78 (left): Presentation of Jesus in the Temple; Simeon and the prophetess Anna recognise in Jesus the Messiah. Joseph walks behind Mary and holds two sacrificial doves in his hand.

the Evangelists in the four spandrels. Among the paintings of better quality is the Descent of the Holy Ghost onto the seated Apostles (southern side of the vault, fig. 76). If this picture is compared with a presentation of the same topic of two centuries later, it will be noticed that the figure in the fore-ground, a personification of the world with sceptre, is flanked in Amasgou by two figures stretching their naked arms upwards. These are personifications of the races and languages. In the later portrayal (fig. 65 p. 82) they are replaced by a cloth which Cosmos, the old world, holds between his two hands, and in which twelve rolls with the Gospel are contained as a symbol of its spread among the peoples of the world.

Medallions showing well-known composers of hymns are also dated as being early thirteenth century: Joseph, Cosmas Melodos and John of Damascus. The

Fig. 79: The Archangel Michael who as usual dominates the niche to the north of the altar.

frescoes from the first half of the fourteenth century, that is to say the third period, are damaged. It is possible to recognise the Communion of St. Mary of Egypt by the saintly monk Zosimos in the lunette on the north-western wall, in addition the Apostles James, Philip and Thomas in the archivolt of the arch of the south-western niche, and unknown prophets in the lunette surrounding this arch. To the south of the west door is St. Barbara.

The fourth period, finally, can be dated exactly through an inscription: the Presentation of the Virgin Mary in the Temple was painted afresh in 1564 with John the Baptist at the lower right side (fig. 77). Cosmas, Damian and Hermolaos are to be seen in the arch. As usual, the saintly bishops, here all Cypriots, take their place in the sanctuary in the apse, but they too are only preserved in fragments. The Virgin is portrayed with the archangels in the apse conch, in the central zone the Communion of the Apostles. In addition, there are also traces of the most varied fragments of more recent date.

The artistic inheritance of Amasgou goes back to several painters. It is not, however, possible to state their exact number or to ascribe works to particular artists. For example, only the austere treatment of the colours in the Presentation of Christ in the Temple, in which blue, purple and red predominate, speaks for the monastic style.

The formerly abandoned monastery has been put back into use again recently as a convent; active construction work is greatly changing the immediate vicinity. Soon an asphalt road will lead to this sight, replacing the unpaved path with its innumerable potholes.

Pelendri: Church of the Holy Cross

Fig. 80: The Church of the Holy Cross stands on a small hillock between houses and gardens in the village of Pelendri.

The Church of the Holy Cross lies some two kilometres below Kato Aminatos in Pelendri, a village on the road to Limassol. Originally – when exactly is not known – it was erected as a single-domed building with a side aisle and niches in the side walls, but only the apse survived. Up to now, we have no indication why and by whom the original church was destroyed. The present building with its Franco-Byzantine arches separating the nave from the side aisles came into being around the turn of the thirteenth to the fourteenth century. Some two hundred years later, a second side aisle was added on the north side. This no longer has an apse today because this would appear to have been damaged in the course of time and was renewed without the vaulting.

It is possible that the frescoes in Pelendri were painted in part in the second half of the fourteenth century and in part in the second half of the fifteenth century. But it is also conceivable that all are from the fourteenth century representing two completely different stylistic trends. Only the completion of the restoration of the frescoes will be able to throw more light on this. What is certain is that the monumental painting of the dome and bema are

Fig. 81: St. Anthony, one of the founders of monasticism.

Fig. 82: St. Simeon Stylites, the monk saint on the pillar.

to be ascribed to the Macedonian school of the Palaiologue period, whereas the western part of the naos and the northern side aisle are decorated in a much more simple and popularistic manner. These areas clearly bear the touch of a master who also worked in Asinou. There he restored frescoes which had been damaged during reconstruction works.

Christ Pantocrator in the dome is just as badly damaged as the Preparation of the Throne directly beneath with the angels and the symbols of the Evangelists – an angel for Matthew, the lion for Mark, the bull for Luke and the eagle for John. The 16 prophets of the Old Testament who prepared mankind for the Incarnation of God by their prophecies take their traditional place between the four windows of the tambour bearing the dome. A sickle emanates from the wrist of one of them, described in the inscription as Zechariah. This method of portrayal goes back to a passage in the Greek version of the Old Testament, the *Septuaginta* which is not to be found in the western version as it was translated from the Hebrew original.

The refined style of the Palaiologan renaissance, which dominated in the Macedonian school, is to be seen best in the Ascension of Christ (fig. 23, p. 50) and a fragment of the Descent from the Cross. Both are to be found on the northern side of the vault, opposite the Descent of the Holy Ghost and the Entombment. On the lunette above the apse conch, one sees the Empty Tomb of Christ, the Touch Me Not scene and Christ sending out His Disciples to preach the Gospel to all nations. The Mary Orans and the censer-swinging archangels in the apse conch itself are slightly squat in size, they are not particularly differentiated in finish. The same may also be said about the figures of bishops beneath.

Fig. 83: Memorial portrait of Nengomia, Basil's wife.

Fig. 84: Memorial portrait of the priest Basil.

The Crucifixion, *Anastasis*, Christ before Pilate, the Mocking, Christ on the Way to the Cross and Christ before Annas, fragments of the Betrayal, the Washing of the Apostles' Feet and Jesus's encounter with the woman of Samaria, in short the remainder of the New Testament cycles has not yet been cleaned and is therefore difficult to assess. Nevertheless, as already mentioned, it is possible to clearly recognise the touch of the painter who also worked in the naos of Asinou. The figures of the saints which fill the bottom zone of painting are devoid of any particular refinement. Among them are unusually arranged or rarely portrayed saints, but also quite traditional ones, such as St. Anthony (fig. 81) or Symeon the Stylite (fig. 82).

The portraits to the memory of deceased persons betray western influence in the clothing. They show French origin. In the north-western niche one sees a man at prayer (fig. 84) below Christ bestowing His blessing. The text in between reads, in translation: "The servant of God, Basil, the son of the noble archon Olimites, son of Madellos, has fallen asleep, and may those who read this pray for him". Archon is a Byzantine title. Basil's wife, Nengomia, is also portrayed in a field in the arch with a similar text about her (fig. 83). She wears a high-necked dress and a then fashionable dark red veil of a type to be found in various portraits of donors of that time.

Although dedicated to the Holy Cross, Christ's Passion does not dominate in the church. Space is taken rather by the detailed portrayal of the life of the Mother of God. It is based on the apocryphal Gospel of St. James taking up the whole western vault, as well as the lunette of the nave. The cycle begins with the prehistory of her birth, the disappointment of Anna

Fig. 85: Mary visits Elizabeth. In the background a trelliswork painted with a love for detail, typical for the anonymous master.

and Joachim about their childlessness. They make sacrifices in the Temple, but their gifts are rejected. Then both search their consciences and seek counsel from God in prayer. Their prayers are heard, Anna and Joachim meet again, and shortly later Anna expects a child; the Birth of the Virgin is portrayed. These scenes are followed by reports on her childhood ending with her betrothal. Joseph the Carpenter leaves his young wife for a journey, the Marian cycle shows them both in conversation before his departure. Then follows a 'double Annunciation', Gabriel promises and explains to Mary, who is shown once in the garden fetching water and then sitting in front of her house with a spindle, the mystery of the Birth of God for which she has been chosen (Gabriel from the latter scene is still to be seen at the left in fig. 85). According to James's report, Mary was one of the virgins who were to weave the curtain for the Temple in Jerusalem, which is why she is shown here spinning red wool. When her pregnancy was well advanced, she seeks support from Elizabeth who lives far away in the mountains. She too bears a child beneath her heart; she will give birth to John the Baptist. Quite unusual for Byzantine frescoes is the portrayal of the two babes who are to be seen in their mothers' bellies, John is shown bowing towards the future Saviour of the World (fig. 85). This detail is to be found more often in the West and in manuscripts. The Marian cycle also deals with Joseph's reaction who finds his wife in her sixth month after his journey: an angel explains to Joseph what has happened, and he lowers the stick again which he had raised in anger.

Trooditissa Monastery

Fig. 86: The entrance to the church from the courtyard.

Dedicated to the Mother of God, the monastery church of Trooditissa was constructed in the wonderful Troodos Mountains at an altitude of 1392 metres above sea level. There are no records of its medieval history; according to oral tradition, it was built shortly after the iconoclastic period, thus in the eighth/ninth century. The first hermit monks might have settled here at that time. They established their monastic communities particularly near the 'Cave of Trooditissa'. The historical details about the monastery from later centuries are also very scanty. The Russian monk Basil Grigorovich Barsky collected some information, describing the church in 1735 as 'small and poor' with just one monk still living there.

The artistic inheritance of Trooditissa is modest. The majority of the icons date from the nineteenth century, just a few from the seventeenth and eighteenth. The monastery's collection includes portraits of the Evangelist John, the Virgin Mary and the Archangels Michael and Gabriel as its most interesting pieces. They show a remarkable degree of influence from Italian art.

The gold-plated iconostasis made of wood was erected in 1856 under Abbot Germanos.

In the course of the past forty years, the monastery has been renovated.

Pedoulas: Archangel Michael

Fig. 87: The western entrance to the church.

An inscription over the north door reveals that the church dedicated to the Archangel Michael in Pedoulas was constructed and painted in 1474. (The text of the inscription is reproduced on the copyright page.) Of interest in this connection is an entry in a psalter now kept in the library of the Greek Patriarchate in Jerusalem; according to it, the church of the archangel already existed at this spot in 1472, even if perhaps not in the same form. The interior is single-aisled. It is protected by a timber ceiling on the outside of which densely arranged layers of roof tiles keep off the inclemency of the mountain weather. In the east it ends in a semi-circular altar niche.

Above the south door is a portrayal of the donors (illustration on the dust cover). They are the priest Basil Chamados and his wife together with their two daughters. Basil hands the Archangel Michael a model of the church and begs him 'for forgiveness of his sins and

Fig. 88: Apse and iconostasis.

those of his family'. Chamados is portrayed kneeling, in a white liturgical vestment which fits in well with the successful portrait: he has heavy eyebrows, large eyes, marked cheekbones, a full beard and long hair. On his chest he is wearing three embroidered medallions, each with a cross. His wife is standing behind him. She is clad in a long purple robe with long sleeves. Behind the mother stand their daughters with their hands raised in prayer. They are both wearing the same type of shoes.

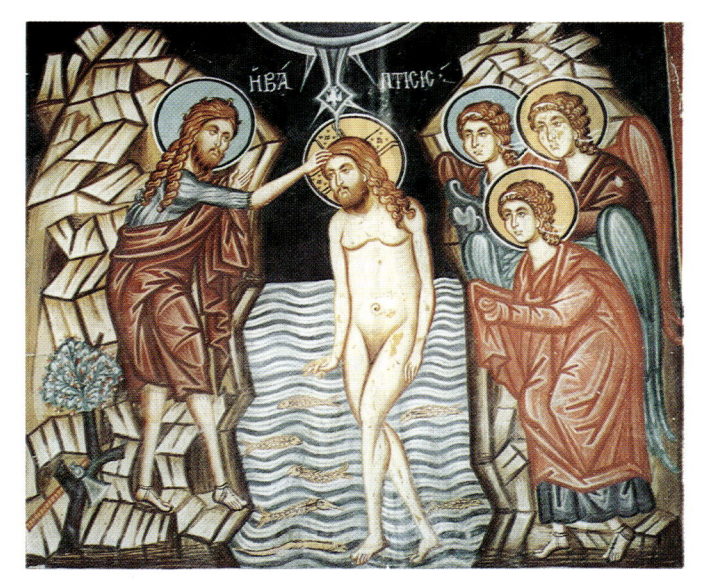

Fig. 89: Baptism of Christ in the Jordan by John the Baptist.

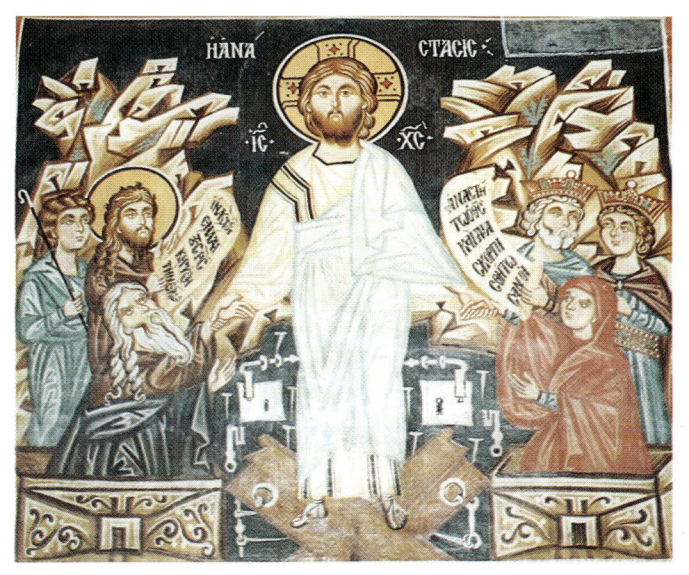

Fig. 90: Anastasis, before His Ascension, Jesus fetches Adam and Eve from Limbo. Fig. 91 (below): The Betrayal of Christ.

The elder daughter is wearing a long, blue dress with a high waistline, similar to that of her sister. These pictures of the Chamados family show us Cypriot clothing of the period in very great detail.

The frescoes are in a good condition (except for some small damage in the portrayal of the Crucifixion and the Ascension in the western and eastern pediment respectively). In the apse conch, the Virgin Mary stands between the censer-swinging Archangels Michael and Gabriel, beneath them the church fathers Nicholas, Epiphanios, Chrysostom, Basil, Gregory and Spyridon. Behind the iconostasis on the north wall is St. Athanasius. In the upper part of the iconostasis are shown the Birth of Christ and His Presentation in the Temple. The Crucifixion is shown in the western pediment. Below it are shown the Baptism in the Jordan (fig. 89) and Judas's Betrayal (fig. 91), on the northern wall of the western side the *Anastasis* (fig. 90) and Ascension. On the eastern side, to the south of the door, is a monumental painting of the Archangel Michael. The portrayals of St. Barbara on the left of the northern wall are exceptionally fine, next to her is St. Kyriaki (fig. 186 p. 183), on the other side Constantine and Helena with the True Cross. The Empress wears a wonderful crown and jewels.

According to the latest findings, the church was painted by Minas, a Cypriot painter from Myrianthousa (the Marathasa valley), whose conservative style of painting remains closely linked with Byzantine tradition. His art is in general quite simple, his style more linear. The composition with the massive figures takes up elements from the paintings of the Macedonian school.

The wooden iconostasis in Pedoulas is one of the loveliest in Cyprus. At the centre of the cornice is a Royal Lusignan coat of arms, symbolically representing the then lords of the Marathasa valley.

Moutoullas: Panagia Moutoulla

Fig. 92: The oldest dated example of a church with a pitched-roof in Cyprus: Panagia Moutoulla.

On a hill above the village of Moutoullas, near Kalopanagiotis, the church dedicated to the Virgin Mary was completed on 4 July 1280. This is to be seen from an inscription. The 'Panagia Moutoulla' has a steeply pitched roof with flat tiles on a timber substructure. From inside one looks directly onto the dark wooden boards. The red roof tiles are held in place on the rafters by clay hooks like our plain roofing tiles. This style of church with pointed gable areas had been used at least a century earlier in the Troodos region under the influence of western architecture and the constraints of the wet climate with its heavy snow falls in winter (e.g. in Panagia Asinou and Amasgou). The inscription stating the year of construction and the portrait of the donors, John Motoullas and his wife Irene above it, decorates the northern wall (fig. 94). John has a carefully trimmed moustache, a pale, olive-green tunic extending below his knee, over it a cobalt green coat and black shoes. His wife's head dress extends over her head, ears and neck. Together they hold a model of the church. A part of the composition on the right side is slightly damaged, the wife's mouth has also been obliterated in the course of time.

Fig. 93: Crucifixion. From the shield of the Just Centurion one can see the influence of the Crusaders.

The interior of the church is small and the cycle of frescoes is reduced accordingly. Its style with the large figures which manage without any plasticity is rather conservative. The form and rhythm are influenced by the mystical artistic sense of the crusaders of the Latin Kingdom of Jerusalem. In the small apse conch there is a portrait of the Virgin Mary done in wonderful colours in the manner of the Blachernitissa with raised hands, the Christ child in a medallion before her breast and the usual guard of archangels. The Virgin's face is round – an important detail – recalling the portrayals of the Mother of God in wall paintings or in what are known as the Crusader icons on Sinai. Below the apse conch are to be found the church fathers Nicholas, Gregory, John Chrysostom, Basil and the Cypriot saints Epiphanios and Auxibios. All are holding scrolls in their hands. The Annunciation is depicted on the spandrels on either sides of the apse arches, between them is the Preparation of the Throne of which only fragments have survived. We find the portrayal of Birth of Christ on the southern wall. Stylistically it belongs to the genre of monumental painting from Crete and Mount Athos. On the western wall one sees the Raising of Lazarus in which Christ stands close to the cave tomb while Mary and Martha kneel at His feet. A young man holds the end of his garment before his nose with one hand, while with the other he holds one end of the winding-sheet of the man raised from the dead after four days. Adjoining this scene is the triumphal Entry into Jerusalem. Christ rides on a donkey, followed on the left side by Peter and John, while two men with long white beards and a woman who has covered her head with a white cloth await him at the gateway to the city. The Crucifixion forms the end at the western side (upper right part damaged, fig. 93). Christ hangs in the middle on His cross, His head inclined to one side. The Virgin Mary and another woman are standing upright and composed, also John the Evangelist who holds a jewel-encrusted book in his left hand and touches his

101

Fig. 94: The donor with the donation inscription.

Fig. 95: The Mother of God as intercessor, part of the deesis.

cheek with his right one. The Good Centurion has lost his head through the damage, he is to be recognised by his chain-mail and the shield. Above the northern door, the death of the Mother of God is shown (badly damaged), while we see an *Anastasis* on the north wall: Christ stands at the broken gates of Hell, one sees the broken hinges and locks. The frescoes on the southern wall are badly damaged: the Virgin enthroned with Christ on her knee, St. Christopher mounted, Theodore, Paul and Cosmas stand. The figures in the lower zone of the western and northern walls are badly preserved. Of interest are the Intercession (fig. 95) and St. Barbara with bejewelled garments, a crown and ear-rings, entirely in the Byzantine tradition, as the thirteenth century interpreted it. A Last Judgement with elements of the Macedonian school from the late period of the Palaiologan dynasty from the fifteenth century decorates the outside of the northern wall. Two frescoes by another painter on the western outside wall can only be recognised with difficulty, especially the Presentation of Christ. Under the mounted St. George there is a very unusual dragon to be seen: half woman, half reptile.

Kalopanayiotis: St. John Lampadistis

Fig. 96: Courtyard of the Monastery of St. John Lampadistis, a place of peace and meditation even today.

Kalopanayiotis, the first large village in the Marathasa valley, is located by the stream Setrarchos. One has to drive some 60 km from Nicosia in order to visit an unusual complex here: two churches constructed after one another with a common narthex added later and a chapel at the north end probably erected for Catholic believers in the Lusignan period. All are covered by a huge roof. The buildings belong to a recently restored monastery which is no longer in use. The older of the churches is on the southern side. Its is dedicated to Herakleidios, a Cypriot saint who was converted by Barnabas and Paul on their missionary journey. Barnabas then ordained him as Bishop of Tamassos; later Herakleidios, is said to have become first Archbishop of Cyprus as successor to Barnabas. However, in the case of this tradition it must be borne in mind that these offices only developed in the second century, this here can only be a retrospective projection. St. Herakleidios is, like St. Nicholas tis Stegis in Kakopetria, laid out with a cross-in-

Fig. 97: Choir of holy men and archprelates. Scene from the Last Judgement in the narthex. Shortly after 1453.

square ground plan (cf. also the meaning of this term p. 66 ff.) and dates from the same period, the eleventh century. A minute fragment of frescoes from the twelfth century has been found in the apse so that it may be assumed that the present ones are overpaintings. There are two layers which have been ascribed to the early thirteenth and the early fifteenth centuries respectively. The first series includes several scenes from the New Testament of which the triumphal Entry into Jerusalem is the best preserved. Together with the Raising of Lazarus opposite, it decorates the barrel vaulting in the western arm of the cross (seen from the form of the ground plan). In the lunette above is the Crucifixion. In this it is possible to observe the influence of Crusader iconography. The oval shield which the Good Centurion is carrying is decorated with the coat of arms of the Lusignan kings. The vaulting of the southern arm is covered entirely by an Ascension. Christ ascends on a throne without a back rest to His Father; His aureole is borne by four angels. As Pantocrator in the dome, Christ is surrounded by eight angels worshipping Him, divided into groups by a cherub at the western point and the Preparation of the Throne at the eastern one. Christ Himself wears an unusual *himation*, unusual because this cloak draped around the body, leaving the chest partially free, is purple-coloured here instead of blue.

The second series are late-Byzantine frescoes which are difficult to classify. There are over 30 New Testament scenes distributed around the two other arms of the cross and the compartments in the vaults. The artists had to accommodate eight scenes per vault instead of the usual two (cf. fig. 99). Both series also include figures of individual saints in each case, including two portraits of the titular saint. In St. Herakleidios there is also a preliminary stage preserved before the iconostasis, what

Fig. 98: Fathers of the Church; c. 1400, St. Herakleidios.

is known as a *templon,* a low barrier between the altar and congregation area. It is painted with heraldic motives. The second church of the whole complex, originally from the twelfth century, is dedicated to a local saint, John Lampadistis from the Marathasa valley, who died already while still a young man. His veneration goes back to the miraculous force of his relics. His grave lies beneath the north-west pillar, the only one to have survived the total renovation of the eighteenth century. The saint's reputation would seem to have drawn so many pilgrims that a new narthex had to be constructed in front of the church in the fifteenth century. A donor's portrait with an inscription reveals to us that the 'Servant of God', the lay reader and choir master of Michael, together with his wife and sons, financed the painting. From the inscription it also becomes clear that the church came into the Catholic rite. The sons are tonsured in the Latin manner, but wear the vestments of Orthodox priests. This was possible in the period after the ecclesiastical union adopted at the Council of Florence in 1439. Quite certainly, the political prerequisites for the implementation of this union were favourable on Cyprus with its Catholic kings; the fact that it also failed to become established here shows how very much it disregarded the needs of the ordinary faithful.

Another inscription shows that the frescoes in the narthex are by a master from Constantinople. He had fled from the Turks in 1453 and must have carried out the painting a short time later. His style is devoid of all the elegance of the capital; without the inscription, one would quite certainly not have hit on this origin. The stories drawn with graphic outlines tell in particular of Christ's Miracles and the Last Judgement, thematically in keeping with the purpose of the narthex. Among the oldest motives is that of the Three Youths in the Furnace which is already to be found in the catacombs in Rome

Fig. 99: Ceiling fresco from St. Herakleidios; shortly after 1453: Arrival of the Three Magi, Presentation of Christ in the Temple, Mary of Bethany meets Jesus, Raising of Lazarus.

Fig. 100: Chapel, c. 1500: Abraham entertains three angels, on the right he washes their feet as a symbol of welcome, on the left he kneels before them; Handing over of the Ten Commandments and the Burning Bush.

and which was very popular in the Byzantine-Russian area. The scene designed in accordance with the account by the Prophet Daniel (Dan. 3) was interpreted as a symbol for the Trinity and the physical resurrection. Many of the New Testament themes in the narthex are accompanied by the appropriate text from the Gospel which was taken from a manuscript, thus underlining the meaning of the illustrations as an open book – or also simultaneously defeating it.

The Latin Chapel, which was extended in the fifteenth century, offers a successful synthesis of Eastern and Western elements. In dynamic, animated scenes, the hymn '*Akathistos*' in honour of the Virgin Mary – so-called because it is sung standing – is portrayed. In addition there are scenes, such as Abraham's Hospitality, the Burning Bush or Moses receiving the Ten Commandments to the right and left of Mary on her throne (fig. 100), saints' portraits, etc. They are all in the Italo-Byzantine style. The artist studied the works of the Italian renaissance with great care and has a perfect mastery of their stylistic devices. If one compares fig. 99 and fig. 100, not only does one notice that 100 years lie between the two cycles, but that a completely different conception determines the artistic approach. The immediately noticeable new feature is the view into the depth of the landscape. There are even people moving around it who have nothing to do with the story proper. Nevertheless, the more recent composition retains the Byzantine pictorial systems in the foreground, but without also retaining the backgrounds.

Kykkos: Panagia Kykkotissa

Fig. 101: The Kykkos Monastery lies in a very lovely valley in the Troodos.

The monastery lies on the western side of the Troodos Mountains at an altitude of about 1200 metres above sea level. The nearest villages are Tsakkistra and Kampos in a south-westerly direction, Melekouri in the south and Moutoullas in the east. To the west of the monastery extends a wonderful valley of cedars through which runs the road to Paphos.

The monastery is known under the name of Kykkos or the 'Mother of God of Kykkos', but it is still not known where this name comes from. According to one tradition, the designation '*kykkos*' or '*kokkos*' is linked with the kermes oak (Latin '*quercus coccifera*') which grew in this area a few centuries ago. Another version ascribed the expression '*kykkos*' to a bird whose call '*kik-ko, kik-ko*' became the name of the monastery.

Historical sources indicate that Kykkos was founded at the end of the eleventh century by the Byzantine ruler Alexios Komnenos I. At that time, Cyprus formed part of the East Roman Empire and the emperor regularly sent his governors to the island. They were given the title of duke. Among them was one of the emperor's most brilliant and highly honoured generals, Manuel Boutoumites. Boutoumites could not endure the oppressive heat and sultriness which prevails in Nicosia in sum-

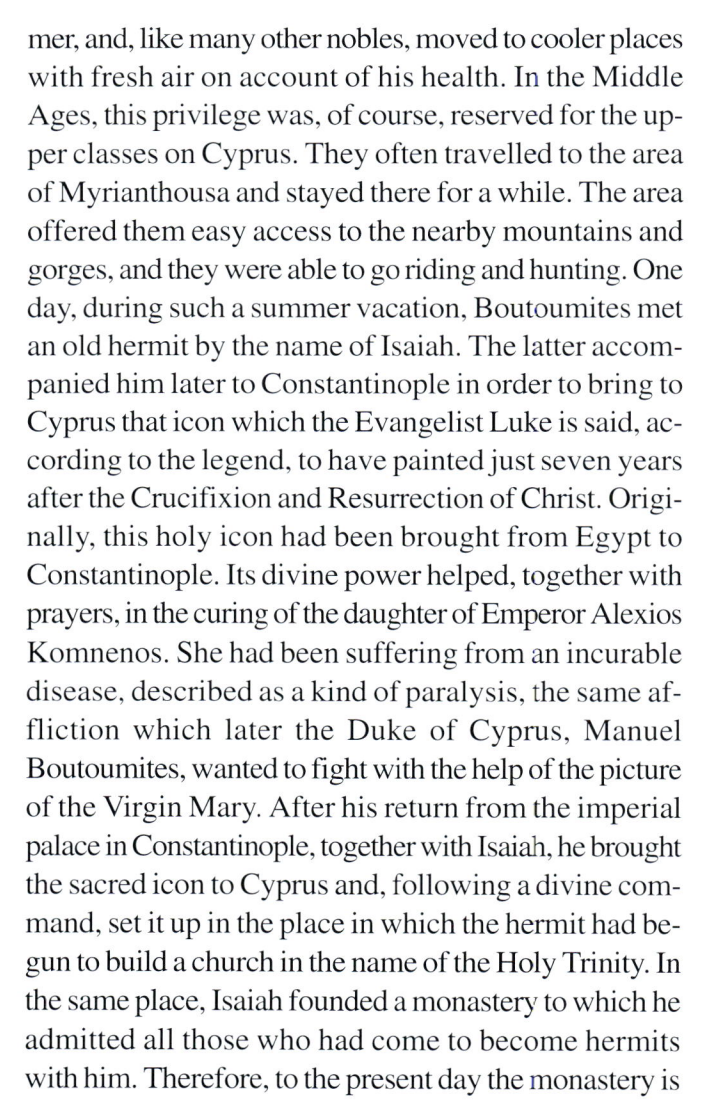

Fig. 102 (left): Entrance with new mosaics.
Fig. 103 (above): Detail from the courtyard, the translation of the Kykkotissa icon from Constantinople to the monastery.

mer, and, like many other nobles, moved to cooler places with fresh air on account of his health. In the Middle Ages, this privilege was, of course, reserved for the upper classes on Cyprus. They often travelled to the area of Myrianthousa and stayed there for a while. The area offered them easy access to the nearby mountains and gorges, and they were able to go riding and hunting. One day, during such a summer vacation, Boutoumites met an old hermit by the name of Isaiah. The latter accompanied him later to Constantinople in order to bring to Cyprus that icon which the Evangelist Luke is said, according to the legend, to have painted just seven years after the Crucifixion and Resurrection of Christ. Originally, this holy icon had been brought from Egypt to Constantinople. Its divine power helped, together with prayers, in the curing of the daughter of Emperor Alexios Komnenos. She had been suffering from an incurable disease, described as a kind of paralysis, the same affliction which later the Duke of Cyprus, Manuel Boutoumites, wanted to fight with the help of the picture of the Virgin Mary. After his return from the imperial palace in Constantinople, together with Isaiah, he brought the sacred icon to Cyprus and, following a divine command, set it up in the place in which the hermit had begun to build a church in the name of the Holy Trinity. In the same place, Isaiah founded a monastery to which he admitted all those who had come to become hermits with him. Therefore, to the present day the monastery is called 'the Imperial and Stauropegial Monastery of Kykkos'. The term '*stauropegial*' designates a cross lying under the foundation stone. After completion of the monastery, Isaiah became the first abbot. Shortly after his appointment, he began to draft rules under which the monks were to live in order to achieve the salvation of their souls.

The iconographic style of the icon of the Mother of God '*Kykkotissa*' differs from all other icon types of the Virgin Mary. It shows her with her child. Christ sits on the right side of the Virgin with his naked legs hanging down. At the beginning of the twelfth century, this icon type – '*Kykkotissa*' – was adopted by the Orthodox Christian world: by Cyprus, Egypt, Greece and larger areas in the Balkans. In the seventeenth century, thanks to the intellectual and cultural links with Cyprus, the '*Kykkotissa*' type was also adopted in Russia.

Since the mid-eighteenth century, the holy pictures in the icon, those of the Mother of God and of the Child Christ, are veiled and not decked out like the rest of the icon. Nobody dares to look them in the face, because many who did so in the past were punished. According to the hagiographic sources, the icon stood open so long as it was in the Emperor's palace. In 1576, it was encased in a silver gilt cover which was replaced by a new one in 1795. At that time, the holy icon stood on the left side of the main portal, before the entrance to the iconostasis. For many centuries it is said to have brought about numerous miracles within the monastery, and right down to the present it is the pride and symbol for the salvation of Cyprus. Therefore, not only Christians, but also non-Christians invoke the 'Holy Mother of God of Kykkos!' when they are in difficulties or danger.

In the course of its long history, the monastery of Kykkos and its residents faced many problems. The first catastrophic fire broke out in 1365. The main church burned down together with many documents and relics. Immediately after, Queen Eleonora, the spouse of the tenth ruler of the French aristocratic family Lusignan, Peter I, had the monastery reconstructed. Conflagrations of similar dimensions took place in 1541, 1751 and 1813. Each time, the interior decorations together with the library were destroyed. That is why only a little written evidence of the early history of the monastery has been preserved.

Scholastic research has shown that Kykkos made a considerable contribution to sacred pictorial art and ecclesiastical literature. This is shown by the large number of manuscripts written on parchment in the twelfth and thirteenth centuries which were used in Kykkos and which are nowadays kept in the French National Library in Paris, the Vatican Library and other major European libraries. Some of these manuscripts furnish valuable information on the abbots and famous persons from Kykkos's past. During Ottoman rule, in Cyprus the old Byzantine tradition of the writing and decoration of books was continued. This can be seen by the numerous liturgical works written by calligraphers and illuminators in an unusual manner which are to be found in the monastery library, the Library of the Patriarchate in Jerusalem, and elsewhere. The illuminations and miniatures in these manuscripts reflect the great influence of the baroque calligraphic schools in Italy which is intermixed with elements of Cypriot popular art (examples in the introduction, fig. 14-16, p. 40 f).

Various pilgrims from the West and the East report important details about the past of Kykkos. In 1683, the Dutchman Cornelis van Bruyn toured Cyprus which at that time was suffering from swarms of locusts. In order to protect the country, Van Bruyn reports, "the inhabitants organised litanies in which they carried round

Fig. 104: Fresco of the Mother of God with the Child Jesus in the apse conch of the type 'Platytera'.

the icon of the Virgin Mary holding Christ in her arms. It is a work of the Apostle Luke which is normally in a monastery called Chicho (Kykkos) with 400 monks. At certain intervals, some monks travelled to Russia and other places in order to carry out the most varied tasks. The monastery is situated on Mount Olympus – the highest on the island. In periods of drought, the icon is carried from the monastery into the church service. The face of the icon is turned to the side from which rain is expected. The same divine service was held against the invasion of locusts, and as soon as the icon was fastened on a pedestal, birds came and descended on the locusts, eating some of them. At that moment, a great gale arose and swept the locusts straight out to sea. The birds which had eaten the locusts had – so it was said –

never been seen on Cyprus before and will never return. At the order of the Pasha, nobody was permitted to kill the birds, and if anyone did nevertheless dare to do so, he was put to death." The Russian monk Basil Grigorovich Barsky, who visited the monastery in 1727 and 1735, left informative reports on Kykkos.

The main church is a basilica; the iconostasis may be dated to the eighteenth century. Some of the icons in the iconostasis come from the seventeenth century. The frescoes in the main part of the restored church were painted recently by the well-known Cypriot painter George Georgiou. The frescoes in the other buildings in the monastery were done a decade ago by Greek, Romanian, Serbian, Bulgarian and Cypriot painters. Impressive are the mosaics, a recent work by the Cypriot artist Philippos Kepolas.

In the church there is a special room in which a large collection of old icons is kept. The small ecclesiastical museum (a new, large museum is due to be completed shortly) is located in the chapel, near the entrance door of unusual design. Here one can view crosses, relics, vestments, golden shrines and other objects of historical value. In addition to all these things, there are numerous old books. The finest among them are the printed Russian gospels decorated with precious stones which were presented to Kykkos in the eighteenth and nineteenth centuries by various Russian church and state dignitaries.

Under the Turks, it was prohibited to call the faithful to divine service with bells. Only at the end of the nineteenth century was it permitted to build a bell tower in which five bells hang. The heaviest one weighs 1280 kilograms, according to an inscription underneath the edge of the bells it was a gift of the Russian Tsar Peter the Great and his wife Catherine.

Kykkos nowadays has a valuable library with some 15,000 printed volumes – some dating from even the early sixteenth century. The monastery collection includes more than a hundred Greek manuscripts. Among them are parchment fragments from the tenth century.

The churchyard in Kykkos is accessible through two entrances from the south and east. The buildings around the main church, including the abbot's residence, were erected, together with those on the eastern side, between 1700 and 1755. The complete restoration of the Kykkos Monastery has been accomplished thanks to the great efforts of the Most Reverend Fr. Nikephoros, the present abbot of Kykkos.

Chrysorrogiatissa Monastery

Fig. 105: View of the picturesque courtyard.

The Chrysorrogiatissa Monastery is about 40 km distant from Paphos. It is located on the peak of Mount Rogia at a height of 844 m above sea-level. '*Rogia*' means pomegranate and '*chryso*' golden, the Panagia Chrysorrogiatissa is thus the Virgin of the Mountain of the Golden Pomegranate. Looking out from it, one has a wonderful view of several valleys.

Regrettably there are no written reports available giving information about the time of the foundation of the monastery, but tradition gives the date of its establishment as the year 1152, during the rule of the Byzantine emperor Manuel Komnenos. The founder of the monastery was the monk Ignatios who found a miraculous icon of the Virgin Mary on the coast near Paphos. An unknown woman is said to have thrown it into the waves on the Isaurian coast (that is the coast of Asia Minor directly facing Cyprus) in order to save it from the iconoclasts.

The icon was brought to Ignatios's hermitage in which it was then discovered that it belonged to the series of 70 icons which the Evangelist Luke is said to have painted. Just like the Virgin Mary of Kykkos ('*Kykkotissa*'), this icon also has a silver cover and is now located on the left side of the main entrance in the iconostatis from 1770.

The monastery complex has the form of an irregular rectangle. The buildings and the monks' cells with their balconies recalling the timber architecture of Mount Athos were constructed on all four sides. The main church is located at the centre of the courtyard, possibly at the same place at which Ignatios's hermitage was located. The Turks destroyed the monastery in 1821 after the monks had participated in actions against the sultan and followed the Greek War of Liberation with too much interest for Ottoman taste. That is why not much has survived from the past.

In addition to the miraculous painting by Luke, there are further icons in the possession of the monastery which is of a certain importance. The oldest picture in the iconostasis shows Jesus Christ. It is dated to the turn of the sixteenth to the seventeenth century. A silver cover was prepared in 1762 for an icon of the Virgin '*Chrysorrogiatissa*', and so it survived well-protected. A portrait of the Evangelist John dates from 1773. The other icons do not date back any further than the eighteenth or nineteenth centuries. In the sanctuary there are some frescoes of an older date to be seen: Abraham's Sacrifice of Isaac and the Birth of Christ. The Birth of the Virgin Mary is resplendent over the north door, and in the lunette over the western entrance the Annunciation and the Assumption.

Thanks to the initiative of the present Abbot Dyonisios the monastery now has a small workshop for the renovation and preservation of icons.

Monastery of St. Neophytos

Fig. 106: St. Neophytos Monastery at the end of a valley near Paphos. Fig. 107: Monks' cells which Neophytos cut into the rock.

In a lovely stretch of country side, about 9 km to the north of Paphos, lies a hermitage dating from the twelfth century. 415 metres above sea level, St. Neophytos found caves which he enlarged by his own labour thus creating his own cell, the church of the Holy Cross as well as a sanctuary. In about 1500, the imposing main building of the monastery was constructed in the church of which nowadays the greater part of his venerable bones are kept to the left of the iconostasis. Other of his relics are to be found in the monasteries of Kykkos, Machairas and in St. Mamas in Morphou. Neophytos is, without doubt, the most famous ascetic among Cyprus's saints. In the past, many miracles have been attributed to his grave which was opened in 1750.

Neophytos was born in Kato Drys, a village near Lefkara, and died in around 1215. He was the most productive ecclesiastical author at the turn of the twelfth to the thirteenth century. A large number of original manuscripts of his writings, mainly theological literature for everyday use, are contained in parchment codices which found their way from the monastery to the National Li-

Fig. 108: The church fathers Basil, Cyril of Alexandria and John the Benefactor, mid-sixteenth century.

brary in Paris and elsewhere. Neophytos's works are, however, an inexhaustible source on the history of the island. This is confirmed by his notes on the conquest of Cyprus by Richard Coeur de Lion and on the end of Byzantium's rule there. He uses just as critical words for the Byzantine usurper Isaac Komnenos as for the king of England. The autobiography of the monastery founder, who was already popular among his contemporaries, does not only provide revealing details on the events of the twelfth century, but also about how the community of monks gathered around him.

The hermitage and main church are part of the large group of Byzantine buildings in the neo-classical style from Constantinople. They were constructed at the productive climax of Byzantinism, thus at a time in which St. Neophytos played a great role. Through the grace of God, with whose help he accomplished his works, he appeared as a teacher of fear of the Lord in accordance with the words of the prophet David: 'Come ye children, and listen unto me: I will teach ye to fear the Lord.'

Already shortly after its completion, the hermitage, in Greek *'enkleistra'*, had become an influential monastic centre. In 1170, Neophytos began to paint the interior of the cave. He is himself portrayed several times in his hermitage. Theodore Apseudes completed the major part of the frescoes in 1183. Apseudes is probably an epithet rather than a surname meaning that he was reliable and trustworthy. He was an excellent Byzantine painter and one of the first whom we know as a person. Very probably, Theodore was also involved in 1192 in two icons and the majority of frescoes in Lagoudera. According to the research results of D. Winfield he may have ended his life as a monk in the monastery Panagia tou Araka.

Back to the Monastery of St. Neophytos: the *enkleistra* is subdivided into two *anachoreses* which were described as the upper and lower hermitage. For us, the lower part is of the main interest in which the naos, bema and the saint's cell are fully painted. Theodore executed the two latter ones in the classical court style of the end

Fig. 109: John the Baptist, David and Solomon, 1196.

Fig. 110: The Last Supper, 1503.

of the twelfth century, whereas the naos was decorated by an unknown painter using what is known as the 'monastery style'. One can gain an idea of the differences by means of the *Anastasis*. The part by Theodore dominates the area above the grave, the monastic variant executed scarcely 13 years later covers the eastern wall of the naos. Whereas Theodore uses gentle, curved lines allowing the garments to flutter extravagantly and giving his figures a mild facial expression, the figures by the unknown painter are drawn with austere and hard lines, in keeping with the humble monks and saints. The *Anastasis* on the eastern wall is regarded as the most remarkable composition. Christ is to be seen before the gates of Hell with Adam, Eve, David, Solomon and John the Baptist who is holding a scroll with the words: 'Behold Him of whom I told you' (fig. 110). One can also compare the 'small Crucifixion' which is painted in the niche above the grave with the second, larger one above the door to the sanctuary showing Christ on the Cross, John and the Good Centurion on the right side in front of the walls of Jerusalem.

On the northern wall, to the left of the grave, the invocation: the donor, Neophytos, is prostrate in prayer before Christ on His throne. To his right one reads: 'Oh Christ, through Thy Mother and John the Baptist who stand in purity and honour by Thy Throne, have mercy on him who is in supplicant prayer at Thy divine feet for now and for ever more.' On the ceiling of the cave, Neophytos, the saintly old man, the guide and teacher on the path of light, truth and eternal life, is portrayed once again, this time with the Archangels Michael and Gabriel who grasp him by the shoulders and accompany him to Heaven (fig. 189, p. 186). Thus he gave expression to his most ardent wish. A third picture of

Fig. 111: Washing of the Feet, 1503, below saints.

Fig. 112: Jesus in Gethsemane, painted by Apseude in 1183.

Neophytos is to be found beneath the *Anastasis*. To the left and right of the door linking the bema and cell is the Annunciation; over the door Christ Emmanuel is placed between the Archangel and Virgin. On the ceiling over the altar the Ascension unfolds, quite close to the Virgin Mary *Orans*. On the same level, instead of below as is usual, are the Fathers of the Church: John Chrysostom, Gregory, Ephiphanios and Nicholas. Theodore banished Ephraim Syrus, Cyriacus the Anchorite, Gerasimos, Theodore, Pachomios, Hilarion and Euthymios to the uneven west wall. The round fresco of Christ Pantocrator on the curved overhang of rock is to be seen on the low, western part of the ceiling (fig. 113). It belongs to the paintings redrawn or renovated by an unknown master in 1503. In the upper southern part of the naos there are numerous scenes from the Passion of Christ: the Last Supper (fig. 110) and the Washing of the Feet (fig. 111)

date from 1503. The Agony in the Garden (fig. 114), the Betrayal, Jesus before Pilate who washes his hands, the Way of the Cross, the Crucifixion, the Deposition, the *Anastasis* already mentioned and the 'All hail' (Matthew 28:9) which the Risen Christ called to Mary Magdalene and the 'other Mary' and then asked them to inform the other disciples of His victory over death (Matthew 28:1-10), were painted in 1196, as mentioned above, in monastic style. The same also applies for the life-size figures of saints in the lower zone: Anthony, Arsenios, Euthymios, Amun the Nitriote, Andronikos, Daniel the Sketiote, Theodosios the Cenobiarch, John of the Ladder, Onouphrios, Makarios, Paisios and Stephen the Younger. The latter is a martyr for his defence of the veneration of icons, and that is why he carries an icon of the Virgin of the '*Glykophilousa*' type

Fig. 113: Christ Pantocrator, fresco from the year 1503.

on his arm. The Hospitality of Abraham is once again from 1503.

Opposite the hermitage, a domed basilica was erected around 1500 with a nave and two aisles, dedicated to the Virgin Mary. The decoration is from the sixteenth century. The cycle begins in the southern aisle with Joachim and Anna Presenting Gifts in the Temple, their Return and Joachim's Prayer. The northern aisle contains 24 pictures on the 24 verses of the hymn 'Akathistos' to the Virgin Mary. They are influenced by the Macedonian school of the Palaiologan period.

Undoubtedly most valuable is the fresco with the Communion of the Apostles in the centre section of the altar apse. The Saviour blesses bread and wine – His Body and His Blood – at the opened altar. Regrettably, only six apostles, led by Peter, are preserved. The portrayal is worthy of the meaning of the holy place and the rite performed here. Beneath it, officiating bishops bow before the Mystery: Saints John Chrysostom, Gregory, Athanasios, Basil, Cyril of Alexandria and John the Almsgiver (fig. 108). The composition varies the Adoration of the Lamb. All these works probably go back to Joseph Houris, a hellenised painter who had come to Cyprus from Syria and left his name on the icons of the great intercession which he painted in 1544.

If one looks once again at the overwhelming Communion of the Apostles, the striking similarity with the treatment of the topic in the Serbian monastery Manasija in Reǎava from the fifteenth century must be mentioned, evidence of a close artistic link. The nearness to the monumental painting in Lagoudera, Kurbinovo in Macedonia or Studenica in Serbia is even more noticeable.

Geroskipos: St. Paraskevi

Fig. 114: The Church of St. Paraskevi nowadays lies in an area exploited too much for tourism.

In Geroskipos, nowadays a suburb of Paphos, a church of St. Paraskevi was constructed in the ninth century. It is one of the finest examples of Byzantine architecture and has the form of a basilica. Five domes forming a cross cover the consecrated area. The three largest ones lie along the centre of the nave, the two smaller ones above the centre of the side aisles to the north and south of the main dome. From outside, the church is similar to St. Barnabas near Salamis, St. Lazarus in Larnaca, the church of the Holy Apostles in Constantinople and St. John in Ephesus. It has still not been clarified up to now whether is stands on the remains of an ancient Greek temple to Aphrodite.

In the past two decades, a great deal of restoration work has been carried out on the frescoes (cf. fig. 116) which were painted at various times in several layers on top of one another. In the course of this, floral and geometric ornaments around a painted cross were discovered in the dome above the altar with forms giving evidence of the influence of early Romanesque and Muslim art. The subdued colours cause one to assume that they are from the iconoclastic period before 843 – inconspicuous and yet in view of their rarity extremely valuable remnants of the markedly modest, non-iconic way of painting. As a result of this, one has one of the main clues with regard to the time when the church was con-

Fig. 115: Paul dictates to a scribe, perhaps Luke.

structed. Palaeographic studies of the form of the letters used for the inscriptions suggest a dating to the ninth century. Some frescoes were destroyed in the past. On the southern arch, supporting the central dome of the nave, figures from the tenth century are to be seen. On the northern lunette below the main dome there is a portrayal of the Dormition of the Virgin Mary from the twelfth century which is covered for the most part by a painting of the Crucifixion from the fifteenth century under the influence of Italian art; various elements could have come from Venice.

The main dome is decorated by a portrayal of the Virgin Mary *Orans*, that is with a picture of Christ in front of her breast. She is surrounded by the twelve prophets of the Old Testament. They are holding scrolls on which one can read their prophetic references to the Virgin Mary – an iconographic synthesis. She bears a title which comes from Byzantine hymnography: 'Prophets have predicted Thee'. In the western dome one sees Christ Pantocrator, surrounded by angels, cherubim and seraphim. The south-east pendentive of this dome bears a picture of the prophet Moses, opposite Abraham's Sacrifice of Isaac is shown. The best preserved scene is to be found in the north-east spandrel. St. Paul dictates a text to a scribe, perhaps the Evangelist Luke (fig. 115). According to the testimony of the New Testament, Paul was indeed linked with the town of Paphos through his apostolic mission – and this is 'documented' in Geroskipos.

In the lower section of the southern lunette, the Gospel cycle begins with the Birth of the Virgin Mary (fig. 116) and her Presentation in the Temple (damaged). These are followed by the Birth of Christ and His Baptism in the Jordan. In this latter composition on the south wall appear a male figure (the personification of the Jordan) and a female one. The latter symbolises the sea; she sits in a shell drawn by two dolphins which, admittedly, look more like sea monsters. The Raising of Lazarus and the Triumphant Entry into Jerusalem have found their place under the western dome (fig. 117) – works recalling the paintings in Mistras, Peloponnese, from 1428 and the Cretan school of painting of the sixteenth century.

The Last Supper and the Washing of the Feet are to be seen in the upper part of the northern lunette under the western dome. The Betrayal scene in which Judas, coming from the left, kisses Jesus is slightly damaged. It contains iconographic elements from Western art. On the northern side of the vault between the western and central domes the Way of the Cross is to be seen (fig. 118). Simon carries the Holy Cross, Christ walks behind him. The Gospel cycle closes with the Crucifixion in the northern lunette under the main dome. As already mentioned, it is painted to a large part over an earlier fresco with the Dormition of the Mother of God.

In Geroskipos there is a valuable Marian icon from the fifteenth century. It is of the type of the Virgin '*Hodegetria*' in which the anonymous painter has taken his lead from Palaiologan models. On the reverse there is a Crucifixion in western style.

Fig. 116 (above): Birth of the Virgin Mary. The pictures have a stripy appearance because at the time of photography they were being prepared for restoration with strips of gauze.
Fig. 117 (right): Triumphant Entry into Jerusalem. The children picking fruit from the fruit tree belong to the usual cast of this scene.

Fig. 118: Via Crucis, the Way of the Cross, here showing Christ going with fettered hands behind Simon of Cyrene while the latter carries the cross for Him for a part of the arduous way – not voluntarily, but because the soldiers had picked him at random out of the crowd (Luke 23: 26).

Vavla: St. Minas

Fig. 119: View of the courtyard.

Fig. 120: Entrance gate to the monastery.

The church of St. Minas lies to the east of the village of Vavla near Lefkara. The exact date of its construction is not known. Some studies of various parts of the structure suggest that it may have been erected in the Middle Ages, perhaps at the end of the Lusignan period. The earliest details about the village and on the divine services in the church date back to the sixteenth and seventeenth centuries; they were discovered in Greek sources which are now held in archives in Paris and Venice.

The church is located within a quadrangle of buildings with twenty former monks' cells. These are distributed over two floors on the southern side where the two main portals are also located. The inscription on the eastern wall from the year 1670 attests that at that time there was an olive-oil mill and various monastic storehouses at this point. In 1730, the Russian monk Basil Grigorovich Barsky visited the monastery and noted in his diary that 45 monks lived in the monastery. Thanks to the endeavours of the then Abbot Parthenios, the church was completely renovated in 1754.

Its frescoes are by a fairly unimportant artist: they were painted in 1757 by Philaretos. We have already encountered him before in the Church of the Archangel near Monagri. The most important part of the portrayal of the titular saint on the southern wall, close to the iconostasis: Minas is sitting on a horse on which he also suffered his martyrdom. Philaretos has painted St. George in the front part of the north wall.

A cave in the monastery garden contains a spring dedicated to the Mother of God. Its blessed water is believed to help with the treatment of diseases of the skin.

In 1965, St. Minas was reopened as a convent. This fact is a sign of the growing spiritual interest on Cyprus in recent times. A similar trend can also be observed in Greece and on Mount Athos.

Kato Lefkara: Archangel Michael

Fig. 121: One clearly sees the difference between the single-aisled, domed old building and the new part added in the west.

The church of the Archangel Michael lies in Kato Lefkara, thus in one of the two parts of the town of Lefkara which is divided into Kato (Lower) and Pano (Upper) Lefkara. The small town is known already from Byzantine times, the period in which the church of the Archangel Michael was constructed. It is a single-aisled building with vaulted niches in the side walls which was mentioned in several documents in the thirteenth and fourteenth centuries. The west wall was removed in 1908 to allow for an extension of the church. Because its style of construction displays great stylistic affinities to the architecture of Constantinople, its origin is dated to the late twelfth century. It is decorated with frescoes from the twelfth, fourteenth and fifteenth centuries.

The fresco cycle begins in the central section of the apse with the Communion of the Apostles (fig. 122). Below this portraits of the early fathers have survived: John Chrysostom, John the Almsgiver and Epiphanius were greatly revered on the island and a series of churches are dedicated to them. All three ascetic figures hold scrolls and are clad in white liturgical vestments decorated with a black cross (fig. 123). The frescoes in the apse were donated by a 'Servant of the Lord': the priest Michael Pileas. In the lunette of the southern central niche one can see in the upper part the Birth of Christ, His Presentation in the Temple, the Baptism of Jesus and the Raising of Lazarus. In the area below, above the south door and to the left of the Archangel Michael is the Headcloth of St. Veronica, slightly damaged (fig. 190 p. 191), to the east of the door John the Baptist. A severely damaged Christ Pantocrator dominates the dome. Also severely damaged are the 16 prophets who enliven the areas between the four windows below the Pantocrator, and the Virgin Mary with the archangels in the apse conch.

Of the remaining paintings, a Resurrection of Christ from the fifteenth century in the west arch and the portrait of St. George on the north side from a much later period are worthy of note.

Fig. 122 (above): Fresco in the middle zone in the apse, the topic of which, relatively freely portrayed, is the Communion of Apostles. Fig. 123 (right): The zone beneath, Chrysostom, John the Almsgiver and Epiphanios (here without his otherwise usual cap). The emphasis on the three ascetes with cloaks decorated with crosses suggests a dating at the end of the twelfth century.

Stavrovouni Monastery

Fig. 124: From the oldest monastery on the island one has a breath-taking view of the plain and sea.

The monastery Stavrovouni was constructed on the peak of the mountain of the same name in the district of Larnaca. In earlier times it had been known under the name of Olympus, nowadays, the highest point of Troodos Mountains further to the west bears that name. Stavrovouni, as the name already says, is dedicated to the Holy Cross; it can be derived from two words '*stavros*' (cross) and '*vouno*' (mountain). According to religious tradition, the monastery was founded by St. Helena, the mother of the Byzantine Emperor Constantine I, the Great. According to the fifteenth century Cypriot chronicler Leontios Machairas, Helena had discovered the three crosses on which Jesus and the two thieves had been crucified on her pilgrimage to the Holy Land. She had them excavated and wanted to bring them to Constantinople. But she is said to have left one of these crosses in Cyprus during an involuntary visit caused by shipwreck, and to have presented it to a monastery. Thus the legend.

Stavrovouni is the earliest documented monastery on the island. The oldest written reference dates from the Byzantine period. It proves that Stavrovouni had been

124

an important religious centre since the fourth century. The relevant information is to be found in the memoirs of a Russian traveller, Abbot Daniel, who stayed on Cyprus in 1106. He recorded that the Holy Cross was located on Mount Olympus with the objective of 'warding off the evil spirits and curing any illness', and he noted: 'This cross is like a meteorite, it is not supported in the ground, because the Holy Ghost holds it in the empty space. I, unworthy man, knelt down before this holy, mysterious object and have seen with my own, sinful eyes the inherent holy grace present in this place.' After its foundation, Stavrovouni was occupied by Orthodox monks living according to the rule of St. Basil. We obtain further historical information from Western visitors to Cyprus in the thirteenth century. Willibrandi de Oldenburg, for example, visited Stavrovouni in 1211 and wrote: 'The cross of the Good Thief is on the highest mountain in Cyprus' – which was wrong, as Stavrovouni is not as high as the Troodos peak. Ludolph von Suchen noted in 1305: 'The mountain is like the Mount Tabor on which the Benedictine monks live. From its peak one can see the Lebanon.' That is true, but the weather must be very clear in order to be able to check this.

In its long history, Stavrovouni went through times of great poverty and hardship caused by the most varied invasions by foreigners on the island. Nowadays, the Holy Cross is no longer there and nobody knows what has happened to it. In 1598, the Bohemian nobleman Kryštof Harant noted: 'Nobody knows what the Turks have done with the Holy Cross.' The walls, the church, the iconostasis and monks' cells in Stavrovouni were almost completely destroyed during a great fire in 1888. The only relic which has been preserved down to the present is a silver cross in which a minute piece of the holy cross is inserted, the only major reliquary which is still kept in Stavrovouni.

Recently, the monastery underwent a complete renovation. Its small church was restored again with frescoes and icons by the well-known painter, Fr. Kallinikos, a monk from Stavrovouni. The legend of the foundation is recorded in these pictures, St. Helena in a brilliant red garment (fig. 125) and the Finding of the True Cross in Jerusalem (fig. 127). By the way, the emperor's mother recognised that she did have the right cross by the miraculous healing of a woman. Colourful, but also not without the skull painted beneath Christ's Cross for centuries is the Deposition (fig. 126). The majority of the frescoes in the church refer to the Cross and the life of St. Helena. In this manner, Stavrovouni is continuing the deeply-rooted Byzantine painting tradition.

The present monks in Stavrovouni live a very strict form of monastic life, similar to that of the monks on Mount Athos. The rule of their first abbot, Dyonisios, forms the basis of this. Perhaps that is why it is still forbidden even today for women to visit Stavrovouni. This is not the case in any of the other monasteries and churches in Cyprus.

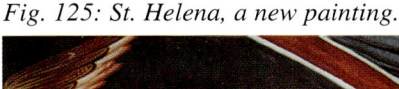

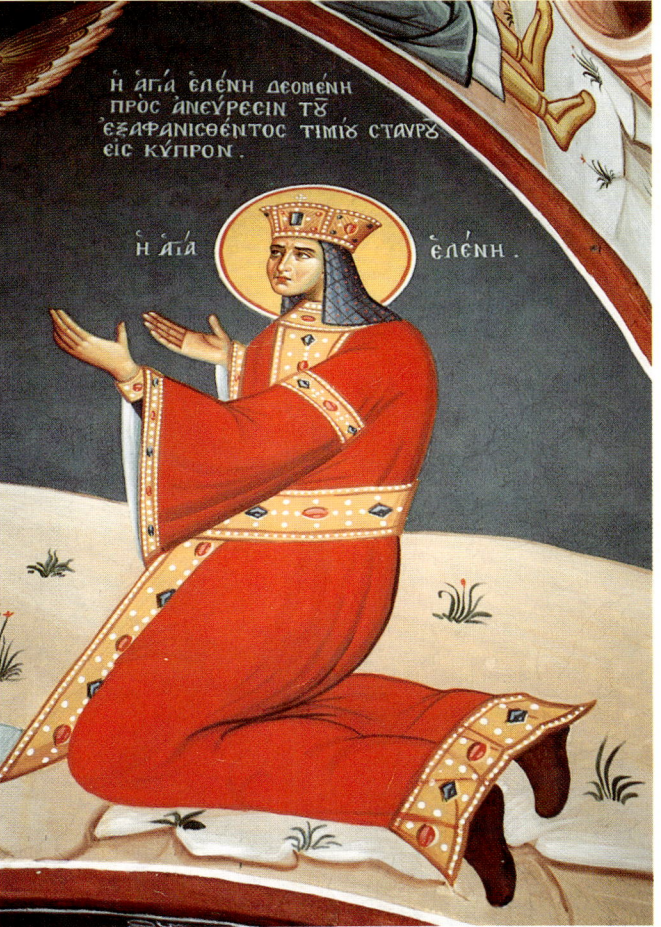

Fig. 125: St. Helena, a new painting.

Fig. 126: The Deposition of Christ.

Fig. 127: Finding of the True Cross.

126

Kiti: Panagia Angeloktisti

Fig. 128: Behind this façade is to be found one of the greatest treasures in the whole of Cyprus: an apse mosaic from the sixth century.

Near to Larnaca, at the north-western end of the village of Kiti, lies a cruciform plan church with dome from the eleventh century (cf. also fig. 17 p. 44). It is dedicated to the 'All Holy One', that is the Mother of God, and bears the epithet '*Angeloktisti*'; according to tradition it was thus 'built by angels'. If not necessarily through divine intervention, nonetheless miraculously enough, remnants of the wall of the early Byzantine basilica destroyed by the Arabs have survived in the apse. The building preserved today was later erected on its ruins. And on the wall remnants of the original basilica, only as recently as the nineteen-fifties was a mosaic discovered, the dating of which is disputed. In particular on account of the ornament frieze last uncovered, which is still very redolent of the Hellenistic spirit towards the end of Antiquity, experts tend towards an early dating in the sixth century. This work of great craftsmanlike and artistic quality is thus the only almost undamaged surviving example of a Byzantine apse mosaic from the period before iconoclasm. This was only possible on Cyprus thanks to the neutrality negotiated between the Arabs and Byzantium. It was not possible for the command of the iconoclastic emperors to completely destroy everything to have effect here.

In keeping with the Orthodox pictorial programme, the mosaic depicts the Virgin Mary between the Archangels Michael and Gabriel with the Child on her arm (fig. 131). As the Mother of God stands facing the beholder on a richly decorated footstool reserved for imperial persons and Jesus is held on her left arm, it is to be regarded as of the '*Hodegetria*' type. *Hodegetria* is one of the many titles of dignity with which Mary is honoured in the East. It means that she shows mankind the right path, guiding them, and goes back to an old Marian hymn. Jesus holds a scroll in His left hand and raises His right hand in a gesture of blessing (fig. 132). Although, as He is on Mary's arm and should really be turned slightly to the side, He is portrayed facing the observer. He is the Ruler who proclaims the True Law. The apse, the end of the room for worship facing towards the east, opening on to it at the same time in a convex curve, is the place of the Appearance of the Lord. Summoned by the divine service, God stays at this place. The fact that now the portrayal of Mary with her Child became canonical for the upper end of the room, the apse conch is closely linked with the violent disputes about the nature of Christ. The depiction of the physical mother of the Son of God Incarnate sets down the theological concept of Orthodoxy in a picture: Christ is man and God, and Mary is the Mother of God, not only of the Mortal Jesus, but also of the Divine Word. In so far, the inscription '*Hagia Maria*', 'Saint Mary', above her halo makes an outdated impression, but we find such anachronisms in East Roman art until well into the middle Byzantine period.

Despite the iconographic treatment of the topic, the scene is full of movement. The buoyant step of the archangels contributes especially to this (Gabriel, cf. fig. 20 p. 47). The unusual peacock eyes on their wings are perhaps meant symbolically. They wear court robes, bear ceremonial staffs and one large, blue orb with a cross on it each; their hair is bound by a headband. The garments drape in soft, plastically elaborated folds. The orbs are a sign of the worldly rule of Christ, but they also characterise the detachment from the world of the scene. The same applies for the green stripes marking the floor line and standing for Paradise. The mosaic is enclosed by a border which takes up and develops the topic of paradise: acanthus leaves alternate with vessels out of which water flows; stags, parrots and ducks are depicted quite naturally. At the top in the crown of the arch the Cross. It was possible to show all these details so clearly, because the artist worked with minute brightly coloured cubes. These cubes are known as tesserae and often they are pieces of glass covered with gold and silver or dipped in paint. Mother of pearl was also included in order to heighten the brilliance of the halos. One must imagine such a mosaic, what sort of an effect it must have had during a divine service lit from below by candle light. Thousands of single elements set at ingenious angles reflect the fitful, flickering light, the figures thus gain a vividness causing one to forget the fixed stare of the faces.

The Angeloktisti was extended in the course of time by two small churches. In the twelfth century, a chapel was added on the north side. It is dedicated to the physicians Cosmas and Damian and decorated with frescoes in two layers one upon the other. The more recent layer shows a portrayal of St. George on horseback and other saints standing; it is attributed to the fifteenth century, whereas it has not been possible to classify the older layer as yet.

In the fourteenth century, a Latin chapel was added at the expense of the French nobleman Gibelet which is provided with the gothic rib vaults of the architecture of southern France. On the west side of the chapel is a gravestone with the names of the members of a French family who were buried here in 1302.

There are frescoes from the thirteenth and fourteenth centuries: in the south-west wing the Annunciation, the Entombment of Christ, the Enthroned Virgin (for the most part destroyed) and John the Baptist. The monumental painting in the dome probably dates from the fourteenth century. In the naos we find several Byzantine icons. The most valuable among them are those of the Archangel Michael and the Evangelist John.

Fig. 129 (left page), 130 (right): The ornamental border around the apse mosaic. Detail from fig. 131.

Fig. 131 (above): The famed apse mosaic of Mary Hodegetria from the pre-iconoclastic period, sixth century. Only the left archangel is damaged, otherwise the work is well preserved. Fig. 132 (below): Detail, the heads of Mary and Jesus with the inscriptions. Above is the designation Hagia Maria, from top to bottom left one reads 'Michael', on the right 'Gabriel'.

Larnaca: St. Lazarus

The most interesting, if not necessarily the oldest church in Larnaca is dedicated to St. Lazarus of Bethany. In St. John's Gospel we hear that Jesus raised the brother of Mary and Martha from the dead (11: 1-57). The unprecedented deed caused the opponents of the Messiah to decide to kill Him; in the biblical story it thus forms the prelude to the events of the Crucifixion.

According to the legend, the raised Lazarus became the first bishop of Larnaca. In the thirty years which he exercised this office he is said to have never laughed – on account of the things he had had to see in Hell. Larnaca, an old Phoenician foundation from the ninth century BC was called Kition in antiquity. The modern name goes back to the discovery of many graves, including that of Lazarus, in the year 890 AD; it is derived from *'larnax',* the Greek work for 'sarcophagus'. The Byzantine Emperor Leo the Wise had the first bishop's remains taken to Constantinople, and in return for the relics had the church dedicated to him in Larnaca constructed in about 900 AD. Later the bones of St. Lazarus were stolen from Constantinople and finished up as a crusaders' trophy in the French city of Marseilles.

Together with St. Paraskevi (Geroskipos) and Sts. Barnabas and Hilarion (Peristerona), St. Lazarus is one of the three Cypriot churches with several domes. The building was originally a basilica which was destroyed and then reconstructed with a new roof. The multiple dome style came to the island already under Justinian I, but nothing has survived in its original form, either because of reconstruction in later centuries or because of serious damage as a result of earthquakes.

The church of St. Lazarus probably stands on the ruins of an older building in a Graeco-Roman necropolis – at the place where Lazarus is said to have been buried. During the last excavations, several grave and sarcophagi were discovered, some of them in the crypt of the church (fig. 135). Behind the holy throne were found the remains of an empty grave on which was inscribed the following in Hebrew: 'Lazaros Tetraemeros and friend of Christ' (according to Kyriatzis). *'Tetraemeros'* stands for the four days which Lazarus was buried in his cave before Christ returned to Judea to call him from his grave. The name 'Lazarus' comes from the Hebrew *'Eleazar'* and means 'God helps'.

Fig. 133: Alongside the bell tower, the church proper looks almost modest.

From western sources we know something of the history of the church. C. Enlart recorded in the late nineteenth century that at the time of the Venetians it was used as a Benedictine monastery. After 1571, under Turkish rule, the Turkish conquerors converted the church into a mosque, a not particularly nice practice which continued into the twentieth century. In 1589, the church was bought back into Christian hands and used jointly by Latin and Orthodox worshippers. Later the Russian traveller Basil Grigorovich Barsky noted in his diary that the church is 'constructed high and imposing, like a king's palace. It was reported that this place was constructed by Lazarus who was raised by the Lord from the dead on the fourth day after his death. As the best evidence of this, we find a coffin in a kind of niche deep below the floor of this church.'

It is possible that the walls were painted in the past, but the frescoes have vanished without trace through the repeated devastation. Some icons which were produced by Michael Proskynites from the Marathasa valley at the end of the eighteenth century have survived. In addition, there is a wonderful icon from the sixteenth century showing St. Lazarus as a single figure, as well as one from the seventeenth century with his Raising from the Dead. Finally, mention should also be made of a picture showing St. George; it dates from 1717 and is a work of the painter Iakovos from Crete.

Portraits of St. Lazarus are to be found in several Cypriot churches. Among the oldest ones is that in Pera Chorio and the one in Lagoudera. In the latter, the saint looks more dead than alive (cf. fig. 187 p. 184). The layer of paintings from the fourteenth century in Kakopetria also contains a picture of Lazarus.

Fig. 134 (above): The interior is high and as a result appears narrow. Fig. 135 (below): Sarcophagi in the crypt, even today, fresh flowers are still often laid on them.

Kellia: St. Anthony

Fig. 136: View of the gallery.

A veritable treasury of early Byzantine painting and architecture has been preserved in the Church of St. Anthony near Kellia. The village lies a few kilometres from Larnaca on the road to Agia Napa; its name is derived from the word *'Keli',* 'monks' cell'.

A three-aisled basilica was probably built here in the ninth century which suffered severe damage already a short time later. In the tenth or eleventh century this was made good, around 1500, repairs were carried out on the middle apse and the vault above the transept. During the most recent restoration works in the seventies of this century, new frescoes were discovered. In some places traces were found of three layers of painting from various middle-Byzantine phases, in others just two. On the east wall there are portraits of St. John Chrysostom and St. Basil (classification not certain) dating from the twelfth century. On the pillar constructed in the south against the west wall, two scenes from the Sacrifice of Isaac are preserved. The first under a layer of a later date might go back to the eleventh century (fig. 137). This magnificent fresco has some fundamental characteristics similar to those in St. Nicholas tis Stegis in Kakopetria. At the same time, the saintly physicians and brothers Cosmas and Damian were painted on the north-west pillar.

The south-western central pillar has three layers of frescoes. The most recent, in which St. Demetrios is portrayed with a spear in his right hand and a large shield decorated with a Byzantine cross in his left one, and

Fig. 137: Abraham's Sacrifice of Isaac, fresco from the eleventh century.

which has been carefully removed in the meantime, may be ascribed to the turn of the twelfth to the thirteenth century. Beneath it a fresco of the Virgin Mary standing with Child from the late eleventh or early twelfth century came to light. After this had also been removed, the wall is now dominated by two figures of saints. Probably the church belonged to a monastery, as its names, Andronikos and Athanasia allow one to presume.

On the north side is the enthroned Virgin Mary with Child which, to judge by the style, probably dates from the close of the twelfth century. Opposite the scene of Abraham's Sacrifice of Isaac there is a further portrayal of the enthroned Virgin Mary, this time dating from the early twelfth century. She holds the Child on her lap. Two frescoes of St. George on horseback have also survived: one in the eastern arch, the other high up on the south side. On the west side of the south-eastern pillar, below the dome, one can see a Crucifixion from the twelfth century and the scene of the Betrayal in which Peter cuts of Malchus's ear.

The characteristic features of this church are evidence of the cosmopolitan origin of the builders who apparently came from Constantinople and whose names will remain a secret for ever.

Pera Chorio: Church of the Holy Apostles

Fig. 138: The compact domed structure of the Church of the Holy Apostles.

The Church of the Holy Apostles stands at the western end of the village of Pera Chorio (Nisou) on the main road from Nicosia to Limassol. It is one of the many small Byzantine monasteries which were established between the rule of Emperor Nikephoros Phocas and the attack on Cyprus by the English King Richard Coeur de Lion. Its architectural style, a domed hall church, is typical for the small and compactly built churches which spread over the whole island in the twelfth century. The dome is borne directly by the pillars without any tambour. The pillars for their part form the vaulted niches in the interior. The best example of this is the Panagia tou Araka in Lagoudera.

The cycle of frescoes in the Church of the Holy Apostles in Pera Chorio begins with Christ Pantocrator in the dome. He is attended by the escort of His angels (cf. fig. 139). The face of Christ shows differences to that of the Pantocrator in Lagoudera; it is more like that in Sicilian

Fig. 139: An angel from the period between 1160 and 1180.

mosaics of the twelfth century. A portrait of the Virgin Mary of the Blachernitissa type – she holds a medallion with a Christ Child before her breast – decorates the apse conch. Mary is flanked by the titular saints of the church, the apostles Paul and Peter instead of by the usual archangels. Paul is on her left, Peter on her right. The same type (with archangels) is to be found in the Theotokos in Trikomo, St. Maura in Rizokarpaso and Christ Antiphonitis near Kalogrea. In addition, the most recent findings show similarities with the Church of the Holy Apostles in Peć (Serbia) from the year 1260, with the difference that the Virgin there is attended once again by two angels. Beneath the Blachernitissa, the Communion of the Apostles is portrayed with their harmonic colours and figures with plastic detailing. This applies for the majority of frescoes in Pera Chorio.

The lowest zone in the apse is dominated, as usual, by the fathers of the Church: Lazarus, Gregory, Chrysostom, Basil, Nicholas, and Athanasios. The fact that Lazarus is included among them here is unusual. Two Cypriot fathers of the Church, Barnabas and Epiphanios, are portrayed in medallions beneath the triple window. Both hold ornamented, dark-brown books with blue-violet edges. In the eastern pendentives, the Annunciation unfolds with Gabriel and Mary as life-size figures. The rest of the cycle is made up of the Anastasis, fragmentarily preserved on the right side of the lunette in the dome arch in the north wall, the Ascension in the altar arch, a picture of Pentecost – the Descent of the Holy Ghost – in the whole western vault and the Dormition of the Mother of God over the north door. In the case of the Birth of Christ, by comparison with the fine frescoes discussed up to now, it is of somewhat crude craftsmanship with a rustic element; it covers the whole lunette beneath the southern dome arch. In contrast to the other pictures, the Presentation of Jesus in the Temple in the eastern half below the Birth of Christ is a work of the fifteenth century. The majority of scenes are bordered by ornaments based for the most part on round forms: formalised acanthus, crennelated rhombuses and arabesques. The other frescoes in Pera Chorio show single figures of saints distributed over several sections of wall.

The monumental art of the Church of the Holy Apostles belongs mainly to the classical style of the Komnenian period in its advanced form which is characterised by its robust 'baroque' style. This style was introduced with the small-domed churches of the twelfth century. And the master who worked in Pera Chorio apparently came directly from a school in Constantinople. The characteristics of the style lead to the conclusion that the church was constructed and painted towards the end of the reign of Manuel I Komnenos, very probably between 1160 and 1180. As little has been preserved from that period, its frescoes represent a milestone in the development of the Komnenian style and refer to the even more pronounced classicism of the pictures by Theodore Apseudes in the Monastery of St. Neophytos (1183) and the Panagia tou Araka near Lagoudera (1192).

Peristerona: Barnabas and Hilarion

Fig. 140: View of one of the three Cypriot multi-domed churches.

About 30 km to the south of Nicosia, on the road leading to the Troodos Mountains, lies Peristerona. This village has the finest church dedicated to the Cypriot Saints Barnabas and Hilarion. It is a basilica, crowned with domes forming the shape of a cross. The architectural style of this church is very similar to that of St. Paraskevi in Geroskipos, both belong to the Constantinopolitan school. It was erected in about 1100 AD, as a survey recently showed, and replaced an earlier building which must have been built in the same form and size. During archaeological examinations of the interior, fragments of the holy throne made of stone and the foundation of the original iconostasis were found. A part of the northern wall of the earlier building has also been incorporated in the new one. The door between the narthex and naos probably dates from the Middle Ages.

Only a few fragments of the monumental painting have survived the ravages of time; they are ascribed to the fifteenth century. In addition, some icons have been preserved from the sixteenth century; among the most important are the icons of Christ, Paul, Barnabas, the Virgin Mary and a Presentation in the Temple. Parts of the iconostasis from the sixteenth century have been included in the new one.

Nicosia: St. John's Cathedral

Fig. 141: St. John's has been the bishop's church since 1720.

Byzantine wall painting and iconography flourished in Cyprus even in the post-Byzantine centuries. This is to be seen in one of the finest examples: in the church erected in Nicosia in honour of the Evangelist John. It was consecrated by Nikephoros, the then archbishop of Cyprus 'on the last day of the year 1662'. Until 1426, the piece of land had belonged to the Benedictines. Their monastery had also been dedicated to the Evangelist. After the Mamelukes drove them out, Orthodox monks moved in. In 1720, Archbishop Sylvester had the building renovated and moved his official residence there. Since then, St. John has been a cathedral. Its origins and renovation during the Turkish period did not permit any larger dimensions. Sylvester's successor, Philotheos, had the interior painted from 1736 on.

The small cathedral is a basilica with a barrel vault carried by five transverse arches. The external pier buttresses are in keeping with the architectural style of the time of its construction. A marble slab from an earlier Latin building was mounted above the west entrance. On it are the coat of arms of Lusignan, alongside hang two gothic tablets.

The naos and bema are separated by a gilded iconostasis. Studded with animals, birds, flowers and scenes from the Old Testament, it is a wonderful example of the art of carving by Cypriot craftsmen in the eighteenth century. On its upper part hang two rows of icons in which events from the life of Christ, the Virgin Mary and the Apostles are depicted. On the lower part are fastened large icons of the Virgin Mary and Christ, works by John Cornaros, a Cretan painter of the eighteenth century. He also painted the icons of the Virgin Mary which we now find in the church 'Agia Napa' in Limassol and the Chrysopolitissa church near Paphos. Under the pulpit stands a portable icon of the Evangelist John from the seventeenth century – a work by Theodore Poulakes, also from Crete, which was displayed for a time in the Orthodox church in Venice.

The frescoes are a document to the survival of Byzantine tradition until well into the Turkish period. Its donor Philotheos is portrayed twice. In one case he is

Fig. 142: The upper row illustrates Psalm 148, 11-13: 'Kings of the earth and all people: princes, and all judges of the earth: Both young men, and maidens: old men, and children: let them praise the name of the Lord'; the lower psalm 150:3-5 'Praise him with the sound of the trumpet; praise him with the psaltery and harp, praise him with the timbrel and dance: praise him with stringed instruments and organs. ...'

standing next to his predecessor Sylvester in the apse in the lower section reserved traditionally for bishops and fathers of the Church. In addition, he is to be seen to the left of the north entrance, namely as a supplicant to the titular saint.

With the rare portrayal of the last psalms, his wish had been fulfilled (fig. 142). The cycle proper begins in the dome with the Pantocrator who is surrounded by angels. Beneath him, the Evangelists Matthew, Mark, Luke and John take their place. In the account of the Life of Jesus, eastern and western elements intermix. It covers the south wall from the Annunciation to a giant Crucifixion. Above the south entrance is a frightening scene from the day of the Last Judgement.

A fresco entitled 'The Privileges of the Church of Cyprus' shows an important topic for the history of the Cypriot church. It is located on the south wall, near the archbishop's throne. For the first time in the history of Cypro-Byzantine art, the discovery of the bones of the Apostle Barnabas in his grave near Salamis is portrayed here. An inscription refers to the autocephalous status of the Orthodox Church in Cyprus which was accorded to the church after this discovery in 488 by the Byzantine Emperor Zeno. Barnabas and Paul were the first missionaries on the island in 45 AD. On the same side, to the West of the entrance, we see a portrayal of the Tree of Jesse. On the north wall opposite is a scene from Genesis. It is a synthesis of several sections: human beings, judges, kings, fishes are to be found in a lake, various animals, all quite simple in style. Beneath it are the seven ecumenical councils, the names of which stand for crucial theological decisions from the early period of Christianity. A portrayal of Christ's miracles is to be found on the west side.

Morphou: St. Mamas

Fig. 143: Bell tower, tambour and colonnade of St. Mamas's.

St. Mamas in Morphou is one of the most important Franco-Byzantine architectural monuments on the island. The church belongs to a monastery of the same name and nowadays lies in the occupied part of Cyprus. Nearby is a modern mosque.

In keeping with traditional usage, the monastery stands on the former site of the cult of the Greek goddess Aphrodite. It was renovated in the twelfth century under the Comnenes. The church dates from the late fifteenth or early sixteenth century. It probably stands on the ruins of an early Christian basilica and a Byzantine church added in the Middle Ages. Some frescoes have been preserved; in addition, a beautiful wooden iconostasis from the sixteenth century (fig. 146) and several icons have also survived the vicissitudes of time: Christ, the Virgin Mary, John the Baptist, the Apostles Peter and Paul, the Archangels Michael and Gabriel, St. George and St. Mamas riding on his lion date from the sixteenth or one of the following centuries.

There is an impressive fresco from the sixteenth or seventeenth century. It shows the Holy Child in a Byzantine goblet between two angels, thus symbolising the

Sacrifice (fig. 144). In the middle of the north wall is the sarcophagus for the saint's relics.

St. Mamas's biography tells us that he was born in Langra, Paphlagonia (a province in the north of modern Turkey). During a period of persecution on account of his faith, Mamas lived with wild animals which fed him. The real reason for his rise to become the most popular saint on the island were his bones which were credited with miraculous curative powers against the plague and other illnesses. In addition, he was the patron saint of shepherds and tax evaders – why becomes clear from his legendary biography which is recounted in rough outline below. He is one of the few saints in Cyprus who were mentioned by western travellers in the Middle Ages. Once myrrh is said to have flowed miraculously from his grave. This event is recorded in the diaries of two visitors – Nicole le Huen (1487) and Tommaso Poracchi (1576). Two Englishmen, Richard Pococke and Alexander Drummond, visited the monastery in the mid-eighteenth century. They considered its church as being in 'the Italian style' and regarded it as the most splendid of all. Between 1727 and 1735, the Russian traveller Basil Grigorovich Barsky visited St. Mamas and made a good sketch of the church. Among other things, he too finds that this is the finest of all the monasteries in Cyprus, it was just strange that it lay in the middle of the village.

St. Mamas is said to have lived in a cave near Morphou. As he, in his own opinion, did not use state institutions, he did not want to pay taxes. The emperor's soldiers were to force him to do so, but on their way to the capital, they encountered a lion chasing a little lamb. The hermit commanded the lion to desist from its prey which he took in his arms, and then used the lion as his mount. On seeing this, the emperor's governor dispensed him from all taxes…

The are numerous legends circulating about Mamas and in the monumental painting and icons on Cyprus there are numerous portrayals of him: the earliest is a fresco from the thirteenth century in the church of the Virgin in Kophinou; in addition, he is to be seen in an icon, also from the thirteenth century, in the church of St. Mamas in Moutoullas and in another now to be found in Pelendri. Portraits from the fifteenth century exist in Platanistasa

Fig. 144: The sacrifice.

and in St. Mamas's church in Louvaras (cf. fig. 188 p. 184).

Usually the saint rides on a lion and holds a lamb in his arm. Research has shown that these pictures have early parallels in Georgian art. The iconographic type itself came to Cyprus from Asia Minor and recalls the goddess Ma venerated in Roman times who sat on a lion. On the other hand, St. Mamas was initially portrayed standing, he has only been linked with the lion since the twelfth century.

Fig. 145: The interior. Tympanum with numerous portraits of martyrs.

Fig. 146: The iconostasis with open middle door.

Myrtou: St. Panteleimon

Fig. 147: St. Panteleimon's lies in a military barracks; the premises are largely destroyed.

The monastery of St. Panteleimon lies in the village of Myrtou, 28 kilometres south west of the town of Kyrenia which was occupied by Turkish military in 1974. Photography is not really permitted here.

The history of the monastery before the eighteenth century is unknown. According to the Russian traveller Basil Grigorovich Barsky, who visited Myrtou in 1735, it dates from a late period. It was constructed on the ruins of an earlier church. After 1710, the inhabitants of the village built some monks' cells around the building; an abbot was appointed and a few monks moved in there. At that time, as until recently, their number in this monastic community remained limited.

In the eighteenth and nineteenth centuries, the monastery was an important destination for pilgrims which was visited not just by Cypriots, but also by numerous believers from Asia Minor who wanted to pray to St. Panteleimon – a saint who was known for his miracles throughout the whole Christian world in the East.

On various occasions the monastery received gifts, including also crosses and wooden icons. Two of these icons on which St. Panteleimon is portrayed are encased in silver and date from the eighteenth and nineteenth centuries. After the events in the course of the violent division of the island, they have probably been lost.

Lamboussa: Acheiropoietos

Fig. 148: A church directly by the sea and located in a military prohibited area ...

Our photographic work in Lamboussa (the ancient Lapithos) was not successful. We had no access to the 'Acheiropoietos' because it lies in the Turkish occupied part of Cyprus. Like other important Cypriot monuments, this monastery is also under the control of the Turkish military.

According to historical and other sources, the building is a very important monument from the end of the eleventh and beginning of the twelfth century. The *Katholikon* was constructed on the nave of a considerably larger preceding basilica which, with its five domes, was probably similar in appearance to corresponding churches in Syria, Palestine and Asia Minor. In the apse, some frescoes from the fourteenth century have been preserved.

The monastery takes its epithet '*Acheiropoietos*' from an icon which was kept here for a long time, traditionally regarded as being one of the 'authentic' portraits of Mary – *acheiropoietos* means 'made without hands'. Shortly after 1735, this famous portrait of the Mother of God was destroyed in a fire which Turks from Karamania had laid. The German traveller Petermann visited the church in 1851. During his visit he noted: 'Ninety years before the Turkish thieves from Karamania had plundered the monastery and burned it down completely together with its library.'

Bellapais Abbey

Fig. 149: The ruins of Bellapais, located in the middle of orange and lemon tree plantations, almond and peach trees.

Bellapais Abbey (the name comes from the French 'Abbaye de la Paix' – Abbey of Peace) was constructed on the north side of the Pentadaktylos, 220 m above sea level and about 10 km to the east of Kyrenia. It is one of the most magnificent examples of Cypriot sacred architecture in gothic style and its location in a wonderful landscape is hardly to be surpassed. Its foundation dates back to the beginning of the Frankish period. Very probably it was erected during the rule of Guy Lusignan, Count of Ascalon and King of 'Outremer', the crusader kingdom in Palestine, and of Amalric, his brother and the first Lusignan to be crowned king of Cyprus. Admittedly, the chroniclers Estienne de Lusignan and Francesco Altar report that it was Hugh III who first gave orders for the construction. At all events, Hugh III is known for his generosity towards the abbey. He died in Tyre, but his body was brought across the sea to Bellapais. His successors, John I, Hugh IV and John II

Fig. 150: Tracery and sarcophagus in the cloister.

Problems with insubordinate monks who refused to obey the archbishop occurred again and again, for the last time under Venetian rule in the first half of the sixteenth century. In 1251, Hugh de Fagiano, a monk from Bellapais, became archbishop of Nicosia. He was a wild zealot for the Roman Catholic church and excommunicated all those Greeks who refused to acknowledge the supremacy of Rome and the leading role of the Latin bishops. Even within the ranks of his own church he wanted to ensure discipline and the independence of the church towards the nobility showing little mercy. He soon became involved in a dispute with Henry I. He remained in office until 1260.

After centuries of peace, the abbey suffered under the destruction through Genoa's invasion. In a report to the Venetian government, Bernardos Segredo, the governor, described the state of the abbey in 1562 which was no longer a religious place, but coarsened in morals and ruined both with regards to the state of its buildings and its economic position. The Ottoman invasion brought about its end; after 1570, the church was reconsecrated for the Orthodox rite.

The main entrance to the abbey lay at the southern end of the west side. In the fourteenth century there was a tower here equipped with the lifting mechanism for the drawbridge attached to the battlemented wall. The triple-domed, rectangular church from the thirteenth century is dedicated to the Virgin Mary. It is constructed in gothic style; remains of frescoes suggest the fourteenth century. Numerous buildings were added to the north of the church. On the north side is a large refectory. Above the door lintel here three coats of arms are displayed, that of the kingdom of Jerusalem (centre), that of the kingdom of Cyprus (left) and the family arms of the Lusignans (right). Other rooms lie on the east side. The largest of these is the crypt, above which are the dormitories and the chapter room in which the monks gathered for certain events. Remains of the cloister show tracery in French flamboyant style. The other buildings have been completely destroyed. The remains of some sarcophagi on the north side date back to the fourteenth century. In them were buried members of the Ibelins, one of the most influential families in Cyprus.

also bestowed generous donations on the monastery. All in all, it may be said that the abbey experienced its heyday under the Lusignans. Some sources record that Austin friars first resided here. After them came the Premonstratensians. Because of the white habit worn by the order, the abbey was called 'Abbaye Blanche' (White Abbey) in the Middle Ages. Under church law, the monks were subject to the jurisdiction of the Latin Bishop of Nicosia. The abbot of Bellapais enjoyed privileges. He lived in Nicosia for a time and had considerable influence on the political life of the royal court. He was treated almost like the bishop.

During the rule of King Hugh IV, the monks of Bellapais revolted against their abbot and the Latin archbishop. Pope Benedict XII and the Catholic bishop of Paphos intervened and were able to resolve the dispute.

Koutsoventis: St. John Chrysostom

The main church of the monastery of St. John Chrysostom and the adjoining single-aisled church of the Holy Trinity are situated in Koutsoventis to the south of Kyrenia. They lie on a slope and offer a breath-taking view to the coast. This location was probably selected less on account of the aesthetic advantages than because of the strategic ones.

Just like elsewhere in the Turkish-occupied parts of Cyprus, it is not possible at the moment to photograph the superb Byzantine frescoes. The monastery lies in a military prohibited area. It is not even allowed to photograph the outside.

According to the legend, a queen established the monastery out of gratitude at being cured of a painful skin disease by the water from a well here. Seen historically, the Church of the Holy Trinity was constructed on the orders of Eumathios Philokales, governor of Cyprus under Alexius I Komnenos. The interior decoration dates from the first or second decade of the twelfth century.

There are links between the frescoes here and those in Asinou and Trikomo. Their painters were probably pupils of the master of the Church of the Holy Trinity who came from Constantinople. Notable similarities suggest this: St. Hilarion (Asinou) can be compared with St. Paul the Simple in the south-western niche, Ephrem the Syrian (Asinou) with Gregory the Thaumaturge, St. Basil in the apse of Asinou with St. Gregory in Koutsoventis. There are great similarities between the faces of the apostles in the Effusion of the Holy Spirit and the Ascension (both Asinou) and those one can see here in the Assumption of Mary. The established Byzantine system of presentation is also to be found in the Church of the Holy Trinity in the portraits of St. Gregory, Archbishop '*ton Homeriton*' in the reveal of the window of the north west niche, Procopios on the arch, as well as Arkadios and Xenophon in the lunette above the window. Only a very few remnants have survived from the other frescoes, the Crucifixion and the Annunciation. All in all, the frescoes in the Church of the Holy Trinity in Koutsoventis represent key elements of Byzantine art of the twelfth century in Cyprus.

Byzantine frescoes were also found in the Church of St. John Chrysostom constructed later during renovation works in 1890. As they were restored in accordance with the understanding of the end of the nineteenth century, they have been destroyed for ever. Only the marble floor in the apse and an architrave survived the 'beautification'.

Fig. 151: A photo of the church from 1958 showing the state before the renovation.

Kalogrea: Christ Antiphonitis

Fig. 152: View through an arch to the church and dome near Kalogrea.

The Church of Christ Antiphonitis near Kalogrea originally belonged to a monastery. The name of the village near which it lies also indicates this. It is derived from '*kalogria*' the Greek for nun. The village lies on the north side of the Pentadaktylos range, a good way from Kyrenia. '*Antiphonisma*', means literally 'to hear the voice from the other side', on which the meaning 'liturgical antiphony' is based, but the link of the epithet to the church lies in the dark.

Regrettably, the period after 1974 through the effects of war and plundering had a disastrous effect on the frescoes which are of such artistic and art historical importance. Clear signs of chisels can be seen on the archangels in the apse conch as a result of the attempt to turn the heads into cash on the international art market (fig. 156f). The illustrations in this book were taken in early summer 1995. Photographs dating from before 1974 show that both Michael and Gabriel were at that

Fig. 153: Christ as the Ruler of Everything, Pantocrator, painted in the dome of which Fig. 152 shows the outside.

time unscathed, in contrast to the Virgin Mary between them which had already been damaged earlier.

The church building itself is the only example still extant in Cyprus of the eight-pillared type from the late twelfth century. The dome, which spans the naos with quite a large diameter, rests on eight irregularly spaced pillars standing almost in a circle and by their very arrangement virtually forcing a pictorial programme which does not always adhere to the traditional Byzantine scheme. In addition, they present the painter with the problem of adapting the often two-dimensional scenes, at best possibly drawn in concave vaulting, to the conditions on convex pillar surfaces. Twelve windows are let into the tambour beneath the dome through which much light can flood in. Between the two eastern pillars one must imagine the iconostasis; the pillars stand detached whereas the other ones are connected by the walls. The narthex and an arcade were added in the Frankish period, as can be seen without much difficulty from the gothic pointed arch form of the loggia.

The frescoes belong to two periods. On account of stylistic features, the older layer is dated to the end of the twelfth century, the time when the church was constructed, while the more recent paintings are ascribed to the late fifteenth century, probably shortly after the extension of the single-aisled church. The monumental painting in the *bema* belongs to the layer painted around 1190. It is in keeping with the late-Komnenian style of the capital of the Byzantine Empire and displays certain parallels to the decoration of the Panagia Araka in Lagoudera. Our attention is taken particularly by the Virgin Mary *Orans* in the apse conch; despite the destruction already mentioned, it is still an overwhelming picture with the suggestive blue in the background and

Fig. 154: Archangel Michael on one of the eight pillars.

Fig. 155: Remains of Gabriel on the pillar opposite.

the brilliant colours of the garments. In the apse arch, parts of the Ascension have survived, admittedly without Christ Himself (for the arrangement, cf. fig. 167 p. 158).

The scenes of His Birth and the Presentation in the Temple are damaged to a greater or lesser extent. One of the best preserved compositions is the Baptism in the Jordan on one of the southern pillars: a naked, elegant Jesus crosses the river, his left leg leading, while John lays his hand on His head. The Messiah blesses a personification of the Jordan at His feet with His right hand, His left one hangs loosely at His side. The adaptation of the proportions to the curve of the pillar is successful. Below, St. Endoxus and St. Paul, that is to say a bishop and an apostle, look at the observer with a serious gaze. On the adjoining wall follow St. Anthony and three further saints who can no longer be identified. Many of the bishops and martyrs who are portrayed traditionally in the lowest painting zone on a level with the congregation and thus with worldly things, have not survived very well as they are exposed to the most wear and tear. The bishops Photios, Polychronios, Triphillios, the physician saints Cosmas and Damian, Demetrian, Bishop of Kythrea, Symeon Thaumaturges and Theodosios are depicted in part as busts in medallions and in part as whole-figure portraits. Like Amphilochios, Nicholas, the stylites Daniel and Symeon, they were painted on the wall with a marked sense of proportions. Below the apse conch, one can recognise the church fathers Gregory, Chrysostom, Basil, Cyril and Athanasios. On the two detached pillars, the archangels are portrayed mirror-inverted to on another, Michael on the northern one (fig. 154), Gabriel with his

Fig. 156 and 157: Mary Orans Blachernitissa, above the whole scene, below detail.

151

Fig. 158: Bird ornament, adjoining Fig. 155.

Fig. 159: A gloomy view into the sanctuary.

head destroyed on the southern one (fig. 155). They hold scrolls.

The other frescoes in the nave date from the late fifteenth century. A carefully detailed Last Judgement extends over two pillars and the niche lying between, in the lunette above, the enthroned Christ surrounded by an aureole. He is flanked by Mary and John the Baptist, the intercessors for mankind behind whom crowd a host of angels. The Choirs of Saints, divided into three groups, and naked children with wings, for the Holy Innocents massacred by Herod, are to be seen below the feet of Jesus. They are moving towards the Preparation of the Throne. Normally, the Instruments of the Passion, the Gospel and the dove for the Holy Ghost are shown on the throne. As the former are here shown over Christ, only the two latter are to be seen here. The Last Judge-ment ends with Peter, who holds the keys to Paradise in his hands and is just about to open the gates for the Just. The Penitent Thief, Abraham, stands before a scene with palms and stylised trees symbolising the Garden of Eden; within Mary sits enthroned, surrounded by the archangels. The Tree of Jesse extends over the south wall showing the lineage of Christ from the origins through Solomon and David to Joachim and Anna, Mary's parents. At the bottom left, the prophet Barlaam rides an ass. The dome is dominated by Christ Pantocrator (fig. 153). The medallion is enclosed by a frame in the colours of the rainbow, and as a concentric circle around this rainbow follows the host of angels converging on a Preparation of the Throne flanked by Mary and John the Baptist. Here too the topic of the Last Judgement is present.

One of the most interesting figures of Byzantine art in

Fig. 160: The entrance area – completely destroyed.

general is St. Romanos Melodos portrayed here on a pillar. Melodos is a description of his profession. Romanos was the writer and composer of the Byzantine hymns which play an important role in the divine service. He is portrayed as a young man with a white tunic and an open book. The page facing the beholder shows a text with the appropriate melody in late-Byzantine notation. Of the scenes from Mary's life, only the Birth with stylistic borrowings from the Italian renaissance is well preserved in Antiphonitis.

Tremetousia: St. Spyridon

The monastery of St. Spyridon in Tremetousia, one of the greatest spiritual centres in Cyprus, has been in Turkish hands since 1974.

The monastery church is a two-aisled building which was erected on the ruins of an early Christian basilica from the fifth or sixth century. As the Russian traveller Basil Grigorovich Barsky noted, it was restored twice, namely in 1729/30 and 1738. During the second renovation, a fresco of the titular saint was painted in the interior – a work by the painter Ioannikios. Regrettably, it is neither possible to photograph it, nor is it even certain whether the fresco still exists; the church lies in a military prohibited area.

Its iconostasis dates back to the year 1634. It was constructed by a *'hierographer'*, that is to say a painter of saints, whose name is said to have been Paul without our having any further information about him. The Crucifixion on the iconostasis is a work from the year 1680. It is by one Leontios, a *'hieromonachos'*, an ordained monk, which is by no means the normal case in the Eastern Church by comparison with the West. The oldest icon in the iconostasis must be dated to the sixteenth century.

After 1966, the premises in the buildings around the church were used as a centre for the restoration of books and icons; these workshops were in operation until the Turkish invasion. The events of 1974 meant the total destruction of the spiritual and cultural inheritance which was kept in Tremetousia. The rare manuscripts stored there have also not survived the brutal incursion.

Spyridon, a Cypriot of the fourth century, was elected bishop; his name is highly respected in the Orthodox world. There are roughly thirty portraits of this saint on the island. Early pictures are to be found in Asinou,

Fig. 161: St. Spyridon, fresco by Philip Goul, Church of the Holy Cross near Platanistasa, late fifteenth century.

Monagri (Amasgou), Pera Chorio, Lagoudera and in the catacombs of the Agia Solomoni in Paphos. In the absence of a picture from Tremetousia, we have a fresco from Platanistasa here. The saint is to be seen here with his characteristic basketwork head covering which makes him unmistakable for Orthodox congregations.

Monastery of St. Barnabas

Fig. 162: The tambour of the dome and the barrel vault of the transept can be clearly seen from the courtyard.

Barnabas is a Cypriot saint. He has been greatly venerated by the island's inhabitants since the fifth century, because he is regarded as the founder and patron saint of its autocephalous church. Parts of his mortal remains which had been found at that time in Salamis and called for the separation of Cyprus from the jurisdiction of the archbishop in Antioch are now in Kykkos and Machairas. According to the New Testament, Barnabas did not belong to the closer group around Christ, but to the 70 disciples. In the early period of Christianity, all the missionaries who spread the message of Jesus among the nations were called apostles. This explains the high number of 70 which only later in the course of the canonising of faith was fixed at twelve again. Barnabas' death as a martyr in about 57 AD is commemorated on 11 June; he is one of the saints in the *Synaxarion,* the calendar of saints in Constantinople. On his feast day, a *synaxis* (the equivalent in the Catholic church is a mass) was held in St. Peter's near the Haghia Sophia in Constantinople. Barnabas is also included in the ecclesiastical calendar of the Western Church.

Four and a half centuries after the death of Barnabas,

Fig. 163: The chapel rises over the crypt with the saint's grave. His bones are long since elsewhere.

the Archbishop of Cyprus, Authemios, founded the church near Salamis with the financial support of the Byzantine Emperor Zeno and some wealthy dignitaries. It is a basilica with two domes. The architecture is like that of St. Epiphanios in Salamis and St. Lazarus in Larnaca. The only difference lies in the fact that St. Lazarus still has all three domes, whereas the eastern dome of St. Barnabas was destroyed. The tambours of the domes each have 16 windows. Earlier the church had three doors only in the west wall. The present entry arrangement and the windows were constructed in 1916. In the same year, a building was added on the east side. The apse also dates from a later period. The first renovation of the church was begun in 1674 under Archbishop Hilarion Kigalas and completed in 1740 at the time of Archbishop Philotheos.

There are hardly any written sources on the history of the church. In 1735, the Russian monk Basil Grigorovich Barsky visited the monastery; the entire collection of icons was stolen in the seventeenth and eighteenth centuries. After the Turkish invasion in 1974, the monastic community was forcibly expelled and the church plundered. Near the church there used to be a well from which pilgrims drew holy water. Alongside was to be found the saint's grave and fragments of frescoes. Originally, the saint was buried in the apse of a basilica which the Cypriot Archbishop Anthemios had had erected for this purpose. This church was still standing when Basil Grigorovich Barsky visited the monastery. Nowadays a small chapel of more recent date stands above the crypt with the grave; swallows nest in its deserted interior.

Portraits of Barnabas are preserved in at least nine churches in Cyprus, including earliest layer in Asinou (1105/1106) and the frescoes of Lagoudera. Both in Asinou and in the pictorial programme in Pera Chorio, which also dates back to the twelfth century, Barnabas and Epiphanios are portrayed below at the middle of the apse.

Trikomo: Theotokos

Fig. 164: View of the apse, dome with tambour, bell tower.

Fig. 165: The iconostasis with open middle door.

Trikomo lies in the Famagusta area and has been occupied by the Turks since 1974. The main church in the village, dedicated to the Mother of God, is a structure from the early twelfth century. It is a single-aisled domed church with vaulted niches in the longitudinal walls. This type is characteristic for the early Komnenian period and is evidence, just like the frescoes, for a markedly close link with the capital of the Byzantine Empire during this period. In the fifteenth century, a vaulted side aisle was added on the north side, a western extension came even later. The bell tower was only constructed in the recent past.

The way the saints are drawn and the architecture in the background with its billowing curtains reveal the origin of this art from Constantinople. Coloured spaces are an important feature of the design in which the alternation from blue, green and ochre is particularly noticeable. Dirt and the passage of time have told severely on the relatively few fresco paintings. In 1966, they were cleaned and secured. After 1974, irresponsible persons

Fig. 166 (above): The Ascension of Christ at the crown of the apse arch, He is carried upwards in an aureole by four angels.
Fig. 167 (left): The Apostles follow the Ascension with astonishment. Detail from fig. 166; the twelve disciples stand in groups of six on either side of the apse arch opposite, each accompanied by an archangel.

Abb. 168: St. Mary Orans, Blachernitissa type, in the apse conch, one of the oldest examples of this type in Cyprus.

attempted to remove the frescoes. As a result, even more damage was caused as was also the case with the mosaics and mosaics in the churches in the villages of Lysi and Lythrankomi.

The work of the greatest importance in Trikomo is Christ Pantocrator in the dome. He is being praised by the choir of angels which stands symbolically for God's infinite wisdom. Their host promises a future celestial liturgy which Christ Himself will hold. They move in two groups towards the Preparation of the Throne in the eastern point of the dome. There the Instruments of the Passion of Christ lie above the Book of the Last Judgement. A dove, symbol of the Holy Ghost, stands with its wings spread before the Cross. To the right and left of the throne with its nimbus stand the Mother of God and John the Baptist as intercessors for mankind (fig. 170). The term 'Pantocrator' – 'Ruler over everything' – goes back to the interpretation by the Early Fathers of Genesis and the Revelation: the 'Almighty', the 'King of saints' (Revelation 1:8; 15:3) will judge the Earth. The strict, almost angry expression of the eyes which fix on the visitor in the nave below remind him that the Day of Judgement will come, that on the one hand blessing and Redemption are promised, but that on the other hand compliance with the Laws is demanded. The inscription around the medallion leaves no doubt: "Mortals, fear the Judge" is to be read there. The iconography follows the scheme developed after iconoclasm. A male face with beard and hair parted at the middle, the hair flows, is gathered together at the neck on the back, the right hand raised in blessing, in the left a Gospel book as symbol for the Law of the World (fig. 169).

During restoration in 1966, three further portraits of Joachim and Anna, including the Birth of the Virgin, from a formerly quite certainly more extensive cycle of the Life of Mary, were discovered. The parents of the

160

Fig. 169 (left, above): Dome with tambour; the prophets of the Old Testament quite certainly originally stood in the spaces between the windows. Fig. 170 (left): Christ Pantocrator in the dome, surrounded by angels paying homage. Fig. 171 (above): Entrance to the icon museum. Fig. 172 (right): In the upper part the Prayer of Joachim, in the lower one Mary listens to the Archangel while she spins wool intended for a carpet which is to decorate the Temple in Jerusalem. Part of the Annunciation.

Mother of God are to be seen during their attempt at bringing their Sacrifice in the Temple, the Prayer of Joachim (fig. 172 top) and Anna, as well as their 'encounter', both are shown cheek to cheek in an embrace. Beneath is a fragmentarily preserved Birth of Christ, attended by a group of shepherds, one of whom is playing a flute (above the heads of Salome and the mid-wife). The Ascension of Christ is in the apse arch (fig. 166f). The scene is stylistically similar to that in Asinou. The same is true of the Annunciation. In Trikomo, admittedly, only Mary has been preserved beneath the Prayer of Joachim (fig. 172 bottom). In addition, one may compare the picture of the Mother of God on the lunette above the west entrance in Asinou with the Mother of God Blachernitissa in the apse conch in Trikomo (fig. 168). It represents quite certainly the best portrayal of the topic which was later copied everywhere in Cyprus. Admittedly, the heads of the two archangels have been severely damaged in Trikomo. The study of the frescoes before 1974 clearly proved that the master at work here, or his pupils, also worked in Koutsoventis and Asinou.

Lythrankomi: Panagia Kanakaria

Fig. 173: View from the West, three domes over the narthex, naos and bema, form a row.

The Church of the Panagia Kanakaria with its famous mosaics stands in Lythrankomi, a village in the northern part of Cyprus. The church was erected in the final years of the fifth century as a timber-roofed triconch structure with colonnades and a narthex on the western side. The name 'Kanakaria' is one of a series of honorific names for the Virgin Mary which particularly laud one of her virtues in each case. The church was destroyed in the seventh century during the Arab incursions and rebuilt again shortly afterwards in the same style as before, although without the narthex. In the twelfth century, the basilica was remodelled with three domes and a narthex. As a result of the reconstruction, it acquired domes with tambours over the narthex and the nave, but on the other hand a dome resting directly on the walls over the bema. In the thirteenth century, a domed

Fig. 174: View into the severely damaged interior.

Fig. 175: There is wanton destruction everywhere.

porch was added. The dome over the naos was renovated towards the end of the fifteenth century without causing any major changes to the building.

In keeping with Cypriot tradition, originally the Orthodox and Catholics shared the church. Roman Catholic chapels in Orthodox churches were widely spread during the rule of the Lusignans, especially in rural areas.

The frescoes in Kanakaria date from various periods, in part far back, however, they are in a deplorable state. Among the earliest fragments is an inscription from the seventh century. Pictures of the Archangel Gabriel and St. Barnabas date from the late twelfth and early thirteenth centuries respectively, a portrayal of the Second Coming of Christ from the fourteenth century. Then follow the frescoes from the fifteenth century: Christ Pantocrator, the Preparation of the Throne, Invocation, Annunciation, Ascension, the Birth of Christ and parts of the Dormition of the Mother of God.

Despite the frequent reconstructions directly affecting the substance of the church, the mosaic decoration of the middle apse from the early sixth century has been preserved, albeit in a very fragmentary state. It shows the Virgin Mary with the Child Jesus on her left arm. With regard to the en face portrayal of Mother and Son,

163

this is known as the 'Cypriot' type of the enthroned Mary. To the right of the Virgin can be seen the Archangel Michael, to her left only the right hand of the Archangel Gabriel has survived. Scholars point to the similarities of this scene with mosaic works from the sixth century in Ravenna and Parenzo.

The Virgin Mary is surrounded by geometric motives, flower patterns and medallions of the twelve Apostles. The medallions of Jesus Christ, Peter, Paul and John have been for the most part destroyed, but we know that those of Andrew, Philip, Matthew, Luke, Jude, James, Mark, Bartholomew and Thomas (fig. 177) did survive until 1979.

The real catastrophe which befell these magnificent works of art took place in 1979, when an organised band tore them out of the apse by force to sell them to art dealers. What ultimately happened to the famous mosaics of Kanakaria in Lythrankomi became known worldwide. In 1979, they were brought to Munich to Ayden Dikman, a Turkish Cypriot. The latter sold them in 1988 for an enormous sum to Peggy Goldberg, a gallery owner from Indiana in the USA, but shortly after the Republic of Cyprus and the Church of Cyprus brought the case before a court in South Dakota. The judge finally awarded the ownership rights to the Kanakaria mosaics to the rightful owner, the Church of Cyprus.

Fig. 176 and 177: Apostle medallions, above James, below Thomas; the mosaics are now in the museum in Nicosia.

The Monastery of St. Andrew

Fig. 178: Nowadays the Turkish flag flies over what was one of the most important Orthodox monasteries in Cyprus until 1974.

Andrew, the brother of Peter and one of Jesus's twelve disciples, is the apostle most revered by the Cypriots: a monastery was erected in his honour on Cape Karpasia, occupied territory since 1974. St. Andrew's Cape, as it used to be known, is the most north-easterly point of the island, it points, like the tip of a finger, to a region which was called Cilicia in Byzantine times. The narrow Karpas peninsula is practically uninhabited after Rizokarpaso, although in the monastery itself one Greek still holds out, cared for by Austrian UN soldiers. Only an unpaved path leads to the cape, the monastery has been accessible already for some time by an asphalt road.

The sources on the foundation of this famous monastery are scanty. According to tradition, the Apostle performed a miracle during his short stay in Cyprus, he opened a spring with fresh water, which still flows today, in the dry, rocky area. A captain is said to have erected a small church at this spot because the Apostle helped his blind son to see again. Another story relates that the drinking water ran out on the ship on which Andrew was also travelling to the feast of the Passover in Jerusalem; the one-eyed captain became very worried. Andrew restored his whole sight again and instructed the sailors to land at that part of the cape which they were just passing. He prophesied to them that they would find a spring there with drinkable water. Instead of accepting a reward, he preached the Gospel and was able to convert many, a true fisher of men as Christ had

Fig. 179: The holy well which the Apostle Andrew is said to have discovered during a journey to Jerusalem still provides fresh water today; for centuries it was a place of pilgrimage.

called for: "And Jesus, walking by the sea of Galilee, saw two brethren, Simon called Peter, and Andrew his brother, casting a net into the sea; for they were fishers. And he saith unto them, Follow me, and I will make you fishers of men" (Matt, 4:18-19). From this can be seen that Andrew alongside Peter, was among Christ's first disciples, and that is of importance for his esteem and rank among the Apostles. To return to the legend: the captain is said to have acquired a portrait of Andrew in Jerusalem which he left behind on his return to the spring. The place would thus have had an 'authentic' portrait of the Apostle. It was never occupied by a monastic community in the strict sense, but was primarily a place of pilgrimage and as such one of the most important in Cyprus.

In the grounds of the monastery stands a small gothic church from the fifteenth century which alone by its style of construction shows that it was constructed during the period of Frankish rule on Cyprus. A Frankish nobleman is said to have financed the chapel, but his name has not been handed down to us. Its entrances were constructed in unworked stones (fig. 181) on the west and south sides. It was repaired and renovated on various occasions in the past. Old Cypriot maps dating from 1465 and 1478 confirm its existence. In these sources, the area is called 'Capo de Santo Andrea' or 'Capo Bonandrea'.

Fig. 180 (above): Still life with candles and votive head.
Fig. 181 (below): An old woman leaves the church with an oil lamp in her hand.

Appendix

Cyprus in the Bible

The community of property of the first Christians

And the multitude of them that believed were of one heart and of one soul: neither said any of them that ought of the things which he possessed was his own; but they had all things common. ... And Joses, who by the apostles was surnamed Barnabas (which is, being interpreted, The son of consolation) a Levite, and of the country of Cyprus, having land, sold it, and brought the money, and laid it at the apostles' feet. (Acts 4: 32, 36)

First Christians in Antioch

Now they which were scattered abroad upon the persecution that arose about Stephen travelled as far as Phenice, and Cyprus, and Antioch, preaching the word to none but unto the Jews only. And some of them were men of Cyprus and Cyrene, which, when they were come to Antioch, spake unto the Grecians, preaching the Lord Jesus. And the hand of the Lord was with them: and a great number believed, and turned unto the Lord. (Acts 11: 19-21)

Begin of the first missionary journey

Now there were in the church that was at Antioch certain prophets and teachers: as Barnabas, and Simeon that was called Niger, and Lucius of Cyrene, and Manaen, which had been brought up with Herod the tetrarch, and Saul. As they ministered to the Lord, and fasted, the Holy Ghost said, Separate me Barnabas and Saul for the work whereunto I have called them. And when they had fasted and prayed, and laid their hands on them, they sent them away.

On the island of Cyprus

So they, being sent forth by the Holy Ghost, departed unto Seleucia; and from thence they sailed to Cyprus. And when they were at Salamis, they preached the word of God in the synagogues of the Jews; and they also had John to their minister. And when they had gone through the isle unto Paphos, they found a certain sorcerer, a false prophet, a Jew, whose name was Bar-Jesus: which was with the deputy of the country, Sergius Paulus, a prudent man; who called for Barnabas and Saul, and desired to hear the word of God. But Elymar the sorcerer (for so is his name by interpretation) withstood them, seeking to turn away the deputy from the faith.

Then Saul, (who also is called Paul) filled with the Holy Ghost, set his eyes on him, and said, O full of all subtilty and all mischief, thou child of the devil, thou enemy of all righteousness, wilt thou not cease to pervert the right ways of the Lord? And now, behold, the hand of the Lord is upon thee, and thou shalt be blind, not seeing the sun for a season. And immediately there fell on him a mist and a darkness; and he went about seeking some to lead him by the hand. Then the deputy, when he saw what was done, believed, being astonished at the doctrine of the Lord. Now when Paul and his company loosed from Paphos ... (Acts 13: 1-13)

The begin of the second missionary journey

And some days after Paul said unto Barnabas, Let us go again and visit our brethren in every city where we have preached, and see how they do. And Barnabas determined to take with them John, whose surname was Mark. But Paul thought not good to take him with them, who departed from them from Pamphylia, and went not with them to the work. And the contention was so sharp between them, that they departed asunder one from the other; and so Barnabas took Mark, and sailed unto Cyprus; ... (Acts 15; 36-39)

The arrival in Jerusalem

... There went with us certain of the disciples of Caesarea, and brought with them one Mnason of Cyprus, an old disciple, with whom we should lodge. ... (Acts 21:16)

The Archbishops of Cyprus

Barnabas the Apostle	around 45
Herakleidios	end 3rd Cent.
Gelasios	around 325
Epiphanios I	368-403
Sabinos I	around 404
Troilos	around 420
Theodoros	?-431
Reginos	431-?
Olympios I	c. 449-451
Sabinos II	around 45/458
Anthemios	around 470, poss. 488
Olympios II	495?
Philoxenos	?
Damianos	6th cent.
Sophronios I	6th cent.
Gregorios	end 6th cent.
Arkadios I	end 6th/beg. 7th cent.
Ploutarchos	around 620-625
Arkadios II	around 630-641
Sergios	around 643
Epiphanios II	around 685
Ioannes I	around 691
Georgios	around 750
Konstantinos	around 783/787
Epiphanios III	around 870
Eustathios	until 890
Basileios	end 10th/beg. 11th cent.
Nikolaos Mouzalon	around 1100
Ioannes II the Cretan	1151-1174
Barnabas II	1175-?
Sophronios II	around 1191
Isaias	1205-1209
Simeon or Hilarion	around 1218
Neophytos	around 1222
Gregorios-Germanos	around 1254
Germanos I Pesimandros	around 1260

(1260-1571 autocephaly suppressed; Latin bishops took the place of the Greek ones)

Timotheos	around 1575
Laurentios	around 1580
Neophytos	?-1592
Athanasios	1592-1600
Beniamin	1600-1605
Christodoulos I	1606-?
Timotheos II	1622-?
Ignatios	1634-?
Nikephoros	1640-1674
Hilarion Kigalas	1674-1682
Christodoulos II	1682-1690
Iakobos I	around 1691-1692
Germanos II	around 1695-1702
Athanasios (administered the archdiocese as Patriarch of Antioch)	1705-1708
Iakobos II	1709-1718
Ephrem	1715?
Silbestros	1718-1733
Philotheos	1734-1759
Paisios	1759-1767
Chrysanthos	1767-1810
Kyprianos	1810-1821
Ioakeim	1821-1824
Damaskenos	1824-1827
Panaretos	1827-1840
Ioannikios	1840-1849
Kyrillos I	1849-1854
Makarios I	1854-1865
Sophronios III	1865-1900
Kyrillos II	1909-1916
Kyrillos III	1916-1933

See vacant and administered by Bishop Leontios of Paphos, the later Archbishop

Leontios I	1947
Makarios II	1947-1950
Makarios III (Kykkotis)	1960-1977
Chrysostomos (Kykkotis)	since 1977

Lists of Rulers

Byzantine emperors

The heirs of Constantine

Constantine	324-337
Constantius	337-361
Julian the Apostate	361-363
Jovian	363-364

The house of Valentinian

Valens	364-378

Theodosian dynasty

Theodosius I	379-395
Arcadius	395-408
Theodosius II	408-450
Marcian	450-457

Leontine Dynasty

Leo I	450-474
Leo II	474
Zeno	474-475
Basiliscus	475-476
Zeno (second term)	476-491
Anastasius I	491-518

Justinian dynasty

Justin I	518-527
Justinian I	527-565
Justin II	565-578
Tiberius I Constantinus	578-582
Maurice	582-602
Phocas	602-641

Herakleian dynasty

Herakleios	610-641
Constantine III and Heraklonas	641
Heraklonas	641
Constans II Pogonatos	641-668
Constantine IV	668-685
Justinian II	685-695
Leontius	695-698
Tiberius II	698-705
Justinian II (second term)	705-711
Philippicus	711-713
Anastasius II	713-715
Theodosius III	715-717

Syrian dynasty

Leo III	717-741
Constantine V	741-775
Leo IV	775-780
Constantine VI	780-797
Irene	797-802
Nikephoros I	802-811
Staurakios	811
Michael I Rhangabe	811-813
Leo V	813-820

Amorian dynasty

Michael II	820-829
Theophilus	829-842
Michael III	842-867

Macedonian dynasty

Basil I	887-886
Leo VI	886-912
Alexander	912-913
Constantine VII 'Porphyrogennetos'	913-959
Romanos I Lekapenos	920-944
Romanos II	959-963
Nikephoros II Phocas	963-969
John I Tzimisces	969-976
Basil II	976-1025
Constantine VIII	1025-1028
Romanos III Argyros	1028-1034
Michael IV	1034-1041
Michael V	1041-1042

Zoe and Theodora	1042
Constantine IX Monomachos	1042-1055
Theodora (second term)	1055-1056
Michael VI	1056-1057
Isaac I Komnenos	1057-1059

Ducas

Constantine X Ducas	1059-1067
Romanos IV Diogenes	1068-1071
Michael VII Ducas	1071-1078
Nikephoros III Botaneiates	1078-1081

Komnenes

Alexios I Komnenos	1081-1118
John II Komnenos	1118-1143
Manuel I Komnenos	1143-1180
Alexios II Komnenos	1180-1183
Andronikos I Komnenos	1183-1185

Angeloi

Isaac II Angelos	1185-1195
Alexios III Angelos	1195-1203
Isaac II (s. term) + Alexios IV Angelos	1203-1204
Alexios V Mourtzuphlos	1204

Laskaris

Theodore I Laskaris	1204-1222
John III Ducas Vatatzes	1222-1254
Theodore II Laskaris	1254-1258
John IV Laskaris	1258-1261

Palaiologans

Michael VIII Palaiologos	1259-1282
Andronikos II Palaiologos	1282-1328
Andronikos III Palaiologos	1328-1341
John V Palaiologos	1341-1391
John VI Cantacuzenus	1341; 1347-1354
Andronikos IV Palaiologos	1376-1379
John VII Palaiologos	1390
Manuel II Palaiologos	1391-1425
John VIII Palaiologos	1425-1448
Constantine XI Palaiologos	1448-1453

Lusignan regents and kings

Guy (regent)	1192-1194
Amalric (Amaury, coronation 1197)	1194-1205
Hugh I (a minor at his succession)	1205-1218
- Walter de Montbéliard, regent	1205-1210
Henry I (a minor at his succession)	1218-1253
- Philip d'Ibelin, regent	1218-1227
- John d'Ibelin, regent	1227-1229
Hugh II (child, never ruled)	1253-1267
- Plaisance, Hugh II's mother	1253-1261
Hugh III of Antioch (regent - 1267)	1261-1284
John I	1284-1285
Henry II	1285-1324
Hugh IV	1324-1359
Peter I	1359-1369
Peter II	1369-1382
James I	1382-1398
Janus	1398-1432
John II	1432-1458
Charlotte	1458-1460
James II (illegitimate son of John II)	1460-1473
James III (dies an infant)	1473-1474
Catharina Cornaro	1474-1489

Ottoman rulers

Selim II	1566-1574
Murad III	1574-1595
Mehmed III	1595-1603
Ahmed I	1603-1617
Mustafa I	1617-1618
Osman II	1618-1622
Mustafa I (second term)	1622-1623
Murad IV	1623-1640
Ibrahim	1640-1648
Mehmed IV	1648-1687
Süleyman II	1687-1691
Ahmed II	1691-1695
Mustafa II	1695-1703
Ahmed III	1703-1730
Mahmud I	1730-1754
Osman III	1754-1757
Mustafa III	1757-1774
Abdülhamid I	1774-1789
Selim III	1789-1807
Mustafa IV	1807-1808
Mahmud II	1808-1839
Abdülmecid I	1839-1861
Abdülaziz	1861-1876
Murad V	1876
Abdülhamid II	1876-1909

Chronological Table

7000-4000 BC Neolithic Period
c. 7000 BC first settlement, Choirokitia Culture, then possibly uninhabited
from 5250 BC Ceramics
4500-4000 BC Sotira Culture
from 4000 BC Cypro-Minoan script
4000-3000 Copper Age
3rd millennium: first states beyond a limited area; first time idea of a world empire
3500-2300 BC Erimi Culture
from 3500 BC cruciform idols made of picrite and steatite
3000-2000 BC Bronze Age
from 2200 trade with Egypt, Syria and Crete
from 1900 contacts with the Aegean area
1600 first fortifications in Cyprus
from 1600 Minoan traders in Cyprus
c. 1500 vassal of Egypt
from 1450 Mycenean traders in Cyprus
c. 1300 Achaean colonisation, Hellenisation of Cyprus
around 1200 Shrine to Aphrodite erected in Paphos
c. 1200 People of the sea catastrophe
1200-750 BC Iron Age
by 1100 Achaean has supplanted the indigenous language
Mid 11th century: earthquake, decline of the cities, only Paphos is continuously inhabited, foundation of Salamis
1000-700 Phoenician immigration
Mid 9th century: Phoenicians found Kition (Larnaca)
c. 900 Hellenisation completed
750-475 BC Archaic period
790-669 Assyrian dominion, the first really foreign rule. In 709 a stele is erected to the Assyrian king Sargon in Kition
669-568 Independence of the 7-10 city kingdoms in Cyprus
569-546 Egyptian rule
546-332 Persian rule
475-332 Classical Age
499/498 Onesillo's uprising, revolt against Persian rule with the Greek cities
490-479 Cyprus fights on the Persian side against the Greek cities
480 Battle of Salamis against the Greeks lost by the Persians
470 Phoenicians expand the area of influence on Cyprus beyond Kition
Mid 5th century, Greek influence has prevailed on Cyprus

459/458 Athenian dominion
457 Persian dominion
450 Renewed Athenian advance fails
449 Peace of Callias, Cyprus remains Persian
around 390 Evagoras I, king of Salamis, unites Cyprus, for about 20 years relatively successful foreign policy, capitulates in 379 before Persia, remains king of Salamis, murdered in 374/373
351 Revolt against the Persians suppressed, 345/344 punitive expedition against Cyprus
332-58 BC Hellenistic Period
332-323 Conquests by Alexander the Great. Cyprus joins in 331
323-306 Age of the Diadochi, struggle for Alexander's inheritance
from 315 Zenon, born around 336 in Kition, teaches in Athens; founder of the Stoa, a school of philosophy
306-296 Demetrios's rule over Cyprus
295-280 Ptolemaic rule
early 2nd century: The capital of Cyprus is moved from Salamis to Paphos, closer to Egypt
168 The king of Syria attempts to conquer Egypt and Cyprus, but is repelled by Rome
80 Ptolemaeans withdrawn from Cyprus
58 BC – 4th century AD, Roman Period
58 BC Marcus Portius Cato annexes Cyprus for Rome
51/50 BC Cicero governor of Cyprus
47 BC Caesar gives Cyprus back to Cleopatra, Roman Civil Wars
36 BC Anthony confirms the return of Cyprus
31 BC Cyprus reconquered by Octavian
27 BC Part of the imperial province of Syria
22 BC Senatorial province
7 AD Birth of Christ
45-48 AD First missionary journey by Barnabas and Paul
42 Second missionary journey by Barnabas
57 Barnabas's death as a martyr in Salamis
78/79 Earthquakes destroy Paphos and Salamis
98-117 Acts of violence against Christians under Trajan
115 Roman Empire at its greatest extent
116 Jewish revolt leads to enormous losses in Cyprus; expulsion of the Jews from the island under Trajan
164 Earthquake destroys almost all cities on Cyprus
249-251 First general persecution of Christians
257/258 Persecution of Christians under Valerian

269 Marauding expedition by the Goths in Cyprus
303-311 Persecution of Christians under Diocletian
313 Declaration of general religious freedom ends the persecutions of Christians and the deification of the emperor as a state cult
324 Emperor Constantine has Byzantium reconstructed as Christian capital of the Roman Empire (in contrast to heathen Rome)
325 First ecumenical council in Nicaea formulates the creed after Athanasius which thus becomes the basis of orthodoxy: Christ has two natures, a divine one and a human one; three Cypriot bishops present
330 Inaugurations of the new Roman capital which is called Constantinople after the Emperor
332 Severe earthquake in Cyprus; the governor, Kalokairos, revolts against Constantinople
4th century: Formation of monasticism. In Cyprus, according to legend, the oldest monastery on the island, Stavrovouni, is founded by the emperor's mother Helena
361-363 Heathen cults renewed under Julian who is therefore given the epithet 'the Apostate'
381 Second ecumenical council in Constantinople confirms the results of Nicaea
391 Heathen cults banned; Christianity becomes the state religion

400-700 Early Byzantine period
395 Division of the Empire after the death of Emperor Theodosios
403 Council in Salamis against Origenes
404-407 Isaurian pirates devastate Cyprus
431 Third ecumenical council in Ephesus; Cyprus receives autocephaly; emphasis on the human nature of Christ (Nestor) declared heretical
451 Fourth ecumenical council in Chalcedon regulates, among other things, the institution of the monastery; by declaration of the equality of rank of Rome and Constantinople schism between both sees; condemns Monophysitism (Christ has only one – a divine – nature)
End of the 5th century: Panagia Kanakaria in Lythrankomi constructed; mosaic remains
6th century: Apse mosaic in Kiti
578 Emperor Tiberius settles Armenian prisoners in Cyprus, presumably to compensate for the losses through the great plague epidemic since 542
609 Emperor Herakleios visits Cyprus on his way from Alexandria to Constantinople
626 Persians and Slavs besiege Constantinople simultaneously, army and administrative reforms in the Byzantine Empire
630 First attack by Arab Bedouin on the Byzantine frontier

700-900 Spread of Islam
632 First incursion by Mohammedans on Cyprus
636 The Byzantine provinces of Palestine and Syria become Mohammedan
642 The Byzantine province of Egypt becomes Mohammedan
647/648 Mu'awiya, Emir of Syria, attacks Cyprus
653-680 Abu al-Awan occupies Cyprus; Constantia destroyed
7th century: Panagia Kanakaria in Lythrankomi destroyed and reconstructed
668, 674 Mohammedans besiege Constantinople
680/681 Sixth ecumenical council opposes Monotheletism (Christ has two natures, but only one will)
692 Attempt at resettling Cypriots in Nea Justinianopolis near Constantinople fails
692 Synod 'in Trullo'; confirmation of the autocephaly of Cyprus
717 Mohammedans besiege Constantinople
726 Iconoclast dispute begins
741, 754 Laws and synod against iconolatry
770 Iconophile monks and nuns exiled to Cyprus
787 Synod of Nicaea, temporary victory of iconolatry
790 Mohammedan incursion on Cyprus under Harun al Rashid
800 Coronation of Charlemagne as Emperor in Rome
806 Mohammedan incursion on Cyprus under Harun al Rashid
around 872 Cyprus under Byzantine rule for about seven years
9th century: Construction of the five-domed basilica in Geroskipos, construction of St. Anthony, Kellia
890 Grave of Lazarus discovered in Larnaca
900 Construction of the church of St. Lazarus in Larnaca
906-911 Himerios occupies Cyprus, the island comes under Byzantine administration
812 Damian, Emir of Tarsus, attacks Cyprus

965-1185 Later Byzantine period
965 Niketas Chalkoutzes conquers Cyprus, the island becomes Byzantine again
early 11th century: The oldest preserved Byzantine frescoes are painted in Nikolaos tis Stegis near Kakopetria, they are ascribed to the Macedonian renaissance, St. Herakleidios near Kalopanagiotis and Panagia Angeloktisti in Kiti are constructed
1042/1043 Theophilos Erotikos, the governor of Cyprus, revolts against the capital
1054 Schism between Constantinople and Rome
1071 Defeat of the Byzantine Empire by the Seljuks at Mantzikert
1092 Rhapsomates, the governor of Cyprus, revolts against the capital
End of the 11th century: Acheiropoietos near Lamboussa constructed, Alexios I Komnenos founds the Kykkos monastery; his governor Boutoumites commissions the hermit Isaiah with the work
1092-1102 Eumathios Philokales, governor in Cyprus; the Cypriot Archbishop Nikolaos Mouzalon calls him the 'Prince of Darkness'; probably because Philokales interfered in the church's financial affairs
1094-1099 First Crusade
1098/1099 Crusader states established in Syria and Palestine
1099 Pisan fleet attacks Cyprus
early 12th century: Theotokos church near Trikomo, St. John Chrysostom near Koutsoventis, Panagia Amasgou near Monagri and Panagia Asinou near Nikitari are founded and decorated with frescoes in Komnenian style; St. Nikolaos tis

Stegis near Kakopetria given second layer of frescoes; Panagia Kanakaria near Lythrankomi is reconstructed with narthex and domes; the second surviving five-domed basilica erected near Peristerona

1103 King Eric I of Denmark dies in Paphos while on a pilgrimage to Jerusalem

1103-1107 Constantine Ephorbenos governor of Cyprus

1105/1106 Oldest layer of frescoes in Panagia Asinou dated, governor's son named as donor

1110-1118 Eumathios Philokales once again governor in Cyprus; monastic foundations in Cyprus are promoted by Byzantium, among other things for military reasons

1145 Two monks, Ignatios and Neophytos, find the icon 'Machairotissa'; shortly after they receive imperial permission to found the Monastery of Machairas

1147 Second Crusade

1148 Alexios I grants Venice trading privileges in exchange for support against the Saracens; they also apply for Cyprus

1152 Chrysorrogiatissa Monastery founded by the monk Ignatios

1156 Renaud de Châtillon, prince of Antioch, plunders Cyprus

1157 Severe earthquakes on Cyprus

1158 Egyptian fleet plunders Cyprus

1160/1180 Construction and painting of the Church of the Holy Apostles in Pera Chorio in Komnenian court style

1184 Isaac Ducas Komnenos usurps Cyprus

1186 Theodore Apseudes paints the *'Enkleistra'* of St. Neophytos near Paphos

1187 Saladin takes Guy de Lusignan, king of Jerusalem and later ruler of Cyprus, prisoner

1190 Third Crusade

1191 Richard Coeur de Lion conquers Cyprus and sells it to the Order of Knights Templar in July

Easter 1192 Revolt by the population against the Knights Templar is bloodily repressed

1192-1489 Frankish period

May 1192 Guy de Lusignan takes over Cyprus from Richard Coeur de Lion

late 12th century: Christ Antiphonitis built in Kalogrea, Archangel Michael in Kato Lefkara; first fresco layer; second fresco layer in Panagia Amasgou near Monagri; founding of the Abbey Bellapais

1192 Late Komnenian frescoes in Panagia Araka, Lagoudera, probably also painted by Theodore Apseudes

1196 Monastic style painter works in the *Enkleistra* of St. Neophytos near Paphos

1204 Fourth Crusade conquers Constantinople, the Byzantine Empire collapses

1209-1326 Construction of the Haghia Sophia cathedral in Nicosia, coronation church of the Lusignans

early 13th century: Frescoes in St. Herakleidios, Kalopanagiotis

1217-1250 Eustorge de Montaigu, Latin Archbishop in Cyprus

1218 Genoa receives trading privileges in Cyprus

1219-1224 Genghis Khan and the Mongols weaken the Islamic states

1220 The papal legate Pelagius organises an anti-Greek ecclesiastical policy in Cyprus

1228 Sixth Crusade. In Cyprus in July battle between followers of Emperor Frederick II and the local aristocratic family d'Ibelin; the latter win

1232 Marshal Filangieri is intended to take Cyprus again for Frederick II, fails at Agridi; Genoa's trading privileges in Cyprus are renewed

1244 Jerusalem comes under Islamic rule again

1246 Pope Innocent IV dispenses the Cypriot king from his oath of fealty to Emperor Frederick II

1248/1249 Seventh Crusade under King Louis IX of France spends the winter in Famagusta

1251-1260 Hugo de Fagiano Latin Archbishop

1253-1260 The Mongols under Hulagu and Kublai Khan again convulse the Islamic states

1260 In Egypt the soldier caste of Mamelukes deposes the Caliph

1260 'Bulla Cypria' from Pope Alexander regulates the institutional relations between the Latin and Orthodox churches in Cyprus

1261 Michael VIII Palaeologos reconquers Constantinople; renewal of the Byzantine Empire

1265-1271 Mamelukes conquer Jaffa, Caesarea, Nazareth and Antioch

1272-1282 Armistice between Crusaders and Mamelukes

1280 Panagia tou Moutoulla constructed and painted

1282-1291 Expulsion of the Crusaders from Palestine by the Mamelukes ends with the fall of Acre

1291-1308 The Order of the Knights of St. John of Jerusalem moves its mother house to Limassol, ensures the banning of the Cypriot King Henry II in favour of his brother

1298-1326 Construction of St. Nicholas's cathedral in Famagusta

1302 War between Genoa/Venice and Constantinople ended; begining of the Ottoman danger

1306 Venice may trade in Cyprus free of customs duties; privilege renewed in 1329 and 1436

1334 Venice, the Pope, the Knights of St. John and Henry II of Cyprus join together in a 'Holy Union' against the Turks

1341-1357 Civil war in Byzantium; struggle about a mystic order of monks (hesychasts)

1365 Eighth Crusade under Peter I of Cyprus fails

1374 Cyprus is obliged to make war reparations and pay tributes to Genoa

around 1400 The second layer of frescoes painted in St. Herakleidios and St. Lampadistis Monastery, Kalopanagiotis

15th century: Gothic chapel constructed in St. Andrew's Monastery, Church of the Most Holy Cross in Pelendri and decorated with frescoes in Palaiologan court style

1422 Ottomans besiege Constantinople

1426 Egyptian sultan invades Cyprus and plunders Nicosia. In addition to the obligations towards Genoa, Cyprus is now also tributary to the Mamelukes; 1427 peasants' revolt as a result of the unbearable burden on the populace

1438 Plague rages in Cyprus

1438/1439 Council of Union in Ferrara and Florence

1449 Genoa has to take measures against the depopulation of Famagusta

29.5.1453 Ottomans conquer Constantinople; end of the Byzantine Empire

shortly after 1453 a refugee painter from Constantinople paints frescoes in the narthex of Lampadistis in Kalopanagiotis

1461 The Ottomans conquer Trebizond, the last part of the Byzantine Empire

1472 Peasants' revolt in Cyprus

1474-1478 Venice prohibits trade with Cyprus in order to eliminate Genoa

1474 Church of St. Michael in Pedoulas built and painted

1489-1571 Venetian period

1494 Frescoes by Philip Goul, Stavros tou Agiasmati, Platanistasa

Turn of 15th/16th century: Second series of frescoes in Christ Antiphonitis, Kalogrea; Metamorphis Sotiros in Palaichori and St. Mamas in Morphou are constructed and painted

around 1500: Katholikon of the St. Neophytos Monastery near Paphos constructed and painted with Akathistos cycle; the Latin chapel in St. Lampadistis near Kalopanagiotis is painted

1502 Panagia Podithou in Galata constructed and decorated with frescoes in Italo-Byzantine style

1502 Frescoes in the Enkleistra of St. Neophytos near Paphos renovated and repainted

1544 Kyrenia expanded as artillery fortress

1558 Famagusta's city walls strengthened

1564 Fourth layer of frescoes in Panagia Amasgou near Monagri painted

1567 Fortified ring constructed around Nicosia, almost all Lusignan buildings destroyed as a result

1571-1878 Ottoman Period

1589 Orthodox clergy entrusted with tax collection

1592 Ahmed Pasha has the harbour castle in Paphos renovated

1625 Mehmed Pasha has Larnaca Castle constructed

1660 Archbishop receives right of intervention in Constantinople

1720 St. John's in Nicosia becomes an episcopal church

1727/1738 Basil Grigorovich Barsky travels throughout Cyprus and leaves notes on the majority of monasteries

1736 Archbishop Philotheos donates frescoes for St. John's in Nicosia

1738 St. Spyridon in Tremetousia is renovated and partially painted

1740/1744 Church of the Archangel Michael in Monagri is restored and painted by Philaretos

1747 Abu Bekir Pasha has an aqueduct built for Larnaca

1754 Archbishop of Cyprus recognised as ethnarch in Constantinople

1757 Philaretos paints St. Minas in Vavla

1764 Revolt against the governor Chil Osman Aga

1766 Uprising by Khalil Aga against Ottoman rule

1777-1783 Bishops bring about the deposition of the governor Hadji Baki

1821 Greeks' War of Independence successful; bloody suppression in Cyprus; execution of the archbishop and about 470 Orthodox Christians in Nicosia alone

1833 Disturbances because of the tax policy of Mehmed Ali

1840, 1856 Attempts at reform in the Ottoman Empire

1969 Suez Canal opened

1878-1960 British Rule

1878 Congress of Berlin; Cyprus comes under British military rule

1880 Responsibility for Cyprus transferred from the Foreign Office to the Colonial Office

1882 Cyprus receives a constitution

1923 Treaty of Lausanne; Turkey waives its claims to Cyprus

1925 Cyprus becomes a crown colony

1931 Rebellion against British rule; London curbs the Cypriots' civil rights

1941 Political parties allowed in Cyprus

1944 Wartime business and the first 'Colonial Development and Welfare Acts' stimulate Cyprus's economy

1949 Malaria eliminated in Cyprus

1950 Makarios III becomes archbishop at the age of 37

from 1955 on: The Greek Cypriot secret organisation EOKA carries out attacks on British military installations in order to achieve union with Greece; it is supported by the Church

30.11.1955 State of emergency proclaimed

1956 Makarios III is deported to the Seychelles

1957 The Turkish secret organisation TMT is founded

1958-1959 Negotiations on independence

1959 Election of the President and Vice-President

Since 1960 Independent State

Winter 1963/1964 Makarios's attempt at amending the constitution fails, fighting between Greek and Turkish Cypriots with over 1000 dead, stationing of UN units along the 'Green Line'

1967 New fighting, crisis settled by diplomatic means

15.7.1974 Putsch against President Makarios

20.7.1974 Turkish invasion; 180,000 Greek Cypriots are driven from the North to the South; 40,000 Turkish Cypriots flee from the South to the North

Since then a divided state

Saints

Without laying any claim to completeness or a comprehensive account, the following articles are intended to present more details on some of the saints just mentioned by name up to now. All that is being aimed at is to give an idea of what spectrum the men and women painted in the lower wall zone in churches represented, how contrary they could be, how fantastic. Many are legendary, historically scarcely conceivable figures or the adaptation of pre-Christian gods, but many are also formative personalities of church history. Often several threads of tradition become intermingled and the results are strangely striking, contradictory conglomerates. Depending on the research approach, one encounters covertly surviving darker sides of the human soul. The explanatory notes presented here do not always apply to the saints mentioned in the text, because often several saints have been handed down under one name who are each venerated according to region. Particularly with respect to the witnesses for their faith there are often great differences between the Eastern and Western Churches; information about Byzantine saints, and especially about Cypriot ones, are only available with difficulty outside of their spheres of activity, the Cypriot saints are often only documented in fragmentary form.

Fig. 182: Auxibios, fresco from Lagoudera, 1192.

Alexios (Gr. 'helper') d. 417. Simple ascetic called a 'man of God', greatly revered by the people. Wandered in voluntary poverty through the countryside. Vita has its origin in Syria in the 6th century.

Ambrose b. Trier 340, d. Milan 4.4.397. Had a classical education in Rome, rose to high office and became Bishop of Milan in 373/374 although not even baptised. Important author; many hymns are ascribed to him, he developed ecclesiastical polity, teaching and divine service further, Latin Father of the Church.

Anastasia (Gr. 'arisen one') d. Sirmium 304, martyr under Diocletian; bones buried in Constantinople during the reign of Leo I. Often shown in Western art too with a jar of ointment for embalming the martyrs. Portrayed in Asinou as a 'healer from poison' (fig. 26, p. 56, on the right next to St. George on horseback, with martyr's cross in her hand). → Andronikos

Anastasios d. 599. Patriarch of Antioch from 559, combated monophysites and was therefore banned by Justin II.

Andrew (Gr. 'manly') Brother of Simon Peter and like him a disciple of Jesus, missionised especially in Asia Minor and Constantinople. According to one legend which arose in the Middle Ages he was crucified in Patras on an X-shaped cross which since then has been known as St. Andrew's cross. This cross may have developed from the sun cross; in addition 'Andros' was a title of the sun god in Patras so that a survival of the old cult is to be presumed. Relics of St. Andrew were translated to the Church of the Holy Apostles in Constantinople in 356 and were there intended to support the claim to primacy over the considerably older patriarchates of Alexandria and Antioch, but also over Rome. That is why Andrew was said to have been the elder brother; he was said to have discovered the Messiah first. The apostle is portrayed mainly as an old man with unkempt white hair. cf. p. 165-167 and bottom right in fig. 167, p. 158.

Andronikos and Anastasia Legendary monastic saints from Asia Minor, a couple who decided on a life in Egyptian monasteries. Later, however, Anastasia disguised herself as a monk and met Andronikos on a pilgrimage to Palestine. She remained with the unsuspecting Andronikos, only on her deathbed was the secret discovered.

Anna (Hebr. 'grace') Mother of Mary and patron saint of mothers. She is clearly derived from the Oriental goddess Anna, mother of Mari. Her (legendary) life became known through the apocryphal St. James's Gospel which was widely spread from about 150 AD on; her feast day has been celebrated in the East-

ern church since the 6th century, in the West 2 centuries later.
Antony 'Father of Monasticism', b. c. 250 in Kome Egypt, d. 356. A son of wealthy parents, he gave away his inheritance after their death and lived as a hermit in the desert. Living in a cave, he had to survive many combats with demons; in the west a favoured topic for artistic portrayal. His fame attracted many disciples, he corresponded, among others, with Emperor Constantine. At the request of his friend Athanasios (who also wrote his life), a few years before his death he preached against the Arians in Alexandria. The T-shaped cross is named after him. His bones 'rested' in Alexandria from 561 on and were brought to Constantinople in 635 on account of the Moslem conquest of Egypt. Like many other relics, after the Crusaders' conquest they were brought to France. cf. fig. 81, p. 94.
Arethas Bishop of Caesarea in Cappadocia. Collected and commented on the works of classical authors, was an exegete and polemicist. Stands with Photios for a renaissance of Byzantine intellectual life in the 10th century.
Arsenios b. 354, d. 455. Hermit. Came from the Roman nobility. Deacon. Called to Constantinople in 383 to educate Emperor Theodosius's sons. Left in the court in 395 and went into the desert.
Athanasios (Gr. 'immortal') b. Alexandria c. 293, d. 2.5.373. Son of Christian parents. Attended the Council of Nicaea as deacon. Since 328 Archbishop of Alexandria, church father, in the dispute with the Arians main representative of the doctrine of Christ's identical nature with God the Father. He had to leave his archbishopric five times up to 366 and spent almost twenty years in exile (Trier, Rome, Egyptian desert). Rejected philosophy for the development of Christian doctrine, gave important impulses for the doctrine of the Trinity and logos.
Auxibios Bishop of Soli, Cyprus, cf. fig. 182, p. 179.
Bacchos → Sergios; cf. fig. 30, p. 59. The name Bacchus is the Roman variant of Dionysos, the god of wine and inebriation.
Barbara (Gr. 'foreign') Legendary martyr. Daughter of a pagan who locked her in a tower and killed her because she had become a Christian. The legend arose in the 7th century at the earliest.
Barnabas (Gr. 'son of consolation' from Hebr. 'son of the prophecy') Christian Levite from Cyprus, companion of Apostle Paul on his first missionary journey, later went with Mark, his cousin, to Cyprus, founded the church there and is said to have been stoned to death in Salamis. Is one of the Apostolic Fathers, an epistle dealing particularly with the question of the succession of the Old Covenant which Israel had made with God is ascribed to him. Was known for his generosity in the first Christian community. cf. p. 155 f.
Bartholomew (Hebr. 'son of the ridger'). The name occurs only in lists of the apostles. His name was probably Nathaniel, and Bar Tolmai was his patronymic, just as Simon Peter is called Bar Jonah in places. According to one tradition, he missionised in India and Asia Minor, according to another in Egypt. He is said to have suffered a martyr's death in Armenia – either crucified or flayed, i.e. skinned and then beheaded. There are pictures in which he holds a sacrificial knife in the form of a crescent of the

Fig. 183: Basil, fresco from Platanistasa, late fifteenth century.

moon.
Basil (Gr. 'royal') b. Caesarea (Cappadocia) c. 330, d. 1.1.379. Studied in Caesarea, Constantinople and Athens, became friends there with Gregory of Nazianzos. Baptised in 356. Important preacher, opposed Arianism, had charitable institutions built and promoted monasticism. Many monks in the east follow the rules he compiled together with Gregory of Nazianzos in 360. 370 Bishop of Caesarea, doctor of the church, one of the 'three Cappadocians' who continued Athanasios's inheritance and further developed the doctrine of the Trinity. cf. fig. 183 above and fig. 108, p. 113.
Catherine (Gr. 'pure') According to the legend, daughter of the king of Cyprus, she died as a martyr in Alexandria. She was broken on a wheel. As a highly educated virgin, she bears features of Pallas Athena; the death by the wheel refers to the cult of the great goddess who dances on the fire wheel and was worshipped particularly in Sinai. The St. Catherine's Monastery was then founded over her grave. The earliest veneration can be shown for the 8th century, the vita to the 6th or 7th century

Constantine → Helena

Cosmas Brother of Damian → fig. 57, 76

Cyprianus (Lat. from Gr. 'man from Cyprus') b. Nikomedeia 304. According to the legend, the pagan magician attempted to seduce a Christian virgin, but converted to her faith after his endeavours remained without success. Was beheaded together with his beloved. The material forms the basis of a medieval Faust legend.

Cyprianus b. Carthage c. 205, beheaded there 14.9.258 as a martyr. Son of rich pagans, famous orator. Soon after his conversion priest, 248/49 Bishop of Carthage. Went underground on account of the persecutions under Decius. 251 disputes about the treatment of those who apostatised during the persecution; at the Council in 251 he supported their re-admission to the church. Came into conflict with the pope in 255 because he rejected the validity of a baptism which was carried out by a heretic. Banned under Emperor Valerian. Important ecclesiastical author, many of whose letters and treatises have survived.

Cyril b. c. 315, d. 18.3.386 (uncertain). 348 Bishop of Jerusalem, came into conflict with his patron, the Bishop of Caesarea, on account of the problem whether God the Father and Son were identical or similar in nature. Repeatedly banned (19 years in exile, 16 years in office). Important for the development of the divine service, especially because of the 24 catecheses of 348/349. They are witness to the early Christian opinion on baptism, confirmation and the real presence of the Redeemer in the celebration of the Eucharist.

Cyril b. c.380, d. 27.4.444. Probably lived for some years among hermits in the desert, very well educated. 403 at the synod of the Oak at Chalcedon with his uncle, Bishop Theophilos, on the side of the opponents of Chrysostom. 412 Patriarch of Alexandria as successor of his uncle. Under his leadership, bloody excesses on the Christian and Jewish sides. Later the disputes moved more into the intellectual sphere: Cyril prevailed in 431 at the Council of Ephesus against Nestorios with the doctrine of the simultaneousness of the divine and human in Jesus Christ and of Mary's motherhood of God (Nestorios had wanted to call her only 'Mother of Christ', not 'Mother of God', 'Theotokos'. Important ecclesiastical author. Fig. 108, p. 113).

Damian Brother of Cosmas, physicians who treated their patients free of charge and were therefore given the epithet 'Anargyroi' – without silver; they are said to have been tortured and beheaded around 305 under Diocletian either in Syria or Cilicia. There are no certain accounts about their lives, but their cult was already widely spread in the 5th century, something regarded as proof of a historical core. However, there is also the opinion that they represent a continuation of the classical pair of brothers Castor and Pollux, because their temple had become a Christian church.

Daniel the Stylite b. Samosata, Syria c. 409, d. Anaplous 493. Entered a monastery at the age of 12, but soon left it again and became a disciple of Symeon the Stylite. Around 460 he mounted a pillar of his own in Anaplous north of Constantinople and preached from it for 33 years. Intervened in contemporary disputes more than other stylites. Emperor Leo I was advised by him.

Fig. 184: Epiphanios, fresco from Kakopetria.

David d. 965 BC King of Israel since his conquest of Jerusalem in 1004 BC. Entertained his predecessor with his cithara playing, vanquished the giant Goliath with his catapult thus gaining the hatred of Saul and the love of the people. Fled into the desert, moved around with a band of robbers and after Saul's death fought hard for power over the 12 tribes of Israel. He led the country to its greatest extent. Created an administrative apparatus with which he consolidated the state. His son Solomon (cf. fig. 37, p. 62) continued his work and built the Temple in Jerusalem which his father had not been allowed to build on account of his crimes – the prophet Nathan had severely reprimanded him, but also prophesied: Thy House shall prevail for ever! Hence the reference to Jesus who is regarded as a descendant of David. cf. fig. 38, p. 62 and fig. 109, p. 114.

Demetrios b. Sirmium c. 304, suffered a martyr's death under Maximian. Soldier saint. In the Middle Ages, his alleged grave

Fig. 185: John Lampadistis, Kakopetria, painted after 1350.

was visited by many pilgrims. The starting point for his cult was Thessaloniki which he is said to have saved from an attack by the Bulgarian Tsar in 1207; since then he is often portrayed on horseback.

Demetrianos Bishop of Chytroi, Cyprus

Dionysios the Areopagite One of the most influential mystics of the Middle Ages who did not, however, ever exist. Rather documents were compiled in the 6th century which were ascribed to the first Athenian bishop who had been converted by Paul. The division of the choirs of angels, among other things, dates back to them.

Dionysios b. 264/265. Disciple of Origen, thus coming from the Alexandrian school of which he was head 231/232-247/248. 247/248 Archbishop of Alexandria, fled from persecution by Decius, was banned under Valerian. Like Cyprianus of Carthage, was mild towards those who had apostatised during the persecutions, unlike Cyprianus he recognised a baptism by a heretic. Few of his writings have survived.

Elijah (Hebr. 'My God is Jehovah') b. Thisbe, Eastern Jordania 8th century BC – itinerant prophet against the cults of heathen gods who gave strong backing to the Jehovah-true Israelites. Among the miraculous tales of his life is that angels fed him and he then went into the Sinai for 40 days and nights where God appeared to him in the whispering of the wind: Jehovah is a God of leniency and patience. He is taken up to Heaven in a fiery chariot on which the belief is founded that he will return at the end of time.

Ephrem (Hebr. 'fruitful') the Syrian b. Nisibis c. 305, d. 9.6.373. Deacon from a Christian family. Since 363, after his home fell to the Persians, hermit near Edessa. Many accounts made him a classic of early Christian theology, renowned for his hymns.

Epiphanios b. c. 315 in Judaea, d. 403. From 367 Archbishop of Salamis on Cyprus (Constantia). Opponent of Origen and fanatical fighter against heretics. cf. fig. 184, p. 181 and fig. 123, p. 123.

Eusebios (Gr. 'pious') d. c. 339. From about 314 Bishop of Caesarea in Palestine. Church father and intermediary in the Arianism disputes. Wrote a ten volume history of the church and biography of Constantine I to whom he was court theologian. He gives the theological justification for the emperor's omnipotence. The equivalent to the one God in heaven is the one ruler on Earth as Christ's regent.

Eustachios (Gr. 'rich in wheat ears') Probably identical with → Eusthatios, Patriarch of Antioch. Martyr. According to the legend, before his baptism a Roman commander by the name of Placidus; converted after he saw the vision of a cross between the antlers of a deer he was hunting.

Eusthatios (Gr. 'steadfast') b. Side, Asia Minor, d. c. 340 in exile in Thrace. Bishop in northern Greece, 323/324 Patriarch of Antioch, probably the historical figure behind the legendary Eustachios. Ardent advocate of the principles adopted at the Council of Nicaea; opponent of the Arians, therefore banned in 331. Many sermons by him have been preserved.

Euthymios (Gr. 'good-hearted') b. 377 Melitene, d. 20.1.473. Became priest at 19 and controlled the monasteries of his native city. Went on a pilgrimage to Palestine in 406, settled down in an eremitic colony near the Dead Sea. Together with Theoktistos he founded his own colony of monks in 411, moved without Theoktistos to Marda by the Dead Sea. There his disciple Sabas later founded a famous monastery. Missionised among the nomads whose territory became a separate bishopric in 425. He lived in the Ziph desert before he gathered followers around him once again in 428/429 near the Theoktistos monastery. About 456 he persuaded the Monophysite Empress Eudokia to accept the Chalcedon Creed.

Floros (Lauros, etc.) Stonemason from Constantinople who was martyred together with his companions on account of his Christian faith and thrown into a well. The time is unknown. They are regarded as the patron saints of horses.

Forty Martyrs of Sebaste According to legend 40 Christian soldiers, members of the Legio fulminata (thunder legion) who c. 320 were made to stand naked on a frozen lake in Armenia with a steaming bath before their eyes. With one exception, they held out to the end and froze to death; impressed by this steadfastness, one of the guards undressed and died with them. They were the patron saints of the higher ranks in the Imperial Army, fig. 47, p. 70.

George (Lat. 'farmer') Cappadocian officer, martyred under Diocletian around 303. The legend is so overwhelming that only the early spread of the cult (e.g. in Syria the oldest churches are dedicated to St. George) guarantees a historic kernel. In Cyprus there were over 60 churches to St. George! In the Greek church he is counted among the great soldier saints alongside Demetrios, Prokopios and Theodoros. The most popular concept of his fight with the dragon arose in the west in the Middle Ages. In the Orthodox area he is portrayed mainly as a warrior on foot, but also on horseback. cf. fig. 26, p. 56 and fig. 48, p. 70.

Gregory (Gr. 'vigilant') of Nazianzos b. c. 329, d. c. 390, church father, friend of Basil, 381 Patriarch of Constantinople. Most important Christian poet of his time.

Gregory of Nyssa, b. c. 334 Caesarea, d. c. 394 Nyssa, brother of Basil. From 371 Bishop of Nyssa in Cappadocia. Church father, important theologian and mystic, the most profound thinker among the 'three Cappadocians'.

Gregory the Thaumarturge ('the wonder-worker'), d. between 270 and 275, disciple of Origen, c. 240 Bishop of Neocaesarea.

Helena (Gr. 'shining') b. Drepanon, Asia Minor, c. 255, d. Nikomedeia (east of Constantinople) c. 330. Daughter of an inn-keeper. Lover of the later Emperor Constantius I, Chlorus (d. 306) by whom she had a son, the later Emperor Constantine I. Repudiated in 289, her son came to the court of Diocletian. After he had been proclaimed Emperor, Constantine brought his mother back in 306. She became a Christian in 312, Empress in 327. She financed charitable activities, churches and monasteries. About 324, pilgrimage to Palestine, found three crosses in Jerusalem and recognised the True Cross of Christ by the miraculous cure of a woman. This legend dates back to Eusebios of Caesarea. Helena is said to have taken the cross with her, suffered a shipwreck on Cyprus, left a piece of the Cross on the island at the advice of an angel who appeared to her in a dream, and founded a monastery here: Stavrovouni cf. fig. 61, p. 79 and fig. 125, p. 125.

Hilarion (Gr.-Lat. 'happy') the Great, Cypriot Bishop, concluded his life near Paphos in Episkopi.

Hilarion Monk in the 10th century, found protection in Cyprus on the flight from the Arabs. Buried directly above Kyrenia in the fortress named after him (originally a monastery).

Ignatios (neologism for Egnatius: 'Man from Egnatia', a port city in Apulia) Bishop of Antioch. Was brought to Rome under Trajan and devoured by wild animals in the Colosseum by 117 at the latest. During the voyage he wrote seven epistles to several communities which Bishop Polycarp collected and published. As a result, Ignatios is one of the most important witnesses for the early church: he represents the monarchic church polity, at the head of which is a bishop with all powers appointed by Christ. From him comes the expression 'Catholic' (all-embracing) Church. In opposition to the opinion that Jesus had only apparently had a body, he emphasises that the

Fig. 186: Kyriake, fresco from Pedoulas, 1474.

Divine had truly become Man, been born of a Virgin, redeemed on the Cross and had risen again; in Jesus the divine and human nature were unmixed and yet united in such a manner that the man Jesus had taken on divine characteristics and the eternal God human ones. Ignatios thus defends the real presence of Christ in the Eucharist.

Ignatios (real name Niketas) b. c. 798, d. 23.10.877. Went into exile with his father, who had been banned by Emperor Michael Rangabe, and his brother in 813, became a monk, founded three monasteries. Empress Theodora appointed him Patriarch of Constantinople on 4.7.847 without an electoral synod. Supported iconolatry, deposed some bishops in 853 who therefore turned to the pope. Ignatios encountered difficulties with the new ruler Bardas and abdicated in 858. His successor was Photios who had to resign again in 858 after radical Ignatios supporters had intervened several times in his favour with the pope and emperor. Admittedly, during his second period of office, Ignatios had difficulties with the clergy who in their majority were loyal to Photios. Became reconciled with Photios who personally canonised him after his death.

John the Almsgiver b. in Amathous, Patriarch of Alexandria, fig. 108, p. 113 and fig. 123, p. 123.

Fig. 187: Lazarus, fresco from Lagoudera, 1192.

John Chrysostom (Gr. 'gold mouth') b. Antioch c. 345 (354?), d. Komana (Pontus) 14.9.407. From 398 Patriarch of Constantinople, 404 deposed by the Emperor, doctor of the church and one of the most important preachers in Christian antiquity. From a theological history aspect, he may be counted as belonging to the Antiochian school which rejected allegorical exegesis and instead developed the historical-grammatical one. Scripture was to be interpreted literally, in accordance with its original meaning. In Christology, this school laid the main emphasis on the human side of Christ who underwent a development and only achieved the unification with God through the Resurrection. Whether the liturgy named after him is in fact by him cannot be proved. Fig. 123, p. 123.

John of Damascus b. c. 650, d. c. 750. Came from an influential Arabo-Christian family, initially worked, like his father, at the court of the Caliph in a high position (father was finance minister). When an anti-Christian course was adopted, they lost their offices. John withdrew to a monastery and became an author commissioned by several bishops, especially on questions of iconolatry. Already recognised by his contemporaries as a theological authority, famous for his sermons, great poet and reformer of ecclesiastical music.

John Climax d. c. 650. Abbot on Sinai with 16 monks there. Hermit for 40 years, then abbot. Wrote many ascetic works; main work 'Klimax tou paradeisu', 'The ladder to Paradise' following Gen. 28, 10-19. In 30 steps he gives instructions to monks on how to achieve virtue.

John Lampadistis Deacon, came from the Marathasa valley. In St. Nicholas's church in Kakopetria alongside his portrait is the addition 'Maratheftis'. cf. fig. 185, p. 182.

John Palaiolaurites d. early 9th century. 'Palaiolaurites' means 'from the old Lavra'. This monastery was founded by Chariton 328/335 in Ain Fara near Jerusalem. It is the very first lavra in which John lived as priest and hermit.

Joseph (Hebr. 'May God add') Hymn-writer, b. 816 Syracuse, Sicily, d. 3.4.886 in Constantinople. Left his homeland on account of the Arab incursions in 830 for Thessaloniki where he became a monk. Shortly after arriving in Constantinople in 841, he had to flee again on account of the iconoclastic persecution. On the way to Rome he fell victim to pirates and lived in Crete for several years as a slave. Later he succeeded in fleeing, in 850 he established a monastery in Constantinople. Sent into exile twice again for his iconolatry, the second time with Photios, the Patriarch of the capital.

Joulitta According to legend, under Diocletian she was persecuted as a Christian with her three-year old son Kyriakos, and beheaded in Tarsus, her child being dashed to the pavement.

Kyriake Martyr from Asia Minor who gained great popularity from the 13th century on in the Slav and Byzantine area. As personification of the days of the week apparently a development which was adopted particularly strongly in Cyprus from models in Constantinople and ultimately goes back to a Hellenistic tradition. cf. fig. 186, p. 183.

Kyriakos (Gr. 'dedicated to the Lord') d. as a martyr probably in 305 under Diocletian with 2 or 5 companions.

Kyriakos → Joulitta

Kyros and John Miracle-workers in Alexandria. They there supplanted the cult of Isis Medica because Bishop Cyril had their relics translated to the old temple. They were therefore soon included among the physician saints alongside Cosmas and Damian. Nothing is known of their lives.

Lawrence d. Rome 10.8.258. Deacon, according to the legend burned on the gridiron, oldest portrayal in the church of Galla Placidia in Ravenna c. 450 shows him with Cross and gospel book in his hand alongside the gridiron.

Lauros → Floros

Lazarus cf. p 131 f. left, fig. 187. Epiphanios does not mention him yet as Archbishop of Cyprus, so that it is very probable that this legend only developed after the 4th century. The southern French church also attempted to defend itself against Rome's claims of primacy by claiming that Lazarus had been its first bishop.

Leontinos d. c. 650. Monk. Bishop of Neapolis on Cyprus. Preacher, hagiographer. Wrote the life of Symeon of Edessa, a 'fool for the sake of Christ' of the 6th century.

Luke Physician, companion of Paul, apostle and evangelist, Author of the Acts of the Apostles. According to legend dies as a martyr, is said to have painted authentic pictures of the mother of God and Christ. Symbol: bull as the sign for the sacrifice of Zachariah; fig. 115, p. 118: the writer bears the ca-

Fig. 188: Mamas on his lion, Louvaras, fifteenth century.

nonical symbols for Luke.
Mamas cf. p. 141 and fig. 188 above.
Mark Also John Mark, nephew of Barnabas, came from a Jerusalem family of priests accompanied Paul and Barnabas on their first missionary journey. Paul later refused to take him with him again. He is said to have worked as an interpreter for Peter and wrote, probably before 70, the oldest preserved gospel (the conclusion 16: 9-20 was added later). He is said to have established a community in Alexandria and to have died there as a martyr.
Mary of Egypt, representative of ascetic nakedness. Converted after a licentious life in Alexandria, she withdrew into the desert on the other side of the Jordan and lived – without clothes – almost half a century in complete solitude. The monk Zosimas discovered her by chance. She told him her life and asked him to meet him on the bank of the Jordan the next year. There he gave her holy communion. A year later he found her dead at the same spot and buried her. From her life one can learn many details about the practices of Alexandrian whores. The earliest portrayal in Cyprus is to be found in Asinou 1105/1106.
Matthew (Hebr. 'gift of God'). Actually Levi, son of Alphaeus from Galilee, tax-collector by profession until he followed Jesus. Apostle, especially in the mission among the Gentiles, and evangelist, symbol man/angel for descent and birth of Christ. The gospel named after him but certainly not written by him was written after 70. From the sixth century on, in the tradition of ancient authors' portraits, his picture was placed in the manuscript before the gospel, just like the other evangelists.

Minas d. 295. Martyr under Diocletian. Suffered martyrdom riding on his horse. Buried by a sacred spring in the desert near Alexandria; most important place of pilgrimage of the Eastern Church in the 5th and 6th centuries.
Mnason Bishop of Tamasos, Cyprus, disciple of Paul.
Neophytos b. 1134, d. 1219. Ascetic, known for his teachings, piety and his strong belief in God. One of the most famous ecclesiastical authors of the 12th century, wrote hymns and psalms, but also left information about the political happenings of his time. Most important work: 'Ritual ordinance'. His mortal remains were found in 1750; nowadays they are kept in a wooden sarcophagus in St. Neophytos; the skull is in a silver receptacle. cf. p. 112-115, fig. 189, p. 186.
Nestor b. 381, d. after 451. 428-431 Patriarch of Constantinople. The Council of Ephesus condemned him as a heretic in 431. Like his predecessor Chrysostom, he lost against the Patriarch of Alexandria in the dispute for predominance in the Church.
Nestor Soldier saint; legend linked with that of Demetrios. Fig. 66, p. 83.
Nicholas One of the few saints venerated equally greatly in the Eastern and Western Churches. The legendary figure developed in the Byzantine sphere of influence and is to be found in Italy since the 9th century, since the 10th also in Germany. It has two historical models: a bishop of Myra and an abbot who dies as Bishop of Pinara in 564. Both lived in Lycia. Fig. 44, p. 67.
Nikephoros I (Gr. 'bringing victory') b. c. 750, d. 5.4.828. 775-797 secretary to the Emperors, then hermit, 802 administrator of a hospital, 806 Patriarch of Contantinople, although initially still a layman. Deposed in 815 because he supported the cult of icons.
Onouphrios According to legend a hermit near Thebes in Egypt. He is portrayed naked, covered just with hairs or leaves. Clothes stand for the ballast of worldliness. Following the model of Elijah in the OT, he withdrew into the desert for 60 years. His history is told by Paphnutios (d. c. 380), the Egyptian monastery founder. He is to be seen at the bottom right in fig. 112, p. 115.
Panteleimon also Pantaleon, martyr under Diocletian in Nikomedeia. According to legend personal physician to Emperor Maximinian.
Paraskevi (Gr. 'preparation', 'Friday') A saint venerated in Cyprus as the personification of Good Friday, portrayed in at least 17 post-Byzantinian church paintings with an icon of the Passion of Christ. cf. fig. 73, p. 89.
Paul (Hebr. called Saul) b. c. 10 AD in Tarsus, Cilicia, d. between 64 and 67 in Rome by the sword, martyr probably under Nero. Tent-maker and prospective rabbi. Persecutor of Christians, converted on the way to Damascus in 34 by a vision. In the mid-forties then beginning of his missionary activity. 58 Roman imprisonment. Most important of the apostles as church organiser and theologian. He is portrayed at many events at which he cannot have been present according to Biblical evidence. Typical for him are a balding pate and a dark, pointed beard. cf. fig. 24, p. 51, fig. 74, p. 89 and fig. 115, p. 118.
Peter (Gr. 'rock') d. between 64 and 67 in Rome, martyr under Nero. Actual name Simon, son of Jonah and brother of Andrew,

Fig. 189: Two angels escort Neophytos to Heaven, fresco from the Neophytos´s monastery.

cf. p. 167. Together with John and James, he was among the closest friends of Jesus, the apostles were under his leadership, to which the first bishops referred. Peter is portrayed with grey hair and a long beard, together with Paul his features were the first to be individually fixed. Fig. 24, p. 51.

Prokopios d. 7.6.303 in Caesarea beheaded under Diocletian.

Sabas or Sabbas b. 429 Cappadocia, d. 5.12.532, founded a monastery south-east of Jerusalem from which many daughter houses were founded.

Sozomenos b. in Palestine, hermit, Cypriot saint.

Spyridon d. 348. Shepherd who was elected Bishop of Tremithos, Cyprus, on account of his virtues. Patron saint of Corfu (because his bones were brought there after the Ottoman conquest of Constantinople), portrayed mainly with a basketwork cap, often with a burning roof tile: at the first Ecumenical Council in Nicaea in 325, he is said to have presented his argument for the indivisible Trinity and to have smashed a tile as proof. Thereupon, fire shot to heaven, water came out of the ground and earth remained in his hand. Just as these three elements had been united in the tile, he said, so also had one to imagine the Trinity of God Father, Son and Holy Spirit. cf. fig. 161, p. 154.

Stephen (Gr. 'crown, wreath') Deacon, the first martyr, stoned to death; story in Acts 7:54-59.

Stephen the Younger Monk from Mount Auxentios, lynched by an angry mob in Constantinople (who were for the iconoclastic emperor) in November 765. Martyr for iconolatry.

Symeon the Stylite d. 459. Archimandrite, called thaumaturge (the miracle-worker). Stylites, ascetic monks, widely spread especially in Egypt from the 5th to 10th century, lived unprotected from wind and weather on a pillar ('stylos'), disciples and admirers brought them food. Symeon the Elder lived from about 422 until his death on top of a 15 m high pillar in Syria; he wanted thus to avoid annoyance by visitors who hoped for a cure for themselves by touching his garments. After his death, Emperor Zeno had a place of pilgrimage erected around his pillar. Symeon's feast day on 1 September coincides with the beginning of the Orthodox ecclesiastical year.

Thekla According to legend converted by Paul to chastity, left her family and was betrayed by her bridegroom, but neither the wild animals in the circus nor the flames were able to harm her.

Theodore of Euchaita d. 306. Martyr because he set fire to the Temple at Amasya. According to legend a soldier.

Thomas (Hebr. 'twin') Apostle, the doubter (John 20: 24 ff). Is said to have missionised in India and among the Parthians and to have died a martyr. Apocryphal writings, including a gospel, have been ascribed to him. Fig. 177, p. 164.

Timothy Disciple of Paul, accompanying him on the second and third missionary journeys. Regarded as first Bishop of Ephesos, martyr under Domitian.

Three Kings In Matthew's gospel there are specialist terms and historical details in connection with the visit of the three wise men from the East that a historical event must have formed the basis of the myth. The Biblical Magi must have been the last representatives of the caste of priests in Babylon who were dying out at that time and who had conducted mathematical and astronomical research with great accuracy. In the year 7 BC, the probable year of Jesus's birth, Jupiter, who as the star Marduk was the highest deity of the Babylonians, and Saturn met three times (29.5, 3.10, 5.12) with the result that the star 'rose', 'went before them' and 'stood still'. This event took place in the Zodiac sign of Pisces which Babylonian interpretation ascribed to Palestine; the rise meant for them that a great king would be born in 'Amurru'. On cuneiform tablets found in 1925 and later, we find sentences such as: "Then a great king will arise in the Western Land, then justice, peace and joy will prevail in all lands and bless all peoples".

Triphillios Bishop of Ledra, Cyprus

Tychikos Bishop of Neapolis, Cyprus

Tychon Bishop of Amathous, Cyprus

Zosimas → *Mary of Egypt*

Glossary

Abbot – (Gr.-Aram. abbas 'father') The superior in sole charge of an abbey of monks. Institutionalised in ecclesiastical law in Justinian's time. Is designated by his predecessor and must be confirmed and consecrated by the bishop of the diocese.

Abbey – Monastery which with its territory is subject to an abbot, but not to a bishop in all cases.

Acheiropoietos – (Gr. 'not made by hands') Designation for pictures that are said to have come into existence as real portraits without human intervention by a miracle – such as the Holy Towel of Veronica. There is the explanation that they had been painted by a contemporary or they are said to have been produced by an imprint. They were regarded already in the 7th century as a second incarnation. Originally, this concept referred only to the portrait of Christ; since the 8th century also to the Mother of God and some saints → Mandylion. Large eyes, austerely parted hair, no neck and frontality are characteristic for a Christ Acheiropoietos.

Agios/Agia – (Gr.) 'saint' (m), 'saint' (f)

Acanthus – Bear's breech, an ornament following the model of the spiny leaves of this herbaceous shrub native to the Mediterranean. Leaf without a petiole with serrated, indented or notched edge.

Adoration of the Lamb – The lamb as the symbol for Christ goes back to several similes in the New Testament emphasising the sacrifice for mankind. After the ban on this symbol at the synod of 692, this motif vanished from Byzantine art.

Akathistos – A Marian hymn with 24 verses linked by an alphabetic acrostic. Is sung on the Saturday of the fifth week of Lent. An introductory verse not included in the numbering celebrates Mary as the victorious military leader, verses 1-12 relate her life from the Annunciation to the Presentation of Jesus in the Temple. Verses 13-24 unfold the Mariology. It is a poetic masterpiece which came into being in the 7th century under the impression made by the Slavonic and Asiatic peoples besieging Constantinople. Romanos Melodos is regarded as the author.

Allegory – (Gr. 'express something by something else') Vivid transposition of abstract links (e.g. the Trinity) or a personification (e.g. the River Jordan or the sea) going beyond a sign (→ Symbol). Often used by theologians as attempts at interpretation and thus seldom directly comprehensible. In contrast to → Typology, it is constructed timelessly.

Altar – (late Lat. 'raised place of sacrifice') Originally, the consecration, the central event of the Eucharist, was carried out on an ordinary table. Soon it became a piece of sacred furniture which was designed accordingly. From the 4th century on, altar cloths appeared, in addition, relics were frequently kept in a case in the table; from the 12th century on that was required by regulation in Byzantine churches. The location adopted in the Eastern Church was the apse, separated from the congregation initially by a barrier, later by the iconostasis. The congregation was able to follow the service through the open curtain of the middle door.

Anachoresis – Eremitic life

Anchorite → Hermit, recluse

Anastasis – Christ → Resurrection and journey to the gates of Hell. Byzantine art avoids portrayal of the Resurrection because the event is hidden from view (the Divine cannot be portrayed). Instead it portrays Christ's descent to the gates of hell, as Redeemer he takes the pious of the Old Testament, especially Adam and Eve, up to Heaven. Just as in the case of the Assumption of Mary, the literary model is to be found in the Apocrypha. The classical myth of Heracles's journey to Hades played a role in the origin of this iconography; it was promoted especially by Ephrem the Syrian.

Antiphonary – Book with the antiphons for the liturgy.

Apex – Highest point of an arch or vault.

Apocrypha – Scriptures written between the 2nd and 9th centuries AD and not included in the canon of the Old and New Testament. Among them are numerous important sources for pictorial presentation; thus many scenes from the Marian cycle are to be found in what is known as St. James's Gospel.

Apostle (Gr. 'appointed messenger') Disciples sent out by Jesus to preach the Gospel to the world. Originally 8, then 12 like the 12 tribes of Israel, led by Peter; Matthew took the place of Judas. Paul also claimed for himself to have been called by God and Jesus through an experience of revelation (Gal. 1). Originally, all missionaries in early Christianity bore this title; the wider group of 70 came about as a result.

Barrel vault – Vault with a round or pointed cross section.

Apse – (Gr. 'added') Semi-circular or polygonal end of the church room facing East; originally the place for the clergy including a throne for a bishop. In Orthodox churches often three apses; one for the consecration, one for the altar utensils and one for the altar itself. The apse is the sanctuary and is hidden from profane view by the iconostasis. Its exceptional position was especially emphasised. In the upper end, the conch, Mary with the escorting Archangels Michael and Gabriel, in the early Byzantine period with ceremonial staffs and orbs, later with censers. Below it the Communion of the Apostles; right at the bottom, bishops and church fathers who vary according to the church.

Archangel – Michael and Gabriel act as the envoys from God who bring messages to humans and pay homage to God, often portrayed as an escort or assistants. → Angel

Archbishop – Originally the chief bishop of an autocephalous ecclesiastical territory for whom from the 5th century on the title of patriarch came to be adopted. Admittedly, there was also the opinion that only the Archbishop of Constantinople should be called patriarch.

Archimandrite – Term adopted in the 6th century for the → Abbot of a monastery which is distinguished by a special spiritual rank; commissioner of the archbishop who is in charge of the monasteries in an area.

Asceticism – (Gr. 'exercise') Setting aside pleasure in favour of a pure life to bring one closer to God. Basis of monasticism which in part practised it in extreme forms.

Assumption – Portrayal of Mary's ascension to Heaven. Mary is said to have gone to Heaven with body and soul, this special point is emphasised in the term assumption. → Anastasis → Ascension

Angels – Characteristic intercessor figures between the heavenly and earthly in all religions which have this dualism. In opposition to the cult of angels in heretical religious persuasions, in the 5th/6th centuries, the Church imposed a clear hierarchy of the powers in which the archangels were in the last rank but one and angels in the final one (→ Seraphim and → Cherubim in the first and second). They performed, so to speak, the direct work of intercession; among monks they were greatly venerated as helpers in asceticism.

Athos, Mount – Also called the Holy Mountain. Greek peninsula already favoured in the early Middle Ages by anchorites. In the 10th century, Athanasios founded the lavra which has remained the largest monastery down to the present. Monks from all Orthodox churches live here. They have joined together to form a religious, autonomous republic.

Attribute – (Lat. 'added', 'ascribed') In the East mainly the signs of holiness, the cross and the halo. The marking of the saints by the instruments of their martyrdom which has become established in the West – St. Catherine is to be recognised by the wheel, etc. – is hardly to be found. Only the stylites are depicted on a hinted pillar.

Aureole – Nimbus surrounding the whole figure

Autocephaly – (Gr. 'with its own head') The independence of the Orthodox national churches whose patriarch or archbishop was elected by the bishops and not appointed by another.

Banderole – (Fr.) A ribbon-like scroll or sculptured band bearing an explanatory inscription in a picture.

Barn church – Typical Cypriot architectural form with a pitched roof

Basilica – (Gr. 'King's hall') Type of church building derived from a Roman administrative building in which the interior is divided into sections with differing importance. In the case of basilicas with several aisles, the main nave has a higher roof than the side aisles, the front end of the room is raised (→ Apse), the area for the clergy is separated from that for the lay people (→ Bema)

Basil, Liturgy of – Basil the Great revised the liturgy of Athanasios and expanded it to include the anaphora before the Eucharist with the complex of ideas concerning the Holy Ghost. This liturgy was used in the early and middle Byzantine periods, but then had to make way for the shorter one by John Chrysostom.

Bema – (Gr. 'step', 'stage') Frequently raised, but at all events separate altar area in Orthodox churches reserved for the clergy.

Bishop – (Gr. 'watcher') Ecclesiastical office which developed around 100 AD in Syria. His leading role is legitimised by reference to the succession of the Apostles.

Bishop's throne – Raised seat of the bishop at official liturgical acts; in early Christian times it stood at the centre of the apse behind the altar. → Throne

Blachernitissa – Special form of the portrayal of Mary in the apse conch, called after a picture in the church to the Virgin founded in 450 in the Blachernai area of Constantinople. The Mother of God faces the observer frontally, before her breast is suspended a medallion (like a shield) with the Christ child. After iconoclasm a special form of the victory-bringer following the model of the Greek goddess of victory, Nike. Further developments → Orans, → Platytera

Caliph – (Ar. 'successor') Title of a Moslem ruler who derives his legitimacy from his succession to Mohammed.

Calligraphy – Art of beautiful handwriting.

Capital – (Lat. 'little head') The topmost element of a pillar, transition point from the bearing to the resting parts. Typical for Byzantium are capitals with impost blocks in which the impost is visible between the arch and capital – consists of necking groove, body and padstone (abacus or impost block).

Chapel – (diminutive of Lat. cappa 'cloak') The cloak of St. Martin of Tours was kept in the Frankish king's palace in Paris in the 7th century, the clerics who watched over it were called chaplains. The name of this room for prayer was used for all such smaller rooms. In contrast to a parish church in which sacraments may also be administered, it is purely a devotional room.

Chapter room – Meeting room for the monks in a monastery.

Cherub, pl. cherubim – (Hebr.) Angels with wings and animals' feet, celestial guards who stand around the throne of Christ; the eighth of the nine choirs of angels. Following Near Eastern models, portrayed as a four-headed being with four wings covered with eyes.

Choir of Saints – In the Byzantine divine service, no organ is allowed, even now, thus the choir as the sole musical contribution plays a greater role than in the West. In any portrayal of the Last Judgment, choirs of saints appear, a symbol for the heavenly Jerusalem.

Clergy – (Lat. 'field share', 'inheritance') In the NT, the community is understood as the 'inheritance' over whom nobody shall rule. Later the hierarchisation, the promotion of a theologically trained person over the layman, developed.

Cloister – (Lat. claustrum, 'bolt') Following the ancient model arranged around a quadrangle from 5th century on. Church mainly on the north side as centrepoint of the whole.

Cloverleaf plan – Arms of the transept end in apses which match the form of the Eastern choir (main apse); i.e. the three, usually equally sized, apses are arranged like a cloverleaf (and not in a line).

Communion of the Apostles – Liturgical interpretation of the Last Supper; Christ is mainly portrayed twice, once with the bread, once with the chalice of wine, in front of Him the disciples in groups of six each. From the 12th century, two angels often stand behind Jesus. Part of the apse decoration.

Conception of St. Ann – Celebrated on 9 Dec. in the Eastern Church, only introduced by imperial decree in 1166. Feast content concentrates on the marriage of Joachim and Ann. Portrayal opens the cycles of Mary's life.

Conch – (Lat. from Gr. 'shellfish'). The upper curvature of the apse, sometime also the whole apse. (→ Cloverleaf plan)

Copyist – Until the invention of book printing, books were copied down, e.g. by monks in the scriptorium, the room in a monastery set aside for the copying of manuscripts. Ecclesiastical institutions were dependent on liturgical books and theological literature. Frequently used texts (e.g. grammars for teaching purposes) were dictated, several scribes would work simultaneously on the same text. However, in most cases a copyist worked on one manuscript. In those days, copying, like reading, was regarded as hard physical work.

Council → Synod

Cruciform plan church with dome – With a ground plan like a Greek cross (like a plus sign with all arms of equal length), central structure and often also side rooms with domes. The form of Byzantine church construction since the 7th century.

Crypt – Underground burial chamber of a martyr; saint's grave under the altar dedicated to the saint.

Deacon – Originally a helper of the poor following Christ, later an office in the Church below that of priest.

Deesis → (Gr.) entreaty

Diakonikon – Also pastophoria; a sacristy by function, the southern part of the altar area or the southern apse in a three-part choir.

Doctor of the Church – Title awarded by a council by which the writings of a doctor of the Church gain a particular conclusiveness.

Dodekaortion → Festival cycle

Dome – Hemispherical vault; if it is to be mounted on a rectangular structure, transitions are necessary: squinches, pendentives

Donator → Founder

Dormition of the Virgin – Originally celebrated in January or December, finally fixed on 15 August by Emperor Maurice (apparently following the celebrations for the ancient oriental mother goddess in accordance with the star in the Zodiac sign of Virgo which goes down on 10.8, and rises on 8.9, the feast of Mary's Birth; Mary is also extolled as the 'Star of Life' and portrayed with a star-shaped emblem on her garment). The iconography of the topic is developed independently in the 6th/7th centuries parallel to the Ascension of Christ after the iconoclast dispute. It belongs in the narthex and usually unites several scenes: Mourning by the bier, Reception of the soul by Christ, the church fathers who report about the Dormition (Andrew of Crete), lamenting women, etc.

Ecumenical councils → Synod

Eleousa – (Gr. 'compassionate') Mary with Jesus on her arm has a premonition of the Crucifixion, the signs of which are mainly shown in the corners.

Enkolpion – (Gr. 'on the bosom') A pectoral cross worn by ecclesiastical dignitaries; the medallion with a picture of the Mother of God used in the liturgy of the Eastern Church.

Entry into Jerusalem – The liturgical prerequisite lies in the Palm Sunday festivities according to Mat. 21:1-11; in combination with the Lazarus Saturday on the day before; the feast celebrates the concealed triumphal character and is connected with the Passion cycle. In the Eastern Church, Christ usually sits en face side-saddle to the observer, the donkey lowers its head and sniffs at coats which children spread out before Him to welcome Him with dignity; often two children have climbed up a tree.

Epiphany – Appearance of the Lord, probably the oldest immovable ecclesiastical feast which developed from the 3rd century on. The theological classification was carried out mainly by Basil, Gregory of Nyssa and Gregory of Nazianzos.

Eucharist – (Gr. 'thanksgiving') The sacrament in which Christ's Last Supper is commemorated by the consecration of bread and wine; distributed since the 2nd century within a ritualised celebration in the morning. → Liturgy

Fasting period – The most important fasting period is Lent, the 40 days preceding Easter. Each week, Wednesday and Friday are regarded as days of fasting.

Father of the Church – Early Christian ecclesiastical author whose orthodoxy was acknowledged by the Church.

Festival Cycle – Sequence of pictures with the great festivals of the Lord: Annunciation, Christ's Birth, Circumcision, Presentation of Christ in the Temple, Baptism, Transfiguration, Raising Lazarus from the Dead, Entry of Christ into Jerusalem, Crucifixion, Anastasis, Ascension of Christ, Pentecost. The number twelve is due to the analogy with the twelve apostles; depending on the church and person commissioning it, the choice of festivals is variable; Dormition of the Mother of God and other Marian festivals may come in addition.

Flamboyant style – Special late-Gothic form, especially in France; name derived from the flame-like structure of the → Tracery.

Founder – Donor of money or in kind for a church or monastery; from the High Middle Ages on, the donors of money often had themselves included in the monumental decoration of a church with a portrait and an inscription.

Fresco – (Ital. 'fresh') Wall decoration applied to moist lime stucco with water colours; when dried, inseparably linked with the stucco; must be painted relatively quickly from top to bottom, i.e. fine details are hardly possibly; mainly painted following preliminary sketches on the wall taken from a painter's manual or miniature.

Gospel – Liturgical book with the gospels according to Matthew, Mark, Luke and John from which readings are made during divine service. Also used as a synonym for Christ's teaching as a whole.

Groin vault – A curved arris where two barrel vaults of the same kind intersect.

Hermit – From the hermits of the 3rd/4th centuries developed, especially in Egypt, monasticism. In part they lived in colonies under the leadership of an abbot. → Lavra

Intercession – Saints request mercy and forgiveness of sins for humans; frequently in connection with donor's portraits, but also as an independent motif; Christ sitting on His throne between Mary and John as intercessors belongs to the group of motifs of the Last Judgment in Byzantine art. Frequently centre part of the iconostasis.

Glykophylousa – (Gr. 'caressing') A honorary title for the Virgin Mary, post-Byzantine, richly varied version of the → Eleousa

Hagiography – Description of the lives of the saints which developed out of the acts of the martyrs; after the end of the persecutions 'Confessors' were added whose lives were written down because of a special exemplariness; in the 8th/9th centuries the campaigners for iconolatry and against Islam were added. In the course of time, many bizarre and exalted vitae were included; they were eliminated around the year 1000 in the course of a thorough revision of the canon.

Hetoimasia – (Gr. 'preparation' [of the throne]) An empty throne stands for the Crucified One, a motif exclusive to Byzantine art. The throne is presented with a purple cloak or book, often also the Instruments of the Passion according to Rev. 22: 1-4; means the testimony of Jesus at the Last Judgment.

Hieromonachos – Monk ordained as a priest. Rarer in the Orthodox church than in the Catholic church.

Hodegetria – (Gr. 'guide') A standing Mother of God with the Child on her arm, both frontal, Christ with a blessing gesture.

Hospitality of Abraham – The visit by three men or angels to Abraham who are entertained by him (generally his wife brings the meal, Abraham sits with his visitors at the table) is understood by the church fathers, especially in the Byzantine field of influence, as typological for the Trinity.

Hymnography – Composition of the melody and text of church hymns; work of Melodos

Icon – (Gr. 'eikon' 'image') Pictures attested since the 4th century on wood or cloth which are regarded as a true portrait of the sacred personage depicted, prepared in accordance with strict rules and consecrated. In the 13th century icon painting had a great influence on the development of Western panel painting.

Iconoclasm – Theological debate in the 8th/9th centuries in which the originally iconoclastic tendencies of Christianity prevailed and almost all religious portrayals were destroyed. As in Islam and Judaism there was a total ban on portrayals with religious content; only in the profane sector were figural portrayals allowed. Main opponents of the ban on pictures were the monks, but also the people.

Iconography – More or less canonical arrangement of picture contents in a room → Picture programme

Iconology – Interpretation of the contents of pictures, in the Byzantine area through the link between the liturgy and the arrangement of pictures in the room.

Iconophiles – Icon venerators, supporters of the veneration of the portraits of saints.

Iconostasis – Screen between the naos and bema; usually with several tiers of icons; with three openings or doorways, the middle one being made prominent; developed from an altar barrier.

Illumination – Decoration in colours, gold or silver in manuscripts.

Illuminator – Painter of miniatures who decorated manuscripts with small pictures.

Incarnation – Central dogma of Christian faith; God's becoming man (flesh) in Jesus Christ.

Jurisdiction – Competence in legal questions.

Katholikon – Main church of a Byzantine monastery

Last Supper – Out of the commemoration of the Last Supper which Jesus celebrated with His disciples has developed the Christian divine service with its liturgy which is centred around the sacrament of the body and blood of Christ. The iconography of the portrayal, which is part of the → Passion cycle, depends on the ancient portrayal of a supper: the disciples sit around a table, in the middle stands a bowl and Jesus, as host, is shown in accordance with Jewish tradition breaking the bread. It forms the beginning of the meal proper which was concluded with a cup of wine which was handed around among the guests. Originally, Judas was missing in Byzantine portrayals, later he was included without a halo and as ugly as possible on the left side. He reaches into the bowl at the same time as Christ. John is portrayed as the favourite disciple at Christ's side, sometimes his head on His lap.

Latin – Roman-Catholic; on the basis of the language used in divine service.

Lavra – Eremitic colony under one common abbot, early form of monastic life, still so today on Mount Athos.

Lent → Fasting period

Levant – (Ital. 'East') The countries along the coast of the Eastern Mediterranean, especially from Asia Minor to Egypt.

Litany – (Lat. from Gk. 'entreaty') Intercession and invocation prayers sung in antiphon, also procession during vespers during which the → Troparia are sung and prayers of intercession are pronounced.

Liturgical books – Books for use in divine service or for the administration of sacraments.

Liturgy – (Gr. 'minister', 'office') The divine service centred on the sacrament of the Eucharist and the form in which it is held canonically.

Luke's paintings – Portraits which Luke the Evangelist is said to have painted of the Virgin Mary and Jesus Christ during their lifetime or shortly after; the legend sprang up in the 9th century.

Lunette – (Fr. 'small moon') Tympanum above doors or windows.

Mamelukes – (Arab. 'taken into possession') Freed slaves who worked in Egypt as soldiers and who formed a dynasty of their own there from the 13th to the 16th centuries.

Mandylion – (Pers. 'small cloak', 'cloth') An → Acheiropoietos which is said to have come from the impression made by Christ's face in a cloth and was found in Edessa; in the course of the 10th century, the motif reached Constantinople and became an important part of fresco painting; usually above the apse.

Manuscript – Document written by hand; until book printing the most important form for distributing literature, prepared in scriptoria by copyists, admittedly less in monasteries in contrast to the West.

Mary Orans → Orans

Mary's death → Dormition of the Mother of God

Martyr – (Lat. from Gr. 'witness') Restricted from 2nd century on to blood witnesses, i.e. persons who die for their faith. The veneration goes back to ancient customs, but it turns from the wise to the pious.

Melodos → Hymnography

Metamorphosis – (Gr. 'transformation') Transfiguration of Christ. Christ appears on Mount Tabor between Moses and Elijah, surrounded by brilliance in a shining garment, at His feet the awe-struck disciples Peter, John and James.

Miniature → Illumination

Miniature painter → Illuminator

Monasticism Goes back to the late 3rd and early 4th centuries. Secluded asceticism of an individual ('monachos') in the desert ('eremos'). Admittedly soon already in the form of a community of monks ('coinobion') with disciplinary rules. In the Eastern Church there was no division into orders, accordingly also no rules binding for a whole series of monasteries. Each monastery had and still has its own rules.

Mosaic – (Arab. 'decorated') With gravel stones as a floor covering since the 5th century BC in Greece, large picture compositions are common since the 3rd century BC. Great flowering in the Byzantine period. Use of minute stones, glass, mother of pearl and sheet gold made it possible to apply them to the wall.

Moufflon – Wild sheep to be found only on Cyprus.

Naos – (Gr. 'temple') Main room for the faithful.

Narthex – First main room in a church, here is the baptismal font, antechamber to naos.

Nave – Section of a church bounded on both sides by arches or outside walls counted in the cross section of the building.

New Testament cycle – Pictures from the Life of Christ as related in the four gospels, including the → Passion cycle.

Nimbus – Halo around the head, the aura of the divine indicated with gold, originally only for Christ later also for Mary and the saints.

Noli-me-tangere – (Lat. 'do not touch me') Mary Magdalene's meeting with Jesus after His Resurrection.

Oktoechos – Liturgical book in which the chants are arranged in accordance with the eight ('oktos') Byzantine ecclesiastical tones.

Orans – Icon type of the Virgin Mary based on Isaiah 7:14:

Fig. 190: Mandylion, fresco from Kato Lefkara.

'Therefore the Lord himself shall give you a sign: Behold a virgin shall conceive, and bear a son, and shall call his name Immanuel.' Mary is portrayed with God as a sign, she wears him like a disc before her bosom. Orans comes from 'orare', the Latin for 'to pray' which was done mainly with raised hands in early Christianity.

Orthodoxy – Term first used by Eusebios in his history of the Church, Athanasios restricted it to a theological-church political designation: correct teaching, perfect life of the fathers, correct liturgy, agreement of emperor and Church.

Outremer – Crusader states in Palestine and Syria.

Palaeography – Science of the forms and means of handwriting and manuscripts in antiquity and the Middle Ages.

Panagia – (Gr. 'all holy') Honorary name for the Virgin Mary.

Parchment – Material for writing on used in Antiquity and the Middle Ages made of the specially treated (not tanned) hide of very young lambs.

Passion Cycle – The Passion of Christ, in particular the Way of the Cross. Begins with the Raising of Lazarus and the Triumphal Entry into Jerusalem, continues with the Last Supper, Betrayal and Denial to the Crucifixion, Descent from the Cross, Lamentation and the Resurrection.

Pastophoria – Diakonikon

Patriarch – Archbishop, especially of Constantinople.

Patriarchate – See and diocese of the archbishop.

Pendentive – Spherical triangle forming the transition from the ground plan format to the basic circle of a dome.

Pictorial programme – In Orthodox churches in the course of the centuries a specific distribution of motives and topics within the sacred building developed. Especially in the period after iconoclasm, a theologically thought-out arrangement was laid down taking account of the liturgical functions. In the narthex which served as a baptismal chapel, preference is given to the Last Judgment. To the East, towards sunrise, the Prophecies are shown: the Annunciation; Gabriel and Mary are almost always portrayed left and right of the apse; beneath them often David and Samuel or other prophets; in the apse the Virgin Mary as a portrayal of the Incarnation of God, beneath the Communion of the Apostles. The west wall is occupied with themes from the Passion, either the Dormition of the Virgin or the Crucifixion, beneath them the cycle of the passion. In domed churches, the dome is dominated by Christ Pantocrator, around Him the Preparation of the Throne, below the prophets in the tambour with their prophecies on banderoles, then the Evangelists make the transition to the earthly happenings of the visible Church, ending right at the bottom in the row of saints. In the churches in the Troodos Mountains, in the side niches indicating the transept something is portrayed in the southern niche which is linked with the consecration of the church, in the northern one, on the other hand, almost always the Archangel Michael in armour.

Platytera – ('more spacious [than Heaven is thy lap]') Designation comes from a Marian hymn. Portrayal similar to Mary → Orans.

Post-Byzantine – From the period after the fall of Constantinople in 1453.

Prelate – (Lat. 'held in special esteem') Holder of high ecclesiastical offices.

Premonstratensian – Religious order following the stricter rules of St. Augustine, founded around 1120 in a French valley called Prémontré, the white habit is intended to emphasise the penitential character.

Preparation of the Throne → Hetoimasia

Prophets – In the Old Testament there are 4 'great' prophets (Isaiah, Jeremiah, Ezekiel and Daniel) and 12 'minor' ones; sometimes all 16, sometimes just 12 are portrayed.

Propylaeum – Portico, entrance (especially to a temple)

Raising of Lazarus from the Dead – The portrayal developed already in the early Church, mainly in funerary art. In the Byzantine period, Jesus is shown with a commanding gesture in front of the open tomb in which Lazarus, wrapped in his shroud, is standing upright. Mary and Martha lie at Jesus's feet, a young man stands next to the tomb and holds a cloth in front of his nose to indicate the cadaverous smell. Often there are some Apostles behind Jesus and a group of astonished Jews.

Relic – Remains of sacred personages or objects, understood as real bearers of a power over which death has no control. Their veneration is known since the 2nd century AD; in the course of the 3rd/4th centuries they took on decisive importance for the founding of churches.

Resurrection of Jesus – According to the New Testament, Jesus returned to life after His death. As the mystery is not depictable, even according to Byzantine opinion, the three women who wanted to embalm the corpse standing in front of the open and empty tomb, or Christ's descent to the gates of Hell in order to ascend with them to Heaven are shown. → Anastasis

Sacrament – An outward sign combined with a specific form of words regarded as conferring some specific grace upon those who receive it, at the same time forming the community of the faithful as a church, i.e. as the 'Body of Christ'.

Sacrifice of Isaac – Abraham's sacrifice of his son is already very early made typological for the Crucifixion of Christ, God's sacrifice of His Son.

Scriptorium – Room in a monastery where manuscripts were written.

Scroll, rotulus – The original form of the book which was the obvious way of storing the early form of material used for writing on, papyrus. In the Christian period superseded by the codex form, thus the form of book familiar to us today.

Seraph, pl. seraphim – (Hebr. 'fiery angel of light') Angel of the Old Testament with six wings in the form of a serpent, often portrayed as a cherub.

Squinch – Small arch, corbelling, etc. across an internal corner of a tower used to support a superstructure.

Stylite – A class of recluse saints living on a high pillar, early special form of ascetic hermits from which monasticism developed.

Symbol – Something that represents or stands for something else, usually by convention or association, esp. a material object used to represent something abstract.

Synaxarion – Church calendar of fixed feasts with the appropriate readings for each one.

Synaxis – (Gr. 'Assembly') Divine service in commemoration of a saint on the day fixed in the synaxarion.

Synod – Assembly of bishops meeting at irregular intervals and as such an organ leading the Church; Christian teaching was developd at Ecumenical Councils (or synods).

Tambour – (Fr. 'drum') Cylindrical or polygonal substructure of a dome, as a rule with windows to illuminate the interior.

Theotokos – (Gr. 'Mother of God') Mary's honorary name since the Council of Ephesus in 431.

Throne – Portrayal of the throne goes back to the seat of judgment at the end of time on which Christ will judge Mankind on the Day of Judgment; the bishops as His deputies on Earth are thus also entitled to use it.

Tracery – Gothic building ornaments constructed using a compass, mainly in door and window openings.

Transfiguration of Christ → Metamorphosis

Trinity – God has one being, but three persons: difficult to portray, polytheism misunderstanding likely. Often shown as a sign or as an allegory. → Hospitality of Abraham

Troparion – Rhythmic chant on the life of a saint.

Tympanum – (Gr. 'drum') Space bounded by an arch and the lintel of a doorway or window below it.

Typikon – (Gr. 'biblion typikon') Book of regulations; book with detailed rules for divine service, monastic life or for the clergy with the moral, ecclesiastic and liturgical obligations.

Typology – Teaching of the predictions in the OT of the NT, presupposes that the NT is the fulfilment of the OT and the OT is full of concealed references to the NT.

Vestments – Ceremonial official clothing.

Vita – Ideal portrait of a saint constructed with literary artistic means; prerequisite for canonisation.

Literature

On the introduction

History of Cyprus

E. Chrysos: Cyprus in Early Byzantine Times, 'The Sweet Land of Cyprus' (Nicosia 1993) p. 3-14
D. Hunt (ed.): Footprints in Cyprus. An Illustrated History (London 1990)
P. Loizos: Cyprus, 1878-1955: Structural Change, and its Contribution to Changing Relations of Authority, Chypre. La vie quotidienne de l'antiqité à nos jours. Actes du Colloque Musée de l'Homme (1985) p. 161-174
S. Mayes: Makarios: a biography (London 1981)
A. Papageorgiou: Cities and Countryside at the End of Antiquity and the Beginning of the Middle Ages in Cyprus, 'The Sweet Land of Cyprus' (Nicosia 1993) p. 27-51
D. Richards: Brief History of Cyprus in Ten Chapters (Limassol 1992)
S. Runciman: A History of the Crusades (3 vols. Cambridge 1951-54)
L. Severis: Ladies of Medieval Cyprus and Caterina Cornaro (Nicosia 1995)
F. Sauerwein: Spannungsfeld Ägäis. Informationen, Hintergründe, Ursachen des griechisch-türkischen Konflikts um Cypern und die Ägäis (Frankfurt/Aarau 1980)
A. Schneider: Zypern. 8000 Jahre Geschichte: Archäologische Schätze, Byzantinische Kirchen, Gotische Kathedralen (4th ed. Cologne 1995)
Übersee-Museum Bremen: Aphrodites Schwestern und christliches Zypern. 9000 Jahre Kultur Zyperns (Exhibition catalogue, Frankfurt 1987)

The Byzantine Empire

J. J. Norwich: Byzantium. Vol. 1: The Early Centuries (London 1990). Vol. 2: The Apogee (London 1991). Vol. 3: Decline and Fall (London 1995)
G. Ostrogorsky: History of the Byzantine State. Trans. J. Hussey (2nd ed. Oxford 1968)
The Oxford Dictionary of Byzantium (Prepared at Dumbarton Oaks) 3 vols. (New York/Oxford 1991)

History of the Orthodox Church

H.-G. Beck: Geschichte der orthodoxen Kirche im byzantinischen Reich (Göttingen 1980)
A. Benoît & A. Kallis et al.: Alte Kirche und Ostkirche. Ökumenische Kirchengeschichte, Vol. I (Mainz/Munich 1970)
J. M. Hussey: The Orthodox Church in the Byzantine Empire (Oxford 1986)
R. Janin: Chypre, Dictionnaire d'histoire et de géographie ecclésiastiques, Vol. 12 (Paris 1953) Col. 791-820

History of Byzantine Art

H. Hunger: Schreiben und Lesen in Byzanz. Die byzantinische Buchkultur (Munich 1989)
C. Ihm: Die Programme der christlichen Apsismalerei vom 4. Jahrhundert bis zur Mitte des 8. Jahrhunderts (2nd ed. Munich 1992)
O. Mazal: Handbuch der Byzantinistik (Graz 1989)
K. Onasch: Lexikon Liturgie und Kunst der Ostkirche unter Berücksichtigung der Alten Kirche (Berlin/Munich 1993)
S. Runciman: Byzantine Style and Civilisation (Harmondsworth 1975)
D. T. Rice: Byzantine Art (2nd ed. Harmondsworth 1968)
S. I. Robinson: Images of Byzantium. Learning about Icons (London 1996)
L. Rodley: Byzantine Art and Architecture. An Introduction (Cambridge 1996)

On the churches and monasteries

Nikitari: Panagia Asinou

V. Seymer & W. H. Buckler: The Church of Asinou, Cyprus, and its Frescoes (Oxford 1934) Archaeologia, Vol. LXXXIII, p. 327-350
A. & J. Stylianou: The Painted Churches of Cyprus (London 1985) p. 114-140
A. Papageorgiou: Asinou, ekklisia Panagias Phorbiotissas, Megali Kypriaki Egkyklopaideia, Vol. 3 (Nicosia 1985) p.14-17
D. Kappais: Ta monastiria tis Kyprou (1994) p. 180-183
M. Sacopoulo: Asinou en 1106 et sa contribution à l'iconographie (Brussels 1966)
Asinou. A Guide (Nicosia 1969)

Galata: Panagia Podithou

A. & J. Stylianou: The Painted Churches of Cyprus (London 1985) p. 98-105
A. Papageorgiou: Podithou i Podythou Panagias monastiri, Megali Kypriaki Egkyklopaideia, Vol. 11 (Nicosia 1989) p. 354-356
—— I palaiochristianiki kai vyzantini techni tis Kiprou, Apostolos Varnavas (Nicosia 1966) p. 54, fig. 38

Kakopetria: St. Nikolaos tis Stegis

A. & J. Stylianou: O naos tou Agiou Nikolaou tis Stegis para tin Kakopetrian, Kypriakai Spoudai, Vol. 10 (Nicosia 1946) p. 95-196

—— The Painted Churches of Cyprus (London 1985) p. 53-75

M. Sotiriou: Ai archikai toichographiai tou naou tou Agiou Nikolaou tis Stegis Kyprou, Charistirion eis Anastasion Orlandon, Vol. 3 (Athens 1965) p. 133-141, fig. XIV-L

—— Vyzantinai toichographiai monastikis technis tis Kyprou, Acts of the 1st International Congress of Cypriot Studies, Nicosia 1969 (Nicosia 1972) p. 247f

A. Papageorgiou: Masterpieces of the Byzantine Art of Cyprus (Nicosia 1965) fig. XXIX

—— Idiazousai vyzantinai toichographiai tou 13ou aionos en Kypro, Acts of the 1st International Congress of Cypriot Studies, Nicosia 1969 (Nicosia 1972) p. 247f

V. Djurić: Peinture mediévale à Chypre et en Yougoslavie, Epetirida Kentrou Meleton Ieras Monis Kykkou, 2 (Nicosia 1993) p. 202

Lagoudera: Panagia Araka

D. C. Winfield: The Church of Panagia tou Araka, Lagoudera: First Preliminary Report, 1968, Dumbarton Oaks Papers, 23-24 (1969-70) p. 377-380, fig. 1-9

—— Reports on work at Monagri, Lagoudera and Hagios Neophytos, Cyprus, 1969-70, Dumbarton Oaks Papers, 25 (1971) S. 259-264, Abb. 1-24

A. Stylianou: Ai toichographiai tou naou tis Panagias tou Araka, Kypros, Acts of the 1st International Congress of Byzantine Studies, Thessaloniki, Vol. I (Athens 1955) p. 459-467

A. & J. Stylianou: The Painted Churches of Cyprus (London 1985) p. 157-185

A. Papageorgiou: Eikon tou Christou en to nao tis Panagias tou Araka, Kypriakai Spoudai, Vol. 32 (1968) p. 45-55

L. Hadermann-Misguich: Fresques de Chypre et de Macedonie dans la seconde moitié du XIIè siècle, Acts of the 1st International Congress of Cypriot Studies, Nicosia 1969 (Nicosia 1972) p. 45, 48f

M. Acheimastou-Potamianou: Elliniki techni - Vyzantines toichographies; Ekdotiki Athinon (Athens 1994) fig. 61-70

V. Djurić: Peinture mediévale à Chypre et en Yougoslavie, Epetirida Kentrou Meleton Ieras Monis Kykkou, 2 (Nicosia 1972) p. 45, 48f

Platanistasa: Stavros tou Agiasmati

A. & J. Stylianou: The Painted Churches of Cyprus (London 1985) p. 186-218

A. Papageorgiou: Agiasmati Stavrou ekklisia, Megali Kypriaki Egkyklopaideia, Vol. 1 (Nicosia 1984) p. 80

N. Kliridis: 25 monastiria stin Kypro, Vol. 2 (Nicosia 1968) p. 89-92

D. Kappais: Ta monastiria tis Kyprou (1994) p. 196f

Lazanias: Machairas

I. Tsiknopoullos: I Iera Vasiliki kai Stavropigiaki Moni tis Theotokou tou Machaira (Nicosia 1986)

A. Papageorgiou: Machaira Panagias monastiri, Megali Kypriaki Egkyklopaideia, Vol. 9 (Nicosia 1988) p. 364-366

D. Kappais: Ta monastiria tis Kyprou (1994) p. 22-27

Palaichori: Metamorphosis Sotiros

A. & J. Stylianou: The Painted Churches of Cyprus (London 1985) p. 256-286

A. Papageorgiou: Metamorphoseos tou Sotiros ekklisia, Megali Kypriaki Egkyklopaideia, Vol. 2 (1985) p. 45f

Louvaras: St. Mamas

A. & J. Stylianou: Donors and Dedicatory Inscriptions, Supplicants and Supplications in the Painted Churches of Cyprus, Jahrbuch der Österreichischen Byzantinisten-Gesellschaft, IX (1960) p. 110

—— A Re-Examination of the Dates Concerning the Painted Churches of St. Mamas, Louvaras, and the Holy Cross of Agiasmati, Platanistasa, Cyprus, Jahrbuch der Österreichischen Byzantinisten-Gesellschaft, XXV (1976) p. 279-282

—— The Painted Churches of Cyprus (London 1985) p. 246-255

A. Stylianou: Some Wall-Paintings of the Second Half of the 15th Century in Cyprus, Actes du XIIè Congres International des Études Byzantines, Vol. III (Belgrade 1964) p. 363 f.

A. Papageorgiou: Masterpieces of the Byzantine Art of Cyprus (Nicosia 1965) p. 30, fig. XXXIV (1)

—— Kyprioi zographoi tou 15ou kai 16ou aiona, Report of the Dept. of Antiquities Cyprus (Nicosia 1974) p. 201, 203

—— Mama Agiou ekklisia, Louvaras, Megali Kypriaki Egkyklopaideia, Vol. 9 (Nicosia 1988) p. 286f

Monagri: Archangel Michael

R. Gunnis: Historic Cyprus (London 1936) p. 347

I. A. Sykoutris: Monastiria en Kypro, Kypriaka Chronika, Vol. II (Larnaca 1924) p. 108-115

N. Kliridis: Monastiria en Kypro (Larnaca 1950) p. 26-29

A. & J. Stylianou: Two Donor-Portraits and Two Dedicatory Inscriptions Concerning Bishop Macarios of Kition (1737-1776) Kypriakai Spoudai, Vol. 31 (Nicosia 1967) p. 65-74, fig. XV-XXX

—— The Painted Churches of Cyprus (London 1985) p. 238

A. Papageorgiou: Archangelou monastiri, Monagri, Megali Kypriaki Egkyklopaideia, Vol. 2 (Nicosia 1985) p. 334f

Monagri: Panagia Amasgou

S. Boyd: The Church of the Panagia Amasgou, Monagri, Cyprus, and its Wall-Paintings, Dumbarton Oaks Papers, 28 (1974) p. 277-349

A. & J. Stylianou: The Painted Churches of Cyprus (London 1985) p. 238-245

Pelendri: Church of the Holy Cross

S. Sophocleous: Icons of Cyprus 7th-20th Century (Nicosia 1994) p. 95, fig. 36

V. Djurić: Peinture mediévale à Chypre et en Yougoslavie, Epetirida Kentrou Meleton Ieras Monis Kykkou, 2 (Nicosia 1993) p. 280

A. Papageorgiou: Stavrou Timiou ekklisia, Pelendri, Megali Kypriaki Egkyklopaideia, Vol. 12 (Nicosia 1990) p. 318f
A. & J. Stylianou: The Painted Churches of Cyprus (London 1985) p. 223-232

Trooditissa Monastery

I. Tsiknopoullos: I Iera Moni tis Trooditissis (Nicosia 1990)
D. Kappais: Ta monastiria tis Kyprou (1994) p. 74-79

Pedoulas: Archangel Michael

A. & J. Stylianou: The Painted Churches of Cyprus (London 1985) p. 331-343
A. Papageorgiou: Archangelou ekklisia, Pedoulas, Megali Kypriaki Egkyklopaideia, Vol. 2 (Nicosia 1985) p. 339f
A. Jakovljević: To kykkotiko Psaltirio tou etous 1472 tis patriarchikis vivliothikis ton Ierosolymon, Epetirida Kentrou Meleton Ieras Monis Kykkou, Vol. 2 (Nicosia 1993) p. 187-219, esp. p.189f; fig. 10f

Moutoullas: Panagia Moutoulla

G. A. Sotiriou: Ta vyzantina mnimeia tis Kyprou (Athens 1935) fig. 85-90
M. Sotiriou: Vyzantinai toichographiai monastikis technis tis Kyprou, Acts of the 1st International Congress of Cypriot Studies, Nicosia 1969, Vol. II (Nicosia 1972) p. 250f
A. Papageorgiou: Idiazousai vyzantinai toichographiai tou 13ou ainonos en Kypro, Acts of the 1st International Congress of Cypriot Studies, Nicosia 1969, Vol. II (Nicosia 1972) p. 202, 206, 209
—— Kyprioi zographoi tou 15ou kai 16ou aiona, Report of the Dept. of Antiquities Cyprus (Nicosia 1974) p. 198, fig. XXX, 4
—— Panagias ekklisia, Moutoullas, Megali Kypriaki Egky-klopaideia, Vol. 11 (Nicosia 1989) p. 58f
D. Mouriki: The Wall-Paintings of the Church of the Panagia at Moutoullas, Cyprus, Byzanz und der Westen. Studien zur Kunst des Europäischen Mittelalters; Sitzungsberichte der Österreichischen Akademie der Wissenschaften, Phil.-Hist. Klasse (Vienna 1984) p. 178f
—— The Cult of Cypriot Saints in Medieval Cyprus as Attested by Church Decoration and Icon Painting, 'The Sweet Land of Cyprus' (Nicosia 1993) p. 243, 247f, 251f
A. & J. Stylianou: The Painted Churches of Cyprus (London 1985) p. 323-330

Kalopanagiotis: St. Lampadistis

A. Paschalidou: Typoi kai syntheseis apo kypriakes toichographies tou 15ou kai 16ou aiona, Kypriakai Spoudai, Vol. 12 (Nicosia 1949) p. 1-12, fig. 1-3
A. Stylianou: An Italo-Byzantine Series of Wall-Paintings in the Church of St. John Lampadistis, Kalopanayiotis, Cyprus, Akten des XI. Internationalen Byzantinischen Kongresses, München 1958 (Munich 1960) p. 595-598
A. & J. Stylianou: The Painted Churches of Cyprus (London 1985) p. 292-320
A. Papageorgiou: Idiazousai vizantinai toichographiai tou 13ou aiona en Kypro, Acts of the 1st International Congress of Cypriot Studies, Nicosia 1969 (Nicosia 1972) p. 202, 207, 210f

D. Mouriki: The Cult of Cypriot Saints in Medieval Cyprus as Attested by Church Decoration and Icon Painting, 'The Sweet Land of Cyprus' (Nicosia 1993) p. 243, 248f, 252-254

Kykkos: Panagia Kykkotissa

N. Kyriatzis: Istoria tis Ieras Monis Kykkou (Larnaca 1949)
A. Stylianou: Ai periigiseis tou Rossou monachou Vasileiou Grigorovich-Barsky en Kypro, Kypriakai Spoudai, Vol. 21 (Nicosia 1957) p. 62-66
Chrysostomos, Abbot of Kykkos: The Holy, Royal Monastery of Kykkos Founded with a Cross (Limassol 1969)
A. Pavlidis: Kykkou Panagias monastiri, Megali Kypriaki Egkyklopaideia, Vol. 7 (Nicosia 1987) p. 350-361
A. Jakovljević & A. Djurova: The Role of Kykkos Monastery in the Production of the 16th-18th Centuries Illuminated Liturgical Manuscripts (Nicosia 1996)
Ephraim the Athenian: A Narrative of the Founding of the Holy Monastery of Kykkos and History of the Miraculous Icon of the Mother of God. Prepared by A. Jakovljević & N. Christodoulou (Nicosia 1996)

Chrysorrogiatissa Monastery

Chrysorroyiatissa Monastery, written and compiled by C. G. Christodoulidis (Nicosia 1979)
I. K. Peristianis: I Iera Moni Chrysorroyiatissis (Paphos 1934)

St. Neophytos Monastery

A. C. Indianos & G. H. Thompson: Wall-Paintings of St. Neophytus Monastery, Kypriakai Spoudai, Vol. 3 (Nicosia 1944) p. 155-224
A. & J. Stylianou: Some Problems Concerning the 'Enkleistra' of St. Neophytos and its Wall-Paintings, Kypriakai Spoudai, Vol. 26 (Nicosia 1962) p. 131-135
I. P. Tsiknopoullos: The Encleistra and Saint Neophytos (Nicosia 1965)
C. Mango & E. J. W. Hawkins: The Hermitage of St. Neophytos and its Wall-Paintings, Dumbarton Oaks Papers, 20 (1966) p. 121-206
D. C. Winfield: Reports on Work at Monagri, Lagoudera and Hagios Neophytos, Cyprus, 1969-70, Dumbarton Oaks Papers, 25 (1971), p. 259-264
M. Sotiriou: Vyzantinai toichographiai monastiriakis technis tis Kyprou, Acts of the 1st International Congress of Cypriot Studies, Nicosia 1969 (Nicosia 1972) p. 249f
A. Papageorgiou: Idiazousai vyzantinai toichographiai tou 13ou aionos en Kypro, Acts of the 1st International Congress of Cypriot Studies, Nicosia 1969 (Nicosia 1972) p. 202, 210
—— Syrie et les icônes de Chypre, Report of the Dept. of Antiquities, Cyprus (Nicosia 1989) p. 171-176
F. G. Maier: Paphos in the History of Cyprus (Nicosia 1987) p. 23f, Abb. 17
D. Mouriki: The Cult of Cypriot Saints in Medieval Cyprus as Attested by Church Decoration and Icon Painting, 'The Sweet Land of Cyprus' (Nicosia 1993) p. 241, 245-247, 256
V. Djurić: Peinture mediévale à Chypre et en Yougoslavie, Epetirida Kentrou Meleton Ieras Monis Kykkou, 2 (Nicosia 1993) p. 278f, 282f

A. Jakovljević: Catalogue of Greek Manuscripts in the Library of St. Neophytos, Cyprus (Nicosia 1997)

Geroskipos: St. Paraskevi

A. & J. Stylianou: The Painted Churches of Cyprus (London 1985) p. 382-394
A. Papageorgiou: Paraskevi Agias ekklisia, Geroskipou, Megali Kypriaki Egkyklopaideia, Vol. 11 (Nicosia 1989) p. 106-108
S. S. Hadji-Kyriacou: The Church of St. Paraskevi Yeroskipou (Nicosia 1991)

Vavla: St. Minas

N. Kyriatzis: Monastiria en Kypro (Larnaca 1950) p. 77f
N. Kliridis: 25 monastiria stin Kypro, Vol. 2 (Nicosia 1968) p. 66-68
A. Papageorgiou: Mina Agiou monastiri, Vavla, Megali Kypriaki Egkyklopaideia, Vol. 10 (Nicosia 1989) p. 59

Kato Lefkara: Archangel Michael

A. Papageorgiou: Archangelou ekklisia, Kato Lefkara, Megali Kypriaki Egkyklopaideia, Vol. 2 (Nicosia 1985) p. 339
A. & J. Stylianou: The Painted Churches of Cyprus (London 1985) p. 447-450
D. Mouriki: The Cult of Cypriot Saints in Medieval Cyprus as Attested by Church Decoration and Icon Paintings, 'The Sweet Land of Cyprus' (Nicosia 1993) p. 240f; 245

Stavrovouni Monastery

Archim. Athanasios: Istoria tis Ieras Monis tou Stavrovouniou (1987) p. 1-73

Kiti: Panagia Angeloktisti

A. Papageorgiou: Angeloktistos, Panagia ekklisia, Megali Kypriaki Egkyklopaideia, Vol. 1 (Nicosia 1984) p. 49f
—— I palaiochristianiki kai vyzantini techni tis Kyprou, Apostolos Varnavas (Nicosia 1966) p. 17, 19, fig. 8
C. Delvoye: Vyzantini techni, L'art byzantin (Athens 1983) p. 84, 122, fig. 24
A. & J. Stylianou: The Painted Churches of Cyprus (London 1985) p. 27, 49-51
N. Chatzidakis: Elliniki techni - Vyzantina psiphidota, Ekdotiki Athinon (Athens 1994) p. 231f, fig. 21f
S. Sophocleous: Icons of Cyprus 7th-20th Century (Nicosia 1994) p. 12, 15, fig. 3

Larnaca: St. Lazarus

J. Hackett: A History of the Church of Cyprus (London 1901, reprint New York 1972) p. 411-415
N. Kyriatzis: Monastiria en Kypro (Larnaca 1950) p. 65-72
A. & J. Stylianou: The Painted Churches of Cyprus (Stourbridge 1964) p. 10, 32, 59, 86, 93, 116, 147
A. Papageorgiou: I palaiochristianiki kai vyzantini techni tis Kyprou, Apostolos Varnavas (Nicosia 1966) p. 27f
—— Lazarou Agiou ekklisia, Megali Kypriaki Egkyklopaideia, Vol. 8 (Nicosia 1988) p. 174f
D. Mouriki: The Cult of Cypriot Saints in Medieval Cyprus as Attested by Church Decoration and Icon Painting, 'The Sweet Land of Cyprus' (Nicosia 1993) p. 244
I. Meadows & L. Efthymiou: Barsky's Cyprus Revisited 1726 . 1989 (Nicosia 1994) p. 12

Kellia: St. Antonios

A. Papageorgiou: Antoniou Agiou ekklisia, Megali Kypriaki Egkyklopaideia, Vol. 2 (Nicosia 1985) p. 227f
A. & J. Stylianou: The Painted Churches of Cyprus (London 1985) p. 433-437

Pera Chorio: Church of the Holy Apostles

A. H. S. Megaw & E. J. W. Hawkins: The Church of the Holy Apostles at Perachorio, Cyprus, and its Frescoes, Dumbarton Oaks Papers, 16 (1962) p. 279-348, fig. 1-56
D. Mouriki: The Cult of Cypriot Saints in Medieval Cyprus as Attested by Church Decoration and Icon Painting, 'The Sweet Land of Cyprus' (Nicosia 1993) p. 242f
A. Papageorgiou: I palaiochristianiki kai vyzantini techni tis Kyprou, Apostolos Varnavas (Nicosia 1966) p. 40f, fig. 28
—— Apostolon Agion ekklisia, Pera Chorio, Megali Kypriaki Egkyklopaideia, Vol. 2 (Nicosia 1985) p. 257f
A. & J. Stylianou: The Painted Churches of Cyprus (London 1985) p. 422-424
V. Djurić & S. Ćirković & V. Korać: Pećka patrijaršija (Belgrade 1990) p. 48f, fig. 23f

Peristerona: Barnabas and Hilarion

A. Papageorgiou: Varnava kai Ilarionos ekklisia, Megali Kypriaki Egkyklopaideia, Vol. 3 (Nicosia 1985) p. 151f

Nicosia: St. John's Cathedral

G. S. Schiemenz: Der 148. Psalm in der Johannes-Kathedrale von Nicosia, Epetirida Kentrou Meleton Ieras Monis Kykkou 3 (Nicosia 1995) p. 163-201
V. Grigoriou: O kathedrikos naos tou Agiou Ioannou sti Leukosia (Nicosia without year)
A. & J. Stylianou: The Painted Churches of Cyprus (London 1985) p. 496-499

Morphou: St. Mamas

C. D. Gobham: Excerpta Cypria (Cambridge 1908) p. 19
S. Gabelić: The Church of the Virgin Mary near Kophinou, Kypriakai Spoudai, Vol. 48 (Nicosia 1984) p. 148, fig. 3
—— Predstave sv. Mamanta u zidnom slikarstvu na Kipru, Zograf, Vol. 15 (Belgrade 1984) p. 69-75
A. & J. Stylianou: The Painted Churches of Cyprus (London 1985) p. 251f
A. Papageorgiou: Mama Agiou ekklisia, Morphou, Megali Kypriaki Egkyklopaideia, Vol. 9 (Nicosia 1988) p. 287-289
I. Meadows & L. Efthymiou: Barsky's Cyprus Revisited 1726 • 1989 (Nicosia 1994) p. 89f, fig. 27
D. Mouriki: The Cult of Cypriot Saints in Medieval Cyprus as Attested by Church Decoration and Icon Painting, 'The Sweet Land of Cyprus' (Nicosia 1993) p. 249-251
D. Kappais: Ta monastiria tis Kyprou (1994) p. 164f

S. Sophocleous: Icons of Cyprus 7th-20th Century (Nicosia 1994) p. 89f, fig. 27

Myrtou: St. Panteleimon

A. Papageorgiou: Panteleimonos Agiou monastiri, Myrtou, Megali Kypriaki Egkyklopaideia, vol. 2 (Nicosia 1989) p. 75

Lamboussa: Acheiropoietos

N. Kliridis: 25 monastiria stin Kypro, Vol. 2 (Nicosia 1968) p. 14-18

A. Papageorgiou: Acheiropoietou monastiri, Megali Kypriaki Egkyklopaideia, Vol. 1 (Nicosia 1984) p. 96f

Bellapais Abbey

L. Durrell: Bitter Lemons of Cyprus (London 1959)

R. Janin: Chypre, Dictionnaire d'histoire et de géographie ecclésiastiques, Vol. 12 (Paris 1953) col. 799, 811, 813

C. P. Kyrris: History of Cyprus (Nicosia 1985), p. 34, 44f, 214f
—— Bella Pais avvaeio, Megali Kypriaki Egkyklopaideia, Vol. 11 (Nidosia 1989) p. 249-252

A. Schneider: Zypern. 8000 Jahre Geschichte: Archäologische Schätze, Byzantinische Kirchen, Gotische Kathedralen (4th ed. Cologne 1995) p. 313-315

Koutsoventis: St. John Chrysostom

C. Mango & E. J. W. Hawkins: Report on the Field Work in Istanbul and Cyprus, 1962/63, Dumbarton Oaks Papers, 18 (1964) p. 333-339

D. C. Winfield: Hagios Chysostomos, Trikomo, Asinou. Byzantine Painters at Work, Acts of the 1st International Congress of Cypriot Studies, Nicosia 1969, Vol. II (Nicosia 1972) p. 285-291, fig. L-LX

A. & J. Stylianou: The Painted Churches of Cyprus (London 1985) p. 456-463

Kalogrea: Christ Antiphonitis

A. & J. Stylianou: The Painted Churches of Cyprus (London 1985) p. 569-485

A. Papageorgiou: Antiphoniti ekklisia, Megali Kypriaki Egkyklopaideia, Vol. 2 (Nicosia 1985) p. 222-224

Tremetousia: St. Spyridon

A. Papageorgiou: Spyridonos Agiou monastiri, Megali Kypriaki Egkyklopaideia, Vol. 2, (Nicosia 1990) p. 295f

D. Mouriki: The Cult of Cypriot Saints in Medieval Cyprus as Attested by Church Decoration and Icon Painting, 'The Sweet Land of Cyprus' (Nicosia 1993) p. 241f

St. Barnabas Monastery

G. A. Sotiriou: O naos kai o Taphos tou Apostolou Varnava para tin Salamina tis Kyprou, Kypriakai Spoudai, Vol. 1 (Nicosia 1937) p. 175-187, fig. 1-3

D. Mouriki: The Cult of Cypriot Saints in Medieval Cyprus as Attested by Church Decoration and Icon Painting, 'The Sweet Land of Cyprus' (Nicosia 1993) p. 240

C. P. Kyrris: Saint Barnabas and Saint Paul in Cyprus, Stasinos (Nicosia 1985) p. 97-125

A. Papageorgiou: Varnava Apostolou monastiri, Megali Kypriaki Egkyklopaideia, Vol. 3 (Nicosia 1985) p. 157-159

Trikomo: Theotokos

D. C. Winfield: Hagios Chrysostomos, Trikomo, Asinou. Byzantine painters at work. Acts of the 1st International Congress of Cypriot Studies, Nicosia 1969, Vol. II. (Nicosia 1972) p. 285-287, fig. LV,2; LVI,2; LVII,2; LVIII,2; LX,2

V. Djurić: Peinture medievale à Chypre et en Yougoslavie, Epetirida Kentrou Meleton Ieras Monis Kykkou, 2 (Nicosia 1993) p. 278

L. Hadermann-Misguich: Fresques de Chypre et de Macedoine dans la second moitié du XIIè siècle. Acts of the 1st International Congress of Cypriot Studies, Nicosia 1969, Vol. II (Nicosia 1972) p. 48

A. Papageorgiou: I palaiochristianiki kai vyzantini techni tis Kyprou, Apostolos Varnavas (Nicosia 1966) p. 37, 40f, fig. 25f
—— Masterpieces of the Byzantine Art of Cyprus (Nicosia 1965) p. 23

A. & J. Stylianou: The Painted Churches of Cyprus (London 1985) p. 486-491

Lythrankomi: Panagia Kanakaria

O. M. Dalton: Byzantine Art and Archaeology (London 1911) p. 367, 384-387

O. Wulff: Altchristliche und byzantinische Kunst, II (Berlin 1914) p. 432, 533, fig. 369

G. A. Sotiriou: Ta palaiochristianika kai vyzantina mnimeia tis Kyprou, Praktika tis Akadimias Athinon (1931) p. 478, 487

A. Papageorgiou: I palaiochristianiki kai vyzantini techni tis Kyprou, Apostolos Varnavas (Nicosia 1966) p. 10f, fig. 9

A. H. S. Megaw & E. J. W. Hawkins: The Church of the Panagia Kanakaria at Lythrankomi in Cyprus, its Mosaics and Frescoes (Washington 1977)

A. & J. Stylianou: The Painted Churches of Cyprus (London 1985) p. 43-48

C. P. Kyrris: The Kanakaria Documents 1666-1850... Report by the Cyprus Research Centre, No. XIV (Nicosia 1987)

The Destruction of the Cultural Heritage in the Turkish Occupied Part of Cyprus, Flagellum Dei (Nicosia without year)

Kanakaria Mosaics - the Trial (Nicosia without year)

St. Andrew's Monastery

A. Pavlidis: Andrea Apostolou monastiri, Megali Kypriaki Egkyklopaideia, Vol. 1 (Nicosia 1984) p. 174-177

D. Kapais: Ta monastiria tis Kyprou (Nicosia 1994) p. 42-45

On the appendix

Cyprus in the Bible

The Bible in the authorised King James's version (Oxford without year)

Archbishops of Cyprus

R. Janin: Chypre, Dictionnaire d'histoire et de géographie ecclésiastiques, Vol. 12 (Paris 1953) col. 809f

Quellenbuch zur Geschichte der Orthodoxen Kirche. Zsgest. u. eingel. v. N. Thon (Trier 1983)

Lists of Rulers

E. Eickhoff: Macht und Sendung. Byzantinische Weltpolitik (Stuttgart 1981)

J. Matuz: Das Osmanische Reich. Grundlinien seiner Geschichte (Darmstadt 1985)

S. Schneider: Byzanz. Oldenbourg-Grundriss der Geschichte, Vol. 22 (Munich 1986)

S. Runciman: History of the Crusades (3 vols. Cambridge 1951-1954)

Saints

W. Härle & H. Wagner (ed.): Theologenlexikon. Von den Kirchenvätern bis zur Gegenwart (Munich 1987)

E. Haustein-Bartsch: Ikonen-Museum Recklinghausen (Munich 1995)

K. Koch & E. Otto & J. Roloff, H. Schmoldt: Reclams Bibellexikon (Stuttgart 1987)

B. G. Walker: Das geheime Wissen der Frauen. Ein Lexikon (Munich 1995)

O. Wimmer & H. Melzer: Lexikon der Namen und Heiligen (4th ed. Innsbruck/Vienna/Munich 1982)

Fotograph

Bibliotheca Apostolica Vaticana: fig. 12
G. Boelmann: fig. 1, 25, 29, 109, 116, 118, 139, 162
P. Chouris: cover
Cyprus Museum: fig. 2
Department of Antiquity, Cyprus: fig. 151, 176, 177
A. Jakovljević: fig. 14, 15, 16, 18
P. G. Schiemenz: fig. 142
All the other photos were taken by E. Hein.

Thank you...

We would very much like to thank Anette Hein for her untiring work in the background, Nina Wenig, Ina Groesdonk, Oliver Funke and Claudia Stevens for the translation and gathering of the texts by A. Jakovljević from English, Thelma Michaelides from the MAM book store in Nicosia who fulfilled our literature requests, Professor P. G. Schiemenz of the University of Kiel for the photo of the interior of St. John´s Cathedral in Nicosia, Ali Yavasoglu who drove us to Northern Cyprus, and not least the many priests, sacristans, nuns and monks who opened the doors of their churches to us and waited with great patience until the photo works were completed.

Further publications by Melina:

Tibet - Der Weiße Tempel von Tholing
(The White Temple of Tholing)
400 years old temple paintings in the west of Tibet with a foreword of Dalai Lama. Comprehensive historical view of Buddhistic development in Tibet.
By Ewald Hein and Günther Boelmann
Hardcover, Book Jacket, 188 p., 52 col. pict., 19 x 24 cm, 1994, 79,00 DM
German ISBN 3-929255-06-5

Ethiopia - Christian Africa
Art, Churches and Culture
In the fissured and in some regions hardly accessible highlands of Ethiopia there are still places of a living Christianity which is older than the Christian churches of Europe. Evidence of old tradition can be found in Axum, the ancient capital of Abyssinia, where they say the Ark of the Covenant is preserved until today. The illustrated book shows the excellent painted churches in this Christian part of Africa.
By Ewald Hein and Brigitte Kleidt
Hardcover, Book Jacket, abt. 210 p., with 200 col. pict., 29 x 24 cm, 79,00 DM
English ISBN 3-929255-28-6
German ISBN 3-929255-27-8
Date of publication end 1998